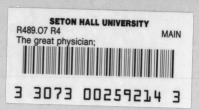

DR. OSLER

From the Sargent portrait at Johns Hopkins

THE
GREAT PHYSICIAN

A Short Life of

SIR WILLIAM OSLER

BY

EDITH GITTINGS REID

OXFORD UNIVERSITY PRESS

LONDON   New York   TORONTO

FIRST PUBLISHED AUGUST 1931
SECOND IMPRESSION AUGUST 1931
THIRD IMPRESSION SEPTEMBER 1931
FOURTH IMPRESSION DECEMBER 1931
FIFTH IMPRESSION DECEMBER 1931
POPULAR EDITION FEBRUARY 1934
SECOND IMPRESSION POPULAR EDITION JANUARY 1936

PRINTED IN THE UNITED STATES OF AMERICA

To

WILLIAM SYDNEY THAYER

Who absorbed the Spirit as he followed
the Methods of the Master

PREFACE

A GREAT number of articles have been written about Sir William Osler, in the medical journals, and in the scientific and popular magazines. The mere list of them, up to 1926, compiled by Dr. Maude Abbott, covers 20 pages. Then there are the two large volumes of Dr. Cushing's "Life," the volume of Tributes on Sir William's 70th birthday and the Memorial Volume published after his death, edited by Dr. Abbott.

I have quoted largely from Sir William's addresses and essays, which, curiously enough, reveal the soul of the man more intimately than his letters. I have also quoted freely from the writings mentioned above, either because a writer recounts his personal experiences, or because an incident is told in language unusually felicitous or because the reputation of the writer gives authority to his opinion.

I must express my appreciation of the help I have received from Dr. W. S. Thayer, who sent me all of Sir William's letters to him, and Dr. W. H. Welch, who made many suggestions; from Mrs. Henry Chapin and Dr. John Fulton, who have sent me letters and memorabilia of Lady Osler; from Dr. W. W. Francis and Dr. Norman Gwyn, who have sent me great numbers of Sir William's letters to children; and from many friends, students and colleagues of Sir William, to whom his name was an open sesame to courtesy and reminiscence. But above all I am indebted to the "Life" by Dr. Cushing, in which he has recorded, year by year, all the events of Sir William's life, and which leaves nothing to be desired by those who knew him personally. But there are those who did not

v

know him who might be deterred by its length, and it has
been thought desirable to publish a shorter " Life." If I
succeed in bringing him for a moment before other eyes
as I myself saw him the reader will turn to Dr. Cushing's
" Life " and live from day to day with this Master and
lover of men.

When Sargent painted the group of the four physicians
he found it comparatively easy to make faithful portraits
of the famous pathologist, Dr. Welch; of the famous surgeon, Dr. Halsted; and of the famous gynecologist, Dr.
Kelly. But when he came to Dr. Osler he was baffled for
a while. Then suddenly he dashed a spirit on the canvas
— and the group was vitalized. It is that spirit we are
seeking in his life.

Baltimore   EDITH GITTINGS REID
   May 1931

CONTENTS

The Formative Years

*And He took the clay in His hand
and said: This is without flaw.
I will mould a vessel that can
stand heat and frost and hold
cool water for parched lips.*

CHAPTER I

THE FORMATIVE YEARS

WILLIAM OSLER, the youngest son and eighth child of Featherstone Lake Osler and Ellen Free Pickton Osler, was born at Bond Head parsonage at Tecumseh, Upper Canada, close to the wilderness, on July 12th, 1849.

There are a few families that seem hand-made by the gods in their best of humours. From such Sir William sprang — an adventurous, religious race — the philosophy of their lives was service, kindness, faith and works, making a strongly matched team in their composition; with initiative to undertake almost any work and power to complete it once undertaken, and to drop it at a moment's notice if something more essential appeared. Masterly controllers of their own habits, the Oslers!

Featherstone Lake Osler and his wife came from Cornwall, England, where their ancestors had long lived. They were for the most part important merchants and ship-owners, and their descendants had a strong urge for the sea and an equally strong urge for the ministry. The gusto of Featherstone Osler's boyhood would delight most boys; when in his teens he was off to the sea and had tremendous adventures; but it would require the grace of God for most boys to understand how, having topped his adventures by becoming sub-lieutenant on a crack frigate, and having an offer of advancement from the Admiralty, he could decide to drop it all at once and return to his father who was in ill health and wanted his son with him during the latter part of his life. This decision ended his career in the Navy. On his return to Falmouth he married Ellen Pickton and began to study for Holy Orders, rapidly advancing in his work and with every prospect of taking honours and having a congenial parish in England. He again dropped certain advancement and comfort for what he felt the call of duty and unhesitatingly took a charge where young men were wanted, who were unafraid of the rigours of the frontier. And so it was that in the summer of 1837, Featherstone Lake Osler and his young wife Ellen Pickton Osler took the long voyage by sea and the long trail by land from Cornwall to their parishes of Tecumseth and West Gwillimbury in Upper Canada, then sparsely settled on the edge of the wilderness.

The hardships these young people encountered in the first years of their mission, their spirited defeat of these hardships and their splendid constructive achievement belong to another story.

When we think of the father and mother of William Osler we can account for much that made him a telling power in his generation. He was the incarnation of the best of his ancestry, whose characteristics were arrestingly good and vital. He and his family were not only affectionate, they were congenial; their life's values were the same.

At the time of his birth Canon and Mrs. Osler's work was well under way. Bond Head parsonage had been built — and a church; much land had been cleared and the seeds of civilization they had sown were bearing abundant fruit. The parsonage was the centre of all the activities for good for miles about; but there were no luxuries and few comforts. We are told that on the day his sister was born little Willie was tethered to a tree along with a calf, and there was a pail of milk close at hand, for which they both struggled, and into which he tumbled and was nearly drowned. In spite of these primitive surroundings the little lad had a proud beginning. No royal palace was more important than that low parsonage. The little black-eyed baby who looked like a papoose, was born under a lucky star; and, what few ever do, he opened his eyes and heart to its light, absorbing and reflecting the best it brought him.

What strikes us so forcibly in William Osler's life is its genuineness. Childhood in the out-of-doors with simple necessary duties — not duties cooked up to meet his psychology — and natural, wholesome play of his own devising, with brothers and sisters as jolly and generous as himself — it was a glad childhood. The most mischievous imp of a boy, his pranks were not taken seriously by his parents. Truth, honour and (where God was spoken of) reverence — these were the things they laid emphasis upon. And, amazing to say, these qualities all their children possessed. Implanted in his early childhood was the vigorous truth of all about him — nature, and people and work — no artificiality anywhere. From a bow so strung the swift arrow of his life sped, undeviating, to its goal.

In 1857 Featherstone Osler felt that he must have better educational facilities for his children, and asked the bishop to transfer him to Dundas.

During the early days at Tecumseth they lived in what was merely a hut, often cold, no doubt often hungry, without a doctor, without a church, with a cure extending over miles and miles of undeveloped country; but they were not appalled.

It is not a picture of Youth and a dream, but of Youth and determination, and spiritedly they undertook an almost impossible job. Now the job is done. Canon Osler writes in his diary: " It was one of the hardest trials of my life to leave the place where I had lived nineteen and a half years and the people with whom I had lived without a jar or discord during the whole period, but I felt that the Church would not suffer by my leaving it. In the neighbouring townships many churches have been built, and in Tecumseh and West Gwillembury, my specially licensed charge, where there had been neither church, parsonage, nor glebe, there are now six churches, two parsonages, and two glebes; the one in Tecumseh being specially valuable, consisting of 200 acres. I had 160 acres cleared."

At Dundas, in the midst of great natural beauty, they found a comfortable parsonage, good schools, congenial, cultivated friends. They had borne the burden in their youth; their adventures and hardships were over. From now on they were to watch with pride and gratification the development of their children; for no family in the dominion has produced so many distinguished men.

Little Willie Osler was put in a grammar school, where he led a group of boys into every conceivable prank until finally he was expelled. He went joyously home to report to his family that " he had the sack." No fear of a wigging. His incomparable mother simply realized that he had better be sent to a boarding school. He was merely, she knew, a fine young colt not yet fitted to harness; he would kick up his heels in the meadow, but if you got behind him he would not kick — so it was nothing to be troubled about. In the autumn of 1864 he was sent to a boarding school at Barrie, and again his spirits soared; he was numbered among a group called " Barrie's Bad Boys " and was, no doubt at all, an insufferable pest to his masters, though among his schoolmates he was a leader. His parents remained untroubled. Their son reverenced God and loved all his creatures; he was still only a colt kicking up his heels. But it was not all mischief. He was, one of his companions tells us, easily the first boy in school, and notably proficient in the Bible, and so kind and friendly. He had already a genius for friendship.

When the school at Barrie seemed on the wane, his parents sent him to Weston, a provincial Eton, and there he suffered from liberal canings and a most unhumorous head master. As you think of it, was there ever a humorous head master? Certainly few, if any, would have appreciated Willie Osler's style of humour. However that may be, it landed him and nine boon companions in jail. Still his mother was not concerned; he would get out. It was only a pity to make himself such a nuisance, and it might hurt the reputation of the school; so she sent him two dollars to pay the costs — and her love.

The incident that landed him in jail was one which he took a never-ending pleasure in relating to children. The matron of their school was detested by the boys. Her crimes reached a climax when she upset a bucket of slops over one of them. As soon as the coast was clear for action Willie Osler, two of the Warden's sons and six others, made a mixture of molasses, pepper and mustard, and put it on the stove so that the fumes would rise to her room through the stove pipe and smoke her out. The indignant and alarmed woman stuffed the hole with clothes; then the delighted boys got pointers and poked out the clothes. To keep from suffocating the victim sat on the register and shouted for help, much to the joy of the boys who poked her from below. Enters the Head Master at the crucial moment, rescues the woman and birches the boys. But that was not the just and happy ending of the incident; the woman, not satisfied, got a warrant against them for assault and battery, and they were duly arrested and spent three days in jail. Featherstone Osler, our hero's elder brother, defended the boys before a magistrate and got them off with a reprimand and the payment of one dollar.

Unquestionably what made his parents so philosophical about his escapades was that they knew their boy. They were soon justified in their faith, for a few years later, a fellow pupil of the school wrote: " A spirit of the highest refinement, culture, and straightforward manliness prevailed everywhere, true in the school and in the general life of all. It was easily recognized that this elevated tone was due to the influence of a small group of older boys, and of these, Osler, then seventeen, stood markedly the leader. His personality was so strong that his influence extended to every department, and his consistent high qualities were such that in every scope of activity he was recognized without bitterness or jealousy of any kind, as the head. This applies not alone to scholarship and sports of every kind, but his strong independence and clear positive character stood out in everything. I do not think his elevating influence in the school can be exaggerated, and it was such that when he went from school to college the effect of his personality remained and was unquestionably a strong element in giving character to the school for many years."

In a letter to his little nephew many years later he gave this version of the transformation:

" Dear Willum — Have you had the taws? Oh my, how they hurt. I had them often when I was Gwyn's age. After that I got good and did not need them."

A most unmodern method of conversion. What, however, seems to have been more effective than the taws was that at Weston he had the great good fortune to come in contact with two men who profoundly influenced his life. In a sense during the last school years at Weston he received the baptism of soul and mind. Father Johnson, priest and naturalist, and Dr. Bovell, physician and naturalist — and later priest — were like two very rare old volumes, first editions, in a bibliophile's library — not for general use. The rollicking eager boy found in them something that

corresponded to himself. It is an old and certain truth
that we only get from life what we bring to it. Were the
biographies of Johnson and Bovell written, upon the fly
leaf of each volume should be:

> Stand still, O man, and consider
> The wonderful works of God!
> We are the priests of the high mysteries.

Their young pupil brought to them and took from them
some of these qualities: the gentleness of their hearts towards suffering, their intense curiosity into natural phenomena, and their mystical and spiritual obsessions. He
did not take their fanaticism or any of the qualities that
made them so pathetically ineffective in their lives. He
far transcended his teachers, but a little of their quality
always remained with him. Father Johnson who was accustomed to read aloud to the boys in his parsonage, often
selected extracts from the *Religio Medici;* he who could
only clumsily fumble with the strings, touched a note on
a supreme instrument that would vibrate to that note all
its mortal life. The second book his pupil bought was the
Religio, the 1862 edition, and it was laid in his coffin fifty-
two years later. People have wondered how a youth of
seventeen could catch an inspiration that came from
scholar saints. Those who years later saw him watch a
voyager on his last journey would know exactly what he
brought to Sir Thomas Browne when, for the first time,
he heard the fascinating words of the *Religio.* But we are
with his youth now and it is a normal youth. His mother
wrote: " I see your name flourishing in the games "
and " I must scribble a line to tell you how proud we
were to see ' Osler first ' so many times in the paper to-
day." He was considered by his companions a fine all-
around athlete without being a champion in any way.
But though athletics had their share, he was almost as

obsessed as his teachers, Johnson and Bovell, over natural history.

A fellow pupil at Weston describes their field days: " It was our greatest treat when ' old Johnson ' could be led to take a squad out for a field day hunting fossils, and he did not need much persuasion. I can see the Warden wielding an old prospector's pick, and Osler, the most eager boy of the lot to secure a perfect orthoseratite or whatever Lower Silurian relic the soft stone about Weston might yield. . . . Osler, however, was the scientist of the expedition. To him was entrusted the delicate work of grinding down and mounting specimens for microscopic slides. Sometimes he might graciously, after the manner of Tom Sawyer, delegate some of his protracted mechanical grinding in the Water-of-Ayre stone to our less skilled hands — it wasn't every day that a boy had a chance to help in the construction of valuable scientific exhibits! Nevertheless experts pronounced them exceptionally fine — after Osler had put the finishing touches."

Fate was weaving fast the permanent threads in the fabric of the boy's life. Father Johnson was to be always a part of him; and now James Bovell comes into the pattern, deepening the colour and strengthening the design. These two men, more than any others, awakened the basic spiritual quality in William Osler.

Dr. James Bovell had been made medical director at the Trinity College School; he was in practice in Toronto and a teacher in the Medical College. But every week-end found him at Weston searching the woods and streams with Father Johnson for specimens, staining and mounting their collection for microscopical study. They genuflected before the mysteries; but as naturalists, they were just as fanatical. There was nothing in Nature that did not arouse in them the passion of the seeker and investigator. Their theology they kept in air-tight cells; Huxley and

Darwin could not break into them; but their religion was tenderly human and knew no bounds. The hunting of parasites, the marvels revealed by the microscope, were an absorbing dissipation and the young boy who was always with them was having a training than which there is none better on earth. Father Johnson's son gives us this reminiscence: " One thing I remember vividly. Old Bovell and my father were (as usual on the days Bovell spent at the rectory) working at the microscope case which had many tempting little drawers in it. And I (boylike) opened one of these drawers — when old Bovell said in his fash, impetuous, yet loving manner: ' Don't take that — that is one of the bones of Nebuchadnezzar's *Cat*. You *must* not have it.' It made a lasting impression on my boyish mind. That most probably occurred on one of those days when Osler and myself were rewarded by being allowed in my father's study for bringing home a good haul of frogs — used by Bovell and my father for studying the blood in the frog's foot."

Osler's powers of concentration were extraordinary; even as a boy he could be aloof in the midst of turmoil. The following story is characteristic: Pandemonium in the room full of fourth form boys when the Master was safely out of sight, and in the midst young Osler with his thumbs in his ears oblivious to everything but his book; then a well-inked paper dart roused him to summary vengeance; that accomplished he resumed his pose of what the boys called the deaf adder — and the remarkable part is that after a while the pose was respected.

At the end of the spring term as head of the class he received the Chancellor's prize; but Father Johnson strongly urged his remaining another year at school though he had passed all the subjects necessary for college. This good advice was taken; he returned in the autumn, worked hard for a scholarship and was interested in games. What, however, absorbed him most was, in conjunction with Father Johnson, collecting and tabulating Diatomaceae, and this was the beginning of his first scientific collection. A little later he became even more absorbed in the fresh-water polyzoa.

Though at this period he fully intended to enter the ministry, he was beginning to find the certainties of the theologian less appealing than the widening possibilities and surprises of the natural world; Dr. Bovell's influence was overshadowing that of Father Johnson. Years later when speaking of the value of Science in the public schools, he said:

" As a boy I had the common experience of fifty years ago — teachers whose sole object was to spoonfeed classes, not with the classics but with syntax and prosody, forcing our empty wits, as Milton says, ' to compose Theams, Verses and Orations,' wrung from poor striplings like blood from the nose, with the result that we loathed Xenophon and his ten thousand, Homer was an abomination, while Livy and Cicero were names and tasks. Ten years with really able Trinity College, Dublin, and Oxford teachers left me with no more real knowledge of Greek and Latin than of Chinese, and without the free use of the languages as keys to great literatures. Imagine the delight of a boy of an inquisitive nature to meet a man who cared nothing about words, but who knew about things — who knew the stars in their courses and could tell us their names, who delighted in the woods in spring-time, and told us about the frog-spawn and caddis worms, and who read us in the evenings Gilbert White — and Kingsley's ' Glaucus,' who showed us with the microscope the marvels of a drop of dirty pond water, and who on Saturday excursions up the river could talk of the Trilobites and Orthoceratites and explain the formation of the earth's crust. No more dry husks for me after such a diet, and early in my college life I kicked over the traces and exchanged the classics with ' divvers ' as represented by Pearson, Browne, and Hooker, for Hunter, Lyell and Huxley. From the study of nature to the study of man was an easy step. My experience was that of thousands, yet, as I remember, we were athirst for good literature. What a delight it would have been to have had Chapman's ' Odyssey ' read to us, or Plato's ' Phaedo ' on a Sunday evening, or the ' Vera Historia ' ! What a tragedy to climb Parnassus in a fog! How I have cursed the memory of Protagoras since finding that he introduced grammar into the curriculum, and forged the fetters which chained generations of schoolboys into the cold formalism of words! How different now that Montaigne and Milton and Locke and Petty have come into their own, and are recognized as men of sense in the matter of training youth."

All his faculties were now aroused; he was playing hard, studying hard. He had found his spiritual associations. Everyone who met him was his friend. His scientific curiosity was growing apace, but not yet did he realize that it was too keen for him to do what he still intended to do — go into the ministry.

In the autumn of 1867, at the age of eighteen, having gained the Dixon prize for Scholarship he went up to Trinity College, Toronto. Most of the teachers in the Arts course were clergymen and it was a good deal on the order of a divinity school. There he spent three months during which he was at Dr. Bovell's every Saturday, and he wrote: " We put up preparations for the microscope and I attend the medical school every afternoon. I am grinding at Lyell's ' Principles of Geology ' in vacation." We see, though he did not, where he was tending. He returned to Trinity for his second year in Arts — but he only endured it for a few days and then wrote to his parents and

the Provost his determination to go into medicine. When
Dr. Bovell heard of his decision he said, " That's splendid.
Come along with me."

This was the important turning-point in his life. It is
a curious paradox that he was diverted from the church
to medicine by the influence of Dr. Bovell who, himself,
was about to give up medicine for the church.

Of this turning-point Dr. Osler wrote later: " In my
school-days I was more bent upon mischief than upon
books — I say it with regret now — but as soon as I got
interested in medicine I had only a single idea and I do
believe that if I have had any measure of success at all,
it has been solely because of doing the day's work that
was before me just as faithfully and honestly and ener-
getically as I could."

Looking back with our present knowledge we see that
at this period his character and the line of his activities
were already determined. He was consecrated to his profession, and brought to it a glowing idealism; but there
was not in him a trace of eccentricity, so one could count
on his reactions to life; the unexpected never happened.

Fifty years later Osler wrote of Dr. Bovell's influence
upon him. " It has been remarked that for a young man
the privilege of browsing in a large and varied library is
the best introduction to a general education. My opportunity came to me in the winter of '69–70. Having sent his
family to the West Indies, Dr. Bovell took consulting
rooms on Spadina Avenue not far away from Mrs. Barwick, with whom he lived. He gave me a bedroom in the
house, and my duties were to help keep appointments —
an impossible job! — and to cut sections and prepare
specimens. Having catholic and extravagant tastes, he had
filled the room with a choice and varied collection of
books. After a review of the work of the day came the
long evening for browsing, and that winter (1869–70)

gave me a good first hand acquaintance with the original works of many of the great masters. After fifty years the position in these rooms of special books is fixed in my mind. Morton's ' Crania Americana,' Annesley's ' Diseases of India ' with the fine plates, the three volumes of Bright, the big folios of Dana, the monographs of Agassiz. Dr. Bovell had a passion for the great physician-naturalists and it was difficult for him to give a lecture without a reference to John Hunter. The diet was too rich and varied, and contributed possibly to the development of my somewhat ' splintery ' and illogical mind; but the experience was valuable and aroused an enduring interest in books. In such a decade of mental tumult as the '60's, really devout students of whom Dr. Bovell was one, were sore let and hindered, not to say bewildered, in attempts to reconcile Genesis and Geology. It seems hardly credible, but I heard a long debate on Philip Henry Gosse's (of to me, blessed memory) ' Omphalos, an Attempt to Untie the Geological Knot.' A dear old parson, Canon Read, stoutly maintained the possibility of the truth of Gosse's views that the strata and the fossils had been created by the Almighty to test our faith! A few years ago, reading ' Father and Son ' which appeared anonymously, the mention of this extraordinary ' Omphalos ' work revealed the identity and, alas! to my intense regret, the personality of the father as Philip Henry Gosse.

" Of this mental struggle the students reaped the benefit — for Dr. Bovell was much more likely to lecture on what was in his mind than on the schedule, and a new monograph on Darwin or a recent controversial pamphlet would occupy the allotted hour. One corner of the library was avoided. With an extraordinary affection for mental and moral philosophy, he had collected the works of Locke and Berkeley, Kant and Hegel, Spinoza and Descartes, as well as those of the moderns. He would joke about the impossibility of getting me to read any of these men, but at Trinity, in '67–68, I attended his lecture on Natural Theology and he really did get me interested in Cousin and Jouffroy and others of the French school. Three years of association with Dr. Bovell were most helpful. Books and the Man! — the best the human mind has afforded was on his shelves and in him all that one could desire in a teacher — a clear head and a loving heart. Infected with the Æsculapian spirit he made me realize the truth of these memorable words in the Hippocratic oath, " I will honour as my father the man who teaches me the Art."

Dr. Nevitt, one of Dr. Osler's contemporaries, gives this account of Dr. Bovell's consulting room: " One afternoon I had some engagement with William Osler and called for him at Dr. Bovell's office. The room was large and bare with a few chairs and a small table — like a kitchen table. Osler opened the drawer of the table — Dr. Bovell had gone out — and said: ' Look here! This drawer has been filled to overflowing with bills two or three times this afternoon and now look! ' One solitary bill lay in the drawer. As the patients paid their fees Osler placed them in the drawer. A needy patient came along and Dr. Bovell reversed the process and handed money out so that the sick man might get his medicine and the food and other things required."

How familiar Dr. Nevitt's account sounds to the later day patients of Dr. Osler! The system of payments was different but the spirit was the same — exactly.

We catch another glimpse of this period from Dr. Bovell's granddaughter:

" He (Osler) was about twenty in those days and literally lived at our house. He adored grandfather and the latter loved him like a son — and they were both crazy about the microscope. Mother (Mrs. Barwick) says her life was a perfect burden to her with parcels arriving, which might contain a rattlesnake, a few frogs, toads or dormice. She found quite a large snake meandering around the study one afternoon, and when she protested violently the two told her she should not have been there." After such an experience it would be trying to see your father conducting services in the chancel. That fate awaited Dr. Bovell's daughter in the future.

The medical schools at this period gave a two-year course in anatomy and fewer specialties were given the students then than now. This method, together with the fact that classes were small and the students in close personal contact with the instructor, led to thorough grounding in the fundamentals. The standards of the medical schools of to-day did not exist. The recollections of some of Osler's fellow-students at this time are that " he was always dissecting." Dr. McDonald, prosector in anatomy, speaks of him as spending more time than any other student in the dissecting room. A great deal of his work was done independently, working out his problem alone, and he found cysts of the *Trichina Spiralis* in a dissecting room cadaver, which had been overlooked by all others.

His study of natural history and his work with the microscope had increased his naturally acute observation. His interest in parasites had long been awakened. It has been said that, at this time, he might, if he had come under other influences, have abandoned medicine for biology; but one thing is quite certain: no career would ultimately have satisfied him that had not human beings for its first aim. He was a born physician, the friend of man.

It is a curious picture that comes to us, the brilliant youth destined to make his influence felt in many parts of the world, and his teachers Father Johnson and Dr. Bovell with their many obsessions — with no genius at all for life — bound together by strong ties of affection, madly hunting parasites and making voluminous notes, a microscope always in use.

Dr. Bovell had realized for some time that it would be wise for his pupil to change from the Toronto School to McGill University at Montreal; for the clinical opportunities there far exceeded those at Toronto. In 1870 Bovell went to the West Indies intending only to spend the summer there. A number of things occurred, however, which influenced him not to return to Toronto, but instead to establish his home permanently in the West Indies. This decision was a heavy blow to the boy who had been his intimate companion and friend, who had lived with him like a loved son, but it had the effect of making it easier for him to leave Toronto for Montreal.

There was something in Dr. Bovell that was always a puzzle to his former pupil, for he tries forever to explain the man; but he does not succeed, and always on the margin of his note-books he scribbles " James Bovell, M.D." Beyond the obvious similarity between pupil and master — their attitude to humanity, their reckless generosity and intellectual tastes — there lies something that is unexplained. We don't quite see what was the fascination. The years that are past leave us with queer memories. We do not always understand why some very little thing opened a window and let in the light — or closed one and left us in darkness. But what is certain, though we cannot see why, is that at this early period Father Johnson and Dr. Bovell brought into William Osler's life a spiritual, religious and mystical atmosphere that had always thereafter to be reckoned with; and at the same time they also set free his scientific interests. The personalities of Father Johnson and Dr. Bovell only survived the life of their pupil, but in him they survived with an almost unaccountable persistence.

In 1870 Osler left Toronto for Montreal, ready for

anything that might come his way. His new associates and friends were of a different type, and he began to work in a very active present world. In the evenings, however, the day's work done, he would return in spirit to Father Johnson and Dr. Bovell, and with them and his Bible and the *Religio,* he would explore the past. This nightly sweeping away from his mind of all things connected with his profession would enable him to start the next day fresh for vigorous work.

Laying the Foundation

Before the gates of excellence the high gods have placed sweat. Long is the road thereto and rough and steep at the first. But when the height is achieved then there is ease — though grievously hard in the winning.

Hesiod — *Works and Days.*

CHAPTER II

LAYING THE FOUNDATION

IN 1870 a group of Barrie schoolmates went up to McGill Medical School together and they made a gay crowd. From the echoes that come down to us we catch Willie Osler leading the laughter. McGill at Montreal was the leading Medical School in Canada. The Montreal General Hospital was in close touch with the School and the students were given unusual freedom in the wards. The School was founded by a Scot and the methods used in Edinburgh were closely followed. Osler became a special favourite of Dr. Howard, Professor of Medicine at McGill, who gave him the freedom of his house where he was generally to be found for Sunday dinner, unless he was at the home of his cousins, Mrs. Francis and Miss Jennette Osler, romping with the children and in intimate contact with women, much older than himself, but of such wit and charm that he was not tempted to go elsewhere. Willie Osler's imagination was instantly fired by Dr. Howard and his loyalty and affection captured. The name Robert Palmer Howard became permanently written on the boy's heart, not superseding but following those of Johnson and Bovell; for, unlike most youths, new enthusiasms did not destroy the old. All ties, local as well as personal, were unusually strong with him; they were often wrenched, they were never broken. His fate was always to move a step higher, and never to look back with regret on a step once taken. He carried with each upward move all the good of his past into the living present; and how alive that present was only those who have been with him could possibly conceive.

"In my early days," he wrote in *The Student Life* (1905) " I came under the influence of an ideal student-teacher, the late Palmer Howard of Montreal. If you ask what manner of man he was, read Matthew Arnold's noble tribute to his father in his well-known poem *Rugby Chapel*. When young, Dr. Howard had chosen a path — ' path to a clear purposed goal ' — and he pursued it with unswerving devotion. With him the study and the teaching of medicine were an absorbing passion, the ardour of which neither the incessant and ever-increasing demands upon his time nor the growing years could quench. When I first, as a senior student, came into intimate contact with him in the summer of 1871, the problem of tuberculosis was under discussion, stirred up by the epoch-making work of Villemin and the radical views of Niemeyer. Every lung lesion at the Montreal General Hospital had to be shown him, and I got my first-hand introduction to Laennec, to Graves, and to Stokes, and became familiar with their work. No matter what was the hour, and it was usually after 10 P.M., I was welcome with my bag, and if Wilks and Moxon, Virchow or Rokitansky gave us no help, there were the Transactions of the Pathological Society and the big *Dictionaire* of Dechambre. An ideal teacher, because a student, ever alert to the new problems, an indomitable energy enabled him in the midst of an exacting practice to maintain an ardent enthusiasm, still to keep bright the fires he had lighted in his youth. Since those days I have seen many teachers, and have had many colleagues, but I have never known one in whom was more happily combined a stern sense of duty with the mental freshness of youth."

Rugby Chapel has put into words the feelings of many youths towards some one who has helped them on the road;

indeed, it has become like a mortuary wreath. So it is not surprising that this supremely generous youth should glorify an attractive, very able and very fine man, who had opened his heart and his home to him, into a Dr. Arnold. But it is amazing that he could minimize all there was unattractive in Father Johnson. There is hardly a young man in the world who would not have been turned off by Dr. Johnson's sharp corners and his ideas of personal cleanliness, which were those of a medieval saint. But Dr. Osler kept his eyes on the saint and the naturalist. You never get a characterization from Dr. Osler, but an appreciation of what was best in the people he cared for; he had a very acute eye but he deliberately closed it to the faults in his fellow men. It was an intuitive attitude in his boyhood and a deliberate creed in his later years.

The three men who so influenced his early life were very unlike except in their integrity. Dr. Bovell, and more especially Father Johnson, were distinctly more concerned with the next world than with this one. Father Johnson, in a letter to the boy, writes thanking him for a gift of a copy of *Preparation for Death* by Defenso, Bishop of Agatha, and goes on to say: " The subject is one of all others I like best; really believing as I do, better is the day of a man's death than the day of his birth."

As he read this William Osler might have recalled the words of that other companion of his spirit, Sir Thomas Browne, who in the *Religio* writes: " The first day of our jubilee is death — and we are in the power of no calamity while death is our own." Strange atmosphere to be so congenial to a youth — and a merry youth — of twenty-one!

The path of his life, however, took a new direction under so capable a man as Dr. Howard. He began to feel that he must add to his equipment the functioning power of the executive, one who, once knowing his work to be right, would also put it over. But none the less, the name of James Bovell, M.D. continued to be written over and over again on the margin of Father Johnson's letter. It was about this time that Carlyle's words caught his eye: " Our main business in life is not to see what lies dimly at a distance but to do what lies clearly at hand." This sentence took him by storm. It was like an obsession. He uses it as a knight buckles on his armor. From this time he kept repeating it to himself and others; and, what is more important, he lived up to it. But if Dr. Howard gave him a more practical outlook for his profession, he could not, even had he so wished, obliterate that deeper hold the others held on what, for lack of a better term, we call his soul.

His mother is not concerned about his soul. She rejoices over his normal development: " I will send one of Willie's photographs as soon as I get them from Montreal where he is going on in a very satisfactory manner. A great favourite with everyone, the leading medical men especially." And from a cousin's letter: " I cannot tell what a pleasure it is to have the dear merry fellow coming in and out. We hear his praises on all sides and from those whose opinion is hard to win and worth having. He is pronounced thoroughly reliable, ' as good as he is clever,' ' the most promising student of the year,' and finally from a learned professor, slow to praise, ' a splendid fellow.' "

He found time in the midst of the hard work necessary for his degrees, to keep a running interest in his entozoa collection. His letters to Father Johnson and Dr. Bovell show him almost as keen in collecting his specimens as he was when they searched the ponds and fields together; but he was turning more and more to clinical work and gradually the active field collecting ceased.

Constantly we hear from his colleagues how remarkable it is that he should find time for general reading and should acquire in the midst of strenuous student work, a wide familiarity with great literature; but it is not surprising; for what we will have we will have, and no amount of necessary work will keep a lover of books away from them. When you hear anyone say: " Alas! no time to read now! " You know that particular dissipation is not his. If young Osler read for any reason at all except that he must, he read for inspiration. At twenty-two the style of his literary work was fixed. Anyone reading his first thesis and not knowing by whom it was written would have said: " That is an early venture of Sir Thomas Browne." And as no one could have been less imitative of others than William Osler — " the style was the man." His love of books began in his seventeenth year when working with Father Johnson. His first book purchase was the *Globe Shakespeare;* his second *The Religio.* Later when he had the freedom of Dr. Bovell's library the germ of the bibliophile grew apace.

From boyhood to young manhood he has shown himself to have the very ecstasy of life — a touchstone that brought out the good no matter in what bog it was hidden. He could drink the wine of life with the gayest and not be intoxicated. A rollicking boy like many boys; a gay youth like many youths; an eager student, a tremendous worker. Enough to fill those that watched him with hope for great things.

He was not a Gold Medalist in his graduating year but he received at the end of the term the following honourable mention: " The faculty has in addition this session awarded a special prize to the thesis of William Osler, Dundas, Ontario, which is greatly distinguished for originality and research and was accompanied by 33 microscopic and other preparations of morbid structure kindly presented by the author to the museum of the Faculty."

Towards the end of his life he wrote his recollections

of these student days: " When I began clinical work in 1870 the Montreal General Hospital was an old coccus-and-rat-ridden building, but with two valuable assets for the students — much acute disease and a group of keen teachers. Pneumonia, phthisis, sepsis and dysentery were rife. The ' services ' were not separated, and a man for three months looked after the medical and surgical patients jumbled together in the same wards. The physic of the men who were really surgeons was better than the surgery of the men who were really physicians, which is the best thing that can be said of a very bad arrangement — Scottish and English methods prevailed, and we had to serve our time as dressers and clerks, and, indeed, in serious cases we very often at night took our share in the nursing. There were four first-rate teachers of medicine on the staff — Howard, Wright, MacCallum and Drake — three of whom had learned at first hand the great language of Graves and of Stokes. The bedside instruction was excellent and the clerking a serious business. I spent the greater part of the summer of 1871 at the hospital, and we had admirable out-patient clinics from Dr. Howard and small groups worked in the wards under Dr. MacCallum. An excellent plan, copied from the old custom of *Lancet,* was for the clinical clerk to report the cases of special interest under *Hospital Practice* in the local medical monthly. My first appearance in print is in the Canadian Medical and Surgical Journal, reporting cases from Dr. MacCallum's wards. Our teachers were men in whose busy lives in large general practice the hospital work was a pleasant and profitable interest. A man like Palmer Howard got all that was possible out of the position, working hard at the hospital, studying the literature, writing excellent papers, and teaching with extraordinary care and accuracy; naturally such a man exercised a wide influence, lay and medical. I left the old General Hospital with a good deal of practical experience to my credit and with warm friends among the members of the staff."

The years of his Canadian apprenticeship came to an end; on July 3, 1872 he sailed for Europe to spend two years at foreign universities. For those who are following him in his life it may seem a dull path at this time, unless they are medical students; but even a lay reader catches a thrill of his eager awakening to the possibilities of his profession. Provinciality slips from him like a cast-off mantle.

He gives the following account of his experience there: "After a short *Rundreise,* Dublin, Glasgow and Edinburgh, I settled at the Physiology Laboratory of University College, with Professor Burdon-Sanderson, where I spent about fifteen months working at histology and physiology. At the hospital across the way I saw in full living the admirable English system, with the ward work done by the student himself the essential feature. I was not a regular student of the hospital, but through the kind introduction of Dr. Burdon-Sanderson and of Dr. Charlton Bastian, an old family friend, I had many opportunities of seeing Jenner and Wilson Fox and my note-books contain many precepts of these model clinicians. From Ringer, Bastian and Tilbury Fox, I learned, too, how attractive out-patient teaching could be made. Ringer, I always felt, missed his generation, and suffered from living in advance of it."

In a note-book of this time is written: Wm. Osler, M.D., London, July 1872, Cash Account, "Be frugal." That worthy resolve must have been instigated by his mother, and also it must have been given with little hope of its being followed. For a while, however, he kept his small accounts — and what a virtuous period it must have seemed to him! It was soon over. He was far from being a spendthrift, but he was a hopeless giver. His scantily filled purse was open to all comers and he was often with empty pockets.

While on the East Coast he visited Norwich and saw the skull of Sir Thomas Browne. He stood in the old Museum of the Norfolk and Norwich Infirmary and held in his young hands that empty skull! Many of the inspirations that were feeding his own soul had emanated from that sad relic, once so full of beauty and far-reaching thought. "Alas! poor Yorick!" The newly dead may reasonably expect a tear or two and a few days' remembrance, but for the ancient dead to find a spiritual son considering their mortal remains with a reverent and full heart — that is to have lived! He tells of this visit in an address at Guy's Hospital in 1906: "The tender sympathy with the poor relics of humanity which Browne expressed so beautifully in these two meditations (*Urn Burial* and *A Letter to a Friend*) was not meted to his own. 'Who knows the fate of his bones or how often he is to be buried?' he asks. In 1840 while workmen were repairing the chancel of St. Peter Mancroft the coffin of Sir Thomas was accidentally opened, and one of the workmen took the skull which afterwards came into the possession of Dr. Edward Lubbock who deposited it in the Museum of the Norfolk and Norwich Infirmary. When I first saw it there in 1872 there was on it a printed slip with these lines from 'Hydrotaphia': 'To be knaved out of our own graves, to have our skulls made drinking-bowls and our bones turned into pipes, to delight and sport our enemies, are tragical abominations escaped in burning burials.' "

When Osler first went abroad it had evidently been his intention to take up the study of Ophthalmology. He had talked over this plan with Dr. Howard before leaving Canada and they both had hoped that he might eventually obtain a position as oculist at McGill. But three months after he had been in Europe Dr. Howard wrote telling him that things had occurred that would make his chances very dubious and strongly advised him to cultivate the whole field of medicine and surgery, paying especial attention to practical physiology. This was a great disappointment to him, as he shows in a letter to Dr. Howard: " I now have to look forward to a general practice and I confess to you it is not with the greatest amount of pleasure. I had hoped in an ophthalmic practice to have a considerable amount of time at my disposal and a fair return in a shorter time. . . ."

Bowman was the most eminent eye specialist of the day and young Osler had a great admiration for him; he felt that he was the order of man who had been able to reach prominence in a specialty because of his thorough grounding in science; but Bowman was also an enthusiast in physiology and he urged that no matter what Osler undertook in the future, he should take a period of work at University College. And Father Johnson, writing in a long letter from Canada full of advice says: " May you not lessen your usefulness and knowledge in passing by general information to pursue a speciality."

The consensus of advice was taken and he spent seventeen months in Sanderson's Laboratory. Thirty-five years later he succeeded Sanderson as Regius Professor of Medicine at Oxford. But there was no prophet to tell him of this destiny; nor would he have listened to any if there had been. He lived as he urged others to live, in the present. A great dreamer but not of the things that are temporal.

In Europe in the '70's there were important advances in anatomy, pathology and physiology: and Dr. Cushing writes: " It was into this situation of physiological investigation for which Burdon-Sanderson, Michael Foster, Lauder Brunton, and E. Klein were chiefly responsible, that Osler was introduced, and it was one of which his early familiarity with the microscope and his growing taste for experimental pathology particularly qualified him to take advantage. The situation, too, explains in a measure, his peculiar fitness despite his youth for the position offered him two years later at McGill as Professor of the Institutes of Medicine, then comprising physiology, histology and pathology. Unless perhaps with Cohnheim in Germany, no more stimulating group could possibly have been found than those who were at work in the '70's in Burdon-Sanderson's laboratory."

Osler wrote to Dr. Howard: " I have a little private work going on under Dr. Sanderson's superintendence connected with the antagonistic action of atropine and physostigmin on the white corpuscles; but whether it will come to anything or not remains to be seen. However, in any case, the practice is helpful. I propose after Christmas taking a thorough course in practical chemistry on your advice for, of course, that is the basis of many physiological investigations."

In May he read a paper before the Royal Microscopical Society which was published in its Journal, and which led to his being elected a member of that body. The result of the summer's work was the discovery of the blood platelets, perhaps his most important contribution to knowledge. The report of his observations was presented by Sanderson before the Royal Society in the following spring. When the news reached Montreal of his discovery there was great rejoicing and Dr. Palmer Howard in the opening address at McGill in October said: " In connection with this new subject of scientific interest, the older students present as well as my colleagues, will be pleased to hear that Dr. Osler who graduated here in 1872, has just made a discovery of great interest and that promises well for the future of our young countryman. I wish that some friend of this University would endow a Chair of Physiological and Pathological Histology and that our young friend might be invited to accept the appointment and devote himself solely to the cultivation of his favourite subject, and at the same time bring honour to himself and Canada."

His young friend was just about to leave England for the Continent and was busy over a letter to the Canadian Medical Journal, decrying the waste of time and money spent by young Canadians grinding to pass the English qualification examinations. He calls them neither degrees nor honours and insists that his young countrymen had far better use their time and money in hospital work. Nevertheless with so conservative a mentor in Canada as Dr. Howard, he did the prescribed thing — and became the Licentiate of the College in this year; and in 1878 he passed his examination of membership in the Royal College of Physicians.

He wrote to his sister that he was sorry to say good-bye to London, not such a bad place for a year and much to be picked up; and with this verdict upon his motherland, he went gaily off to Berlin.

Berlin in 1873 he found unattractive in appearance and deficient in drainage; but " the Berlinese have, however, at last roused themselves, and the council has voted two millions sterling for sanitary purposes, so that a striking reduction in the present high death-rate from typhoid and kindred diseases may be shortly expected. It would be superfluous to speak of the advantages here offered for medical studies. The names of Virchow, Traube and Frerichs in medicine and pathology; of Langenbeck and Bardeleben in surgery, of Du Bois-Reymond and Helmholtz in physiology and physics are sufficient guarantees; all of these men, who though they have been prominent figures in the medical world for a long time, are still in their prime as teachers and workers. In contrast to

London, where the teaching is spread over some twelve
schools, it is here centralized and confined to the Royal
Charité — for though there are several small hospitals in
the city, yet they have no schools in connection with them,
but are used chiefly for training nurses. . . . There are
only three or four Americans here, and the same number
of Englishmen. They go chiefly to Vienna, where they
have greater advantages in all specialities. The native students are a hard-working set." He remarked on the great
number who wore glasses; he spoke of the diminution in
attendance and attributed it to the increased cost of living;
and he added, "from a six-weeks' experience, I find it
quite as dear as London. Field sports, such as cricket and
football are unknown among the students, but they have
a curious habit of forming small societies of ten or twelve,
who have a room at some restaurant where they meet to
drink beer, smoke, and discuss various topics. If tobacco
and beer have such a deteriorating effect on the mind and
body, as some of our advanced teetotallers affirm, we ought
to see the signs of it here; but the sturdy Teuton, judging
from the effects of the past few years, has not degenerated
physically, at any rate, while intellectually he is still to
the fore in most scientific subjects; whether, however, in
spite of — or with the aid of the ' fragrant weed ' and the
' flowing bowl ' could hardly be decided. Drunkenness is
not common, or at least not obtrusively so, but they appear to get a fair number of cases of delirium tremens in
the Charité. But it is the master mind of Virchow and the
splendid Pathological Institute which rises like a branch
hospital in the grounds of the Charité, that specially attracts foreign pupils to Berlin. This most remarkable man
is yet in his prime (52 years of age) and the small, wiry,
active figure looks good for another twenty years of hard
work; when one knows that in addition to the work at the
Institute, given below, he is an ardent politician, evi-

dently the leader of the Prussian Opposition, and a member on whom a large share of the work of the budget falls, an active citizen, member of the Council, and the moving spirit in the new canalization or sewerage system; an enthusiastic anthropologist as well as a working member in several smaller affairs, some idea may be formed of the comprehensive intellect and untiring energy of the man. On Monday, Wednesday and Friday from 8:30 to 11:00 he holds his demonstrative course on pathology; the other mornings of the week the course on pathological histology, while on the fourth day at one o'clock he lectures on general pathology. Virchow himself performs a post mortem on Monday morning making it with such care and minuteness that three or four hours may elapse before it is finished. The very first morning of my attendance he spent exactly half an hour in the description of the Skull-Cap. On Wednesday and Saturday the demonstration takes place in a large lecture room accommodating about 140 students, and with the tables so arranged that microscopes can circulate continuously on a small tramway let into them. Generally the material from 10 to 12 post mortems is demonstrated, the lecturer taking up any special group and enlarging on it with the aid of sketches on the black board and microscopical specimens, while the organs are passed round on wooden platters for inspection. A well provided laboratory for physiological and pathological chemistry also exists as well as rooms where men may carry on private investigations, and a library and reading room is now being fitted up."

These lessons learnt in the experience of seeing genius at work, he absorbed and they became a part of his own equipment. And the notes he took at that time were to be of inestimable value later on.

As he whistled along those dreary Berlin streets and by the depressing Spree, he must have looked something like

a beloved vagabond but it was entirely on the surface;
his pleasures and only dissipation at that time were work.
January finds him in Vienna. After recounting a number
of things in the city he had found interesting, he notes:
" 7th, Wednesday, Commenced work with Bamberger at
8:30. Neumann at 10. Wiederhofer at 11, and Braun from
12 to 2. Much pleased with this my first introduction to
Vienna teachers and material." Berlin, however, held the
first place for him. He speaks of Bamberger as " a splendid
diagnostician, but is, I think, inferior to those Berlin
giants, Traube and Frerichs." He adds that " midwifery
and skin diseases are the specialities in Vienna, while in
general medicine and pathology it is infinitely below
Berlin. . . . After having seen Virchow it is absolutely
painful to attend post mortems; they are performed in so
slovenly a manner and so little use is made of the material."

Osler's chief interest lay in pathology but he was aiming
at a broad grounding in general medicine and the specialties.

In 1908 he revisited Vienna and he gave the following
charming account of his visit: " As a medical centre,
Vienna has had a remarkable career, and her influence,
particularly on American medicine, has been very great.
What was known as the first Vienna School in the eighteenth century was really a transference by van Swieten of
the School of Boerhaave from Leyden. The New Vienna
School, which we know, dates from Rokitansky and Skoda,
who really made Vienna the successor of the great Paris
school of the early days of the nineteenth century. But
Vienna's influence on American medicine has not been so
much through Skoda and Rokitansky as through the group
of brilliant specialists — Hebra, Sigmund and Neumann
in dermatology; Arlt and Jaeger in ophthalmology;
Schnitzler and von Schrötter in laryngology; Gruber and
Politzar in otology. These are the men who have been

more than any others responsible for the successful development of these specialties in the United States. Austria may well be proud of what Vienna's School has done for the world, and she still maintains a great reputation, though it cannot be denied, I think, that the Æsculapian center has moved from the Danube to the Spree. But this is what has happened in all ages. Minerva Medica has never had her chief temples in any one country for more than a generation or two. For a long period at the Renaissance she dwelt in northern Italy, and from all parts of the world men flocked to Padua and to Bologna. Then for some reason of her own she went to Holland, where she set up her chief temple at Leyden with Boerhaave as her high priest. Uncertain for a time, she flitted here with Boerhaave's pupils, van Swieten and de Haen; and could she have come to terms about a temple she doubtless would have stayed permanently in London where she found in John Hunter a great high priest. In the first four decades of the nineteenth century she lived in France, where she built a glorious temple to which all flocked. Why she left Paris, who can say? But suddenly she appeared here, and Rokitansky and Skoda rebuilt for her the temple of the new Vienna School; but she did not stay long. She had never settled in northern Germany, for though she loves art and science, she hates with a deadly hatred philosophy and all philosophical systems applied to her favourite study. Her stately German shrines, her beautiful Alexandrian home, her noble temples, were destroyed by philosophy. Not until she saw in Johannes Müller and in Rudolph Virchow true and loyal disciples did she move to Germany where she stays in spite of the tempting offers from France, from Italy, from England, and from Austria.

" In an interview most graciously granted to me, as a votary of long standing, she expressed herself very well satisfied with her present home where she has much honour and is much appreciated. I boldly suggested that it was perhaps time to think of crossing the Atlantic and setting up her temple in the New World for a generation or two. I spoke of the many advantages, of the absence of tradition — here she visibly weakened, as she has suffered so much from this poison — the greater freedom, the enthusiasm, and then I spoke of missionary work. At these words she turned on me sharply and said: ' That is not for me. We Gods have but one motto: Those that honour us we honour. Give me the temples, give me the priests, give me the true worship, the old Hippocratic service of the art and of the science of ministering to man, and I will come. By the eternal law under which we Gods live I would have to come. I did not wish to leave Paris, where I was so happy and where I was served so faithfully by Bichat, by Laennec and by Louis! ' — and the tears filled her eyes and her voice trembled with emotion — ' but where the worshippers are most devoted, not mark you, where they are the most numerous; where the clouds of incense rise highest, there must my chief temple be, and to it from all quarters will the faithful flock. As it was in Greece, in Alexandria, in Rome, in northern Italy, in France, so is it now in Germany, and so it *may be* in the New World I long to see.' Doubtless she will come, but not until the present crude organization of our medical clinics is changed, not until there is a fuller realization of internal medicine as a science as well as an art." This is written in Sir William's happiest vein — so whimsical and so charming, not unlike Oliver Wendell Holmes.

His student days abroad contain only an entire devotion to work; London, Berlin, Paris, Vienna, held no allurements, seeing them for the first time, except in the vistas they opened up to him in his profession. He seems to have closed his mind to all outside diversion. This tremendous concentration relaxed only momentarily now and then to play some practical joke on a colleague or romp with a child. His home letters, except when they touch on his work, are the extreme of the commonplace. You always learn of him in a dead house or in a laboratory or attending a clinic, lapping up information on tiptoe to catch a fresh impression; or making his own experiments.

The results are interesting enough. He returned to Canada with the enlarged outlook that made him a vital factor in the great changes that were taking place in Medicine. He brought back with him the onsweeping wind of the new era. His days of apprenticeship were over; and from this time, though always a student, he was a leader.

Montreal

Knowledge and Wisdom, far from being one,
Have ofttimes no connection. Knowledge dwells
In heads replete with thoughts of other men;
Wisdom in minds attentive to their own.
Knowledge is proud that he has learned so much,
Wisdom is humble that he knows no more.

Cowper.

CHAPTER III

MONTREAL

THE young doctor, home from abroad seems to have accomplished a good deal even in the first few weeks. He reports " speck in the cornea, 50 cents." And we hear that he acted as *locum tenens* for Dr. Charles O'Reilly, Resident Physician at the City Hospital in Hamilton. This undertaking brought him $25 and a pair of elastic boots, which were thrown in with the money as they were too small for Dr. O'Reilly. These ventures into financial independence he greatly delighted to recount; but the Bohemian frolic for a living lasted a very short time. On July 6, 1874, Dr. Palmer Howard wrote informing him of his appointment as Lecturer upon Institutes at McGill University, Montreal, to succeed Dr. Drake who had resigned because of ill health. After expressing his own pleasure in this appointment for his young friend and giving him some good advice he writes: " Please present my congratulations to your father upon this gratifying recognition of your merits by the oldest medical school in Canada."

Dr. Osler replied: " I do not accept without some diffidence; still I hope to be able to work up a decent set of lectures. I am glad it is only a lectureship. It not only sounds better (as I am young) but to my English friends, Sanderson, Sharpey, Klein, *etc.*, it will seem more in keeping with what they know of my attainments. It now remains to be seen whether with teaching (and private practice) I can follow up my original work. Of course I shall try hard."

When in Dundas and Hamilton during these weeks after his return from abroad, he was not only making $25.50 and shoes, but he was meeting relatives and friends and cementing friendships with the older medical men. The size of his fees and the size of his friendships were very much out of proportion. His friends were of all grades from the leading surgeons in the district to the humblest — and the humblest never failed to receive the greater part of his attention.

Dr. Osler some years after, in an address about doctors' signs, gives a charming account of Dr. Case, a physician of the old school: " Happy the man whose reputation is such or whose local habitation is so well known that he needs no sign! This is sometimes the case in country places and small towns, not often in cities. We know of one such in a prosperous Canadian city. Grandfather, father and son have been in ' the old stand ' so long that to the inhabitants of the locality the doctor's house is amongst the things that have always been. The patients' entrance is in a side street and a small porch protects the visitor. The steps are well-worn and the native grain is everywhere visible in the wooden surroundings. There is neither bell nor knocker and the door presents interesting, and, so far as we know, unique evidences that votaries to this Æsculapian shrine have not been lacking. On the panels at different heights are three well-worn places where the knuckles of succeeding generations of callers have rapped and rapped and rapped. The lowest of the three, about three feet from the floor, represents the work of ' Tiny Tim ' and ' Little Nell,' so often the messengers in poorer families. Higher and of less extent is a second depression where ' Bub ' and ' Sis ' have pounded, and highest of all, in the upper panels a wider area where the firmer fists

of the fathers and brothers have as years rolled on worn
away the wood to nearly half its thickness. Such a testimony to the esteem and faithfulness of successive generations of patients is worthy of preservation." As a matter
of fact when the old house was demolished in 1894 the
door was saved and is now in the Hamilton Museum in
Dundurn Park.

The calls that came upon his own heart could have
registered just such a story. No. 1 West Franklin Street
in Baltimore, and No. 13 Norham Gardens in Oxford
needed no sign.

In August he went to Montreal, found a room at 20 Rad-
gonde Street below Beaver Hill in the lower part of the
town, and hung out his shingle. His office was conducted
after the fashion of Dr. Bovell's — as fast as a fee came
in from a well-to-do patient it went out to a poor one.
Few, however, ever came to the door or found him there
when they came. Even in those early days when a good
deal out of pocket he was averse to general practice, and
he fully realized the advantage of not having anyone de-
pendent upon him. He writes that preparing lectures
was a " ghastly task "; but if writing the lectures bored
him he felt it essential that they should not bore his students. One of them referring to these lectures, writes:
" From that hour physiology was an attractive study and
the lectures like unto the Gods." His intuitive sense of
psychology that awoke the moment he looked at you, was
almost in every case sympathetic. And he could give a
sparkle to any subject so that the dullest ears heard and
caught a little. Dr. Osler often said that his " only talent
was industry "; but great as that was, his real power over
others was that of inspiration — no sails meaninglessly
flapped to the wind when he took the tiller. Another thing
that endeared him even to the wrecks in his pathway was
that he took not the least pleasure in pricking their bub-

bles. No blower of bubbles himself and with a sad certainty that most he saw floating in the air would never be landed but would break into vapor — he was sorry.

With his coming to McGill a renaissance began in which he was the moving spirit. They had, however, a strong group of young men — Ross, Roddick, Shepherd and Gardner — men of the highest professional type. Dr. Palmer Howard had something of the insight that was so marked a quality in the late Daniel Coit Gilman, first President of Johns Hopkins: of knowing the right men and knowing them when they were young. When our young lecturer made his first address to his students the rules of life he urged upon them were the ones lived by himself, never changing with the passing years. In substance they were: You must always be a student. You must treat the man as well as the disease. The poor you have always with you and you must consider them beyond all others. He quotes Sir Thomas Browne: "No one should approach the temple of science with the soul of a money-changer." He urged his students to keep in close and friendly touch with physicians, coöperating with them, writing frequently for the medical journals, attending meetings, *etc.* His own "consuming zeal for his fellow creatures" shone out very clearly from the beginning. In spite of all the worry of preparing lectures and doing conscientiously what he must do, he took on voluntary work in the pathological laboratory. The visiting physicians and surgeons were accustomed to perform their own autopsies but gradually they began to look to Dr. Osler and it became evident that sooner or later the position of pathologist would be created for him. In the spring of 1875 he was appointed to Dr. Drake's chair as Professor of the Institutes of Medicine.

Needing far more money than he had, if he was to make his department what he felt it should be, and to equip

it with the necessary microscopes, he undertook, for a
small salary, work in the smallpox ward of the Montreal
General.

This hospital held about 150 beds. It was ill-lighted
and ill-ventilated. The nurses seem to have been in about
the same stage as they were when in 1854 Florence Nightingale described them in no uncertain voice: " They were
untrained and many of them drank." Florence Nightingale's " Agitate! agitate! " had succeeded in England as
far back as 1860 when the Nightingale School for Nurses
was established. But in Montreal the campaign for better
things was only beginning and smallpox in a particularly
malignant form was rife. Though it was epidemic everywhere it was particularly serious in the seaport towns. Vaccination was not compulsory; re-vaccination was rare;
quarantine infrequent. The Montreal General had made
efforts to revoke a law requiring all hospitals receiving
grants from the legislature to accept smallpox patients. In
Boston, Massachusetts, only one case was reported in
twelve months whereas in the Montreal General there
were always 100 cases at a time. While the journals were
bringing before the public the seriousness of the situation, Professor Osler was having his first chance to have
hospital patients under his control and was perhaps too
enthusiastically at work to enter into the civic side. He
could not have chosen a better time for active service as
the epidemic was at its height during the summer. In
September there was an anti-vaccination riot and great
agitation everywhere, but he was so absorbed in his work
that he did not seem to have noticed the excitement. He
had post mortem material at hand and was making the
most of it.

Many papers were inspired by this experience, on the
pathology of the miners' lung, on the pathology of smallpox, on the development of vaccine, on the initial rashes

and on the hæmorrhagic form of smallpox, which is the most virulent form of the disease known. In regard to the latter he wrote: " The epidemic which has raged in this city for the past five years has been remarkable for the prevalence of this variety of disease and the present paper is based on 17 cases, 14 of which came under my own observation, chiefly at the General Hospital; while the remaining 13 were under the care of my predecessor, Dr. Simpson, to whose kindness I am indebted for permission to utilize them. In the smallpox department of Montreal General Hospital there were admitted from December 14th, 1873 to July 21st, 1875 — one year and seven months — 260 cases. Of these 24 died of the variety under discussion, or 9.23 per cent."

Dr. Osler contracted the disease in a very light form; he had been vaccinated several times, and he always referred to his experience as showing that, though re-vaccination was imperative, it did not make immunity certain.

One day when at his Club, Dr. Osler noticed that an attractive young Englishman, a stranger in Montreal, with whom he had often talked, seemed ill. On questioning him, his suspicions were aroused, and he advised him to go at once to his home and to bed. It soon developed that he had malignant smallpox and in a few days he died. Dr. Osler's letter to the boy's father shows the strong sympathy with suffering which was so characteristic of him.

" My dear Sir:

No doubt before this, the sorrowful intelligence of your son's death has reached you, and now when the first shock has perhaps to a slight extent passed away, some further particulars of his illness may be satisfactory. On the evening of Thursday the 22nd and on the following day I discovered unmistakable evidence of the nature of the disease. On Saturday in consultation with Dr. Howard, the leading practitioner of the city, his removal to the small-pox hospital was decided upon. I secured a private ward and took him there in the evening. Even at this date was seen the serious nature of the case and I sent for Mr. Wood at his request. At 10 P.M. I found him with your son, and we left him tolerably comfortable for the night. He was easier Sunday morning, but well aware of his dangerous state. He spoke to me of his home and his mother and asked me to read the 43d Chapter of Isaiah which she had marked in his Bible. I spent the greater part of the evening talking and reading with him. Mr. Wood called in three or four times in the day and at 9.30 P.M. I found him there again. Mr. Norman had also been in just previously. He was still sensible and requested to see Dr. Howard again in consultation with Dr. Simpson, the attending physician in the smallpox hospital. After 11 o'clock he began to sink rapidly and asked me not to leave him. He did not speak much but turned round at intervals to see if I were still by him. About 12 o'clock I heard him muttering some prayers but could not catch distinctly what they were — ' God the Father, Son and Spirit.' Shortly after this he turned round and held out his hand which I took and he said quite plainly: ' Oh, thanks! ' These were the last words the poor fellow spoke. From 12:30 he was unconscious, and at 1:25 passed away without a groan or a struggle. As the son of a clergyman and knowing well what it is to be a ' stranger in a strange land,' I performed the last office of Christian friendliness I could and read the commendatory prayers at his departure.

" Such, my dear Sir, as briefly as I can give them are the facts relating to your son's death."

This letter is so gravely important, so sweet, so very young. In later years Osler the Man was very chary of speaking of religion. He was very chary of *any* words; but a later day patient would know what a boy in a strange land, on the brink of a far stranger land, would have felt with his hand in Osler's. There are people whose features set free their personality. Dr. Osler's vivid face released a spirit, wholly irresistible. The effect of his debonair manner and ready banter, his quick step and radiant vitality were like oxygen in a sick room. But the ill patient never felt him gay; he felt only that a strong hand was stretched out to help him and, curiously, he felt the room empty of all except his physician and himself and power. Patient after patient in one form or another has expressed something to this effect.

His work at the bedside was twofold. He brought insight and, in execution, a brilliant ability to cope with disease — and then when everything that was human had failed — he brought something less tangible but enduring. The memory comes back of him standing at the bedside of a patient for whom he had done all that he could — one hand upon his patient's heart, his watch in the other, counting the slowing, slowing, slowing beat — then stillness. The look that would come in his eyes cannot be forgotten: intent, far-off, following the spirit in its flight. Drawing the cover about the dead as gently as for a sleeping child, he would turn away — perhaps whistling. There never could have been a student so dull as not to have caught that look or one who, knowing him and hearing his whistle, would have thought him unfeeling. To a physician who did not know him and who had once spoken almost in rebuke of some seeming frivolity in his manner. Dr. Osler's answer was: " If I laugh at any living thing 'tis that I may not weep."

The temperament of a man who feels as he did generally goes with the introspective type — with often a touch of sentimentality and a dramatic eye but he was entirely unsentimental; and dramatizing a situation was an im-

possible thing for him to do. It gives a biographer a hard
task to catch him in an event or after an event — generally
he is only caught by a snap shot — he is so quickly out
of an incident — and one was always surprised that the
effect endured so long.

Dr. Barker in his " Note on Osler as Chief of a Medical
Clinic" gives us this insight: " Much might be written
were there space, of the ways in which he overcame ob-
stacles and met important emergencies, of the motives he
appealed to when he desired to excite men to action or to
arrive at a decision, and in general, of those traits of
character ' that act directly by presence, and without
means,' or what is sometimes called ' personal magne-
tism.' Many of the qualities that make for successful management, though easy enough to recognize when they exist,
are difficult of analysis and perplexing to the understanding. Some men are able to secure control without contest;
' whether they stand or walk or sit or whatever thing they
do,' they can place men under their power. Of such char-
acter-control and of prestige-control Professor Osler had
his full share." The psychological instinct of Dr. Osler
was entirely intuitive, unsought; and in contrast to his
pathological work, not laboriously developed.

Early in the spring of 1876 a smallpox hospital was provided in Montreal, and the position of pathologist to the
hospital was created and given to Dr. Osler. In the autopsy
room of the hospital he laid the foundation of his career
as a great clinician. A three months' summer session was
offered to the students of the Montreal General, and the
announcement, after enumerating the lectures, concluded
with " and last but not least we have Dr. Osler who is an
enthusiast in his department, who will give a course of
twenty-five lessons in Practical Histology, and also a course
of Practical Pathological Demonstration in the post mortem room."

All this immense amount of painstaking work, which gave a permanent structure to his mind, cannot be too strongly emphasized for there was such enchantment about the man that those near him became absorbed in the glamour and charm of his personality and the Christ-like quality of his nature, and in realizing what he was, overlooked what he had accomplished. Rapid and meteorlike his grasp of a subject but no dullard had ever spent a more laborious apprenticeship. That he had unusual eyes to see, and ears to hear, and heart to feel, only meant for him an increase of labour. He made post mortems, preserved specimens of diseased tissue, mounted them for the microscope, labelled them, studied them, and filed them away for future use. Dr. Abbott tells us: " The fact is not so well known, that during these years, and even earlier, in his student days, he was not only a pathologist, but also, essentially and to a remarkable extent, a museum collector. Just as he was, throughout his life, to use his own words, a note-book man, jotting down for future reference, every point of interest as it occurred, so it was natural for him to set aside for preservation, as a permanent record of important facts, any remarkable material which he came across in his autopsies which illustrated points of teaching value, or which were to him of interest as a basis for intensive study. In this way he quickly assembled a collection which, while especially rich in specimens of cardiac and arterial, gastric and lung diseases, is representative also of the whole range of human morbid anatomy, as well as significant of his activities in veterinary and medico-legal medicine. Each specimen has been neatly chiselled down to show the lesion freed from encumbering details, and remains of scientific interest to-day, bearing silent but emphatic witness to his skill in dissection and selective faculty. All are fully described in his hospital protocol of the seven hundred and eighty-seven autopsies performed by him here, which filled five large volumes. Of these, two have come down to us. Written almost entirely in his own flowing hand, every page gives evidence of his powers of clear diction and minute observation. Viewed in the light of these records, these specimens undoubtedly present, in visible and tangible form, the first stepping stones in a great career. As such they are of the utmost biographical interest, and an asset of immense value in the history of modern medicine. . . . The origin of much of his later work is to be traced here, notably that on typhoid fever, angina pectoris, aneurysms and cardiac lesions. His *Practice of Medicine* is literally built up out of his rich memories of these and similar cases, and the foregoing clinical histories, accumulated both here and in his later Philadelphia experience, and it abounds in direct references to ' that beautiful healed aneurysm,' ' that wonderful parchment heart,' *etc.*, which apply not only or always to his own material, but also to the older collection placed here by earlier members of the Montreal General Hospital staff before his time, with every specimen of which he was most intimately familiar. How deeply this familiarity had sunk into his consciousness, and become, as it were, a part of his personality and affections, is realized only by those who were privileged to share the daily round of his work in later years, and who had heard the quotations from McGill experiences constantly on his lips."

Dr. Osler began at this time his serious studies as a morbid anatomist and continued them for thirteen years until he went to the Johns Hopkins. He had been greatly influenced by Dr. Palmer Howard who realized the importance for the would-be successful clinician to make his own post mortem examination; and he had seen Virchow in Berlin, for whom his enthusiasm knew no bounds. Virchow had put before him the ideal of perfection in pathological work. Dr. Osler's familiarity with the microscope was unusual at that time and put him in advance of his fellow-students in modern methods, enabling him to make minute study of the processes of disease; and, as Dr. Cushing observes, " aside from all this, in unravelling the mysteries of a fatal malady he felt the same profound fascination that had kept Bichat, Laennec, and many other brilliant and industrious young men for years at the autopsy table."

Dr. Cushing writes further: " His industry became proverbial. . . . The three large quarto volumes in Montreal of these manuscript notes, with the cases numbered and fully indexed, remain a monument to his genius — his capacity for work. . . . It is doubtful whether anything more than a great love of the work led him to study this material in detail; he could hardly have realized until his later years that a long apprenticeship in the laboratory always has been and always will be the only way to reach the very top either for surgeon or physician. . . . He had, moreover, the imaginative type of mind which made him prompt to grasp the problem laid bare by whatever he touched, and with this visualization, came the desire to make some record thereof. It was this characteristic, handed on in goodly measure to his pupils, that made him (and them in turn) so prolific; and in the end, owing to his abundant and well-chosen general reading, he acquired a literary style admirably suited to his purposes."

It is amazing that a young man of twenty-seven with a passion for work, keen about pathology — in this year 1876–1877 there were 100 autopsies worked up — the great Virchow his model, could, at the same time feel what he did for humanity. The Christmas of 1876 he spent visiting an old physician, Dr. James Hamilton. " On my visits home," he writes, " I had been in the habit of calling on the dear old man. I have always loved old men — and I enjoyed hearing anecdotes about Edinboro — . This time

I could see that he was hard hit, with the broad arrow on his forehead. He spoke pathetically of his recent losses, of which I had not heard and quoted the well-known verses beginning ' Naked I came into the world,' *etc.* The scene made an enduring impression. The veteran, after sixty years of devoted work, beaten at last by a cruel fate. ' Call no man happy till he is dead.' "

We get an intimate portrait of Dr. Osler during the McGill days. As he did then, in all fundamental things, he continued to do until the day of his death; living virtually abreast of his times, his purpose and ideals never changed — a young modern and an ancient saint. His cousin Marian Osborne tells the following story which in substance could be repeated many times every year of his life: " One day we were walking down the street together. He found it difficult to walk in the accepted sense of the term; his nature seemed too buoyant to allow him to place one foot before the other, as done by more humdrum individuals. He would dance along humming or whistling. His was the true *joie de vivre* that never left him in spite of work and sorrow and years. On this day we were dancing along St. Catherine Street hand in hand, when an old and very seedy-looking man accosted us and asked for money. Uncle Bill looked at him with his penetrating brown eyes and said with a laugh — ' You old rascal, why should I give you money to drink yourself to death? ' ' Well Sir, it lightens the road going.' ' There is only one thing of value about you and that is your hobnailed liver.' ' I'll give it to you, Sir. I'll give it to you.' Dr. Osler laughed and putting his hand in his pocket drew out some silver which he gave to the old man saying: ' Now, Jehosaphat, promise me you will get some soup before you start in on the gin.' The old fellow eagerly agreed and went away with infirmity in his step. The doctor looked after him with a thoughtful expression. ' Pretty cold for that poor fellow,' he murmured and then I found we were running after the beggar. ' Here, take this. I have a father of my own,' said the doctor pulling off his overcoat and putting it on the astonished old man. ' You may drink yourself to death and undoubtedly will, but I cannot let you freeze to death.' ' Tell me your name, Sir.' ' William Osler, and don't forget to leave me that liver.' With a wave of his hand we continued on our dancing way. Virtue was rewarded two weeks later. The old man, before he died in the hospital made his last will and testament, leaving his ' hobnailed liver and his overcoat to his good friend William Osler! ' It was well, for his ' good friend ' would have had to save for many moons before he could have got the wherewithal to buy another coat, and after it was thoroughly disinfected it was as good as new." His cousin ends her account with, " My intimate association with him as guide, philosopher and friend from earliest years until his death, leads me to the belief that he was of all men the most Christ-like in his life and the most God-like in his attributes." It is singular how all who were thrown with him felt his likeness to Christ. Always before them they saw the divine Physician. They could not see the one without thinking of the other; and yet about the one apparently is the *joie de vivre;* and on the other, the sad young Christ, not so much as a smile. Dr. Osler with his silk hat and a flower in his buttonhole, and the Galilean in his sandals and simple robe, how can they fit in the same canvas? Yet the ages that roll between them seem but as yesterday.

During the April recess, 1877, he spent a week in Boston, where Charles Eliot at Harvard College was making sweeping changes in the matriculation requirements and in the methods of teaching, trying to fix a higher standard of education for the men who aspired to be her graduates. Among many interesting demonstrations and lectures he listened to a recitation on Anatomy by Oliver Wendell Holmes. It is a pleasure to look down a vista of fifty-four years and see, standing on the platform, Oliver Wendell Holmes, 68, and looking up to him from the audience, William Osler, 28. The sweet kindly face of the old man and the dark glowing one of the youth mirrored much the same ideals. Holmes was the greater writer and his humour was the deep-seated humour of genius. Osler was the greater physician and his whimsical humour and boyish fun were more on the surface; but these two were singularly alike in spirit. The young man's small bedside library held the *Autocrat* — and when Osler gives advice to the students it might be Holmes speaking to them. Listen to a part of Oliver Wendell Holmes's lecture, delivered in 1867: " A medical school is not a scientific school, except just so far as medicine itself is a science. On the natural history side medicine is a science; on the curative side, chiefly an art. This is implied in Hufeland's aphorism: ' The physician must generalize the disease and individualize the patient.' " And compare with the expression in Dr. Osler's address, *Teacher and Student*. " The practice of medicine is an art, based on science. Working with science, in science, and for science, it has not reached, perhaps never will the dignity of a complete science with exact laws, like astronomy and engineering." And as a rubric to his *Practice of Medicine* he quotes the words of Plato: " And I said of medicine that this is an art which considers the constitution of the patient, and has principles of action and reasons in each case."

In 1878 Dr. Osler was appointed Physician to the Montreal General. Many years afterwards he wrote in regard to the appointment: " Four years in the post mortem room of the General Hospital with clinical work during the smallpox epidemic seemed to warrant the Governors of the General Hospital in appointing me in

1878 full physician over the heads — it seems scandalous to me now — of the assistant-physicians." But the Governors knew their man. Even to the unimaginative the actual facts of his life were convincing. On the day of his appointment he left for London to take his membership of the College of Physicians and to do some work in clinical medicine.

Years later he wrote of this visit to London: " For three months we had a delightful experience. Murchinson, whom I had seen before in 1873, was most kind and I do not think we missed one of his hospital visits. He was a model bedside teacher — so clear in his expositions, so thorough and painstaking with the students. My old friend Luther Holden introduced us to Gee, in whom were combined the spirit of Hippocrates and the method of Sydenham. Fred Roberts at University College Hospital showed us how physical diagnosis could be taught. We rarely missed a visit with Bastian and Ringer, and at Queen Square I began a long friendship with that brilliant ornament of British Medicine, Gowers. With my old comrade Stephen Mackenzie we went to Sutton's Sunday morning class at the London — his ' Sunday School ' as it was called — and we learned to have deep respect for his clinical and pathological skill. I mention these trivial details to indicate that before beginning work as a clinical teacher I had at least seen some of the best of the day." He returned to Canada late in September.

As Registrar of the Medical School he met the entire student body as they were admitted. His memory for names and faces was remarkable; and not only for names and faces, for he caught and held in his mind the dominant note in the character of the people he met. Innumerable enthusiastic accounts of him come to us from his once-young students who were warmed and cheered by his personal touch. And when he began to work in the wards as attending physician enthusiasm for him was great indeed.

Dr. Rogers gives an account of his first coming as physician to the Montreal General Hospital. "When, therefore, his time came to take charge of a section of the hospital, older doctors looked at him with bated breath, expecting disastrous consequences. He began by clearing up his ward completely. All the unnecessary semblance of sickness and treatment was removed; it was turned from a sickroom into a bright, cheerful room of repose. Then he started in with the patients. Very little medicine was given. To the astonishment of everyone, the chronic beds instead of being emptied by disaster, were emptied rapidly through recovery. Under his stimulating and encouraging influence the old cases nearly all disappeared, the new cases stayed but a short time. The revolution was wonderful. It was one of the most forceful lessons in treatment that has ever been demonstrated."

Dr. Osler had so absorbed the lessons of his experience that they had become a part of himself, and they gave him unusual self-confidence. Nevertheless for him, a young man of 29, completely to revolutionize, on his own initiative, the whole *régime* of the hospital, with the older doctors, who had directed it before, looking on, showed an extraordinary degree of assurance and boldness. These qualities, but without conceit, can be recognized all through his life.

Dr. Osler believed that the use of too many drugs was one of the great errors of the day; and he was fond of saying that Hahnemann had done more good than anyone else in the medical profession because he had shown that the natural tendency of disease was towards recovery.

From May to June he had his first practice of bedside instruction in the wards of the Montreal General. "We worked together," he wrote later, "through Gee's *Aus-*

cultation and Percussion, and in the ward visit, physical-diagnosis exercises, and in a clinical microscopy class the greater part of the morning was spent. I came across the other day the clinical note-book I had prepared for the students with the motto from Froude: ' The knowledge which a man can use is the only real knowledge which has life and growth in it, and converts itself into practical power. The rest hangs like dust above the brain, or dries like raindrops off the stones.' "

He persuaded Dr. Buller, with whom he was living, to take into their *ménage* a young first-year student who had been attending his lectures, Henry V. Ogden. " I can and do," writes Ogden, " see him perfectly as he came up to my room on the third floor of 1351 Catherine Street, the second or third night after I moved in. I happened to be sitting up in bed reading at physiology. He broke out at once in praise of the habit of reading in bed, but heartily disapproved of the physiology — only literature, never medicine. He walked across the room standing with his back to me, his hands in his trousers, tilting up and down on his toes, and inspecting the little collection of about twenty or thirty books I had ranged on two small hanging shelves; and taking down the *Golden Treasury* came over, sat on the foot of the bed, and half-recited, half-read, interjecting a running comment, a number of poems. Then tossing the book to me he said: ' You'll find that much better stuff than physiology for reading in bed.' That same evening, too, he spoke of Sir Thomas Browne and *The Religio* and probably for the first time, for I don't remember his making any reference to the subject in the lectures at the College. His enthusiasm rose as he spoke, and running downstairs he brought up his copy, pointed out and read several passages and left me." Dr. Rogers, the other student who lived with them at Dr. Buller's, St. Catherine Street, recalled that " he had the greatest contempt for the doctor who made financial gain the first object of his work and even went so far as to think that a man could not make more than a bare living and still be an honest and competent physician."

In the year 1880 occurred the death of his two friends and teachers, Dr. Bovell and Father Johnson. Dr. Bovell died on January 15, a few days after a paralytic stroke, in his seventy-fourth year; Father Johnson followed him later in the year, aged sixty-four. The latter died of a disease contracted in Weston in handling a dead body infected with black smallpox which all but he and his clerk had refused to touch. With the death of these two dearly loved friends, you feel a momentary but very significant pause in the life of their former pupil — almost like a Moslem call to prayer, and for a time he wandered about over the old paths hunting for new specimens. In 1881 he published the result of his zoological studies with which they had been so closely associated. He wrote many papers that year, and attended numerous meetings, and made several addresses. He read before the New York Pathological Society a paper on Ulcerative Endocarditis. It was the first important paper on the subject in America. It was published in the Archives of Medicine, New York, February, 1881, under the title of *Infectious* (so-called ulcerative) *Endocarditis*. He believed that his attendance at medical meetings was a professional obligation and when in late years he could not go himself he would send some of his assistants — his department must always be represented.

In 1881 the great International Medical Congress was held in London under the presidency of Sir James Paget. Dr. Osler and Dr. Howard attended the meeting together. It was a stunning affair. Two years had been spent in preparation for this one week of enormous work. 120,000 notices had been sent over all the world and more than

3,000 men from America, Germany, France, England, and other European countries were present when Sir James Paget delivered the inaugural address, a soul-stirring one; but the epoch-making event of the Congress was Pasteur's account of the anthrax test-inoculation that he had made at Pouilly-le-Fort, and the discussion on vaccination in relation to chicken-cholera and splenic fever — and so opened the door of preventive medicine through which the medical world was to follow him later.

This was the time of violent discussions on the question of spontaneous generation. Pasteur, whose thesis was that life comes only from life, was supported at the Congress by such men as Sir James Paget, Lister, Koch, Tyndall, Huxley, Darwin, Virchow, Jenner, Langenbach, Charcot, Volkmann — truly the medical aristocracy. But he had many opponents, of whom Bastian was the leader in England, who held that germs could develop spontaneously in diseased tissue. Dr. Osler did not enter the lists, and seems not to have appreciated the importance of the subject, for he dismissed it with the casual statement that there was an abundant discussion of germs in the Pathological Section. The fact that he had had little training in bacteriology, and his high esteem for Bastian may have had something to do with his indifference. But later, after making many tests, he convinced himself of the truth of Pasteur's ideas. He gave his important paper on Endocarditis before the Pathological Section and it was sufficiently notable for Dr. Gross, Jr., who was present, to say that it was one of the best papers given, and he hoped that some day the young Canadian might be secured for Philadelphia. It is interesting to know that many years later Stephen Paget, the distinguished son of Sir James, recalling in the memorial of his father, famous persons present at the meeting, mentions Osler's name among those that had become household words, since that

great week of August 3, 1881, when as a young man of
thirty-two, he had been a little scornful of germs.

In the year 1882 Dr. Osler was made a Fellow of the
Royal College of Physicians, London. The Canadians appreciated this honour and were full of felicitations. From
their journals of the period we learn that it was " a distinction which few men of Osler's age attain and is now held
by only two Canadians of any age." It seems almost superfluous to mention such honours. As a rule he cared little
for a visible hall mark for himself; for others, a student or
even an acquaintance, he cared much.

In the spring of 1884 he took a short vacation in Europe
to brush up his outlook and get rid of the drudgery of
teaching. He tells of the great improvements in Berlin
since his last visit in 1873. He again writes enthusiastically
of Virchow, " the central figure of the Berlin faculty." And
his letter on the Semitic invasion of Berlin is good to read:
" The modern ' hep, hep, hep ' shrieked in Berlin for
some years past has by no means died out, and to judge
from the tone of several of the papers devoted to the Jew-
ish question there are not wanting some who would gladly
revert to the plan adopted on the Nile some thousands of
years ago for solving the Malthusian problem of Semitic
increase. Doubtless there were then, as now, noisy agita-
tors — prototypes of the Parson Stöcker — who clamoured
for the hard laws which ultimately prevailed, and for the
taskmasters whose examples so many Gentile generations
have willingly followed, of demanding where they safely
could, bricks without straw of their Israelitish brethren.
Should another Moses arise and preach a Semitic exodus
from Germany, and should prevail, they would leave the
land impoverished far more than was ancient Egypt by
the loss of the ' jewels of gold and the jewels of silver ' of
which the people were ' spoiled.' To say nothing of the
material wealth — enough to buy Palestine over and over

again from the Turk — there is not a profession which would not suffer the serious loss of many of its most brilliant ornaments and in none more so than in our own. I hope to be able to get the data with reference to the exact number of professors and docents of Hebrew extraction in the German medical faculties. The number is very great, and of those I know their positions have been won by hard and honourable work; but I fear that, as I hear has already been the case, the present agitation will help to make the attainment of University professorships additionally difficult. One cannot but notice here in any assembly of doctors the strong Semitic element. At the local Societies and at the German Congress of Physicians, it was particularly noticeable, and the same holds good in any collection of students. All honor to them! "

He was fascinated with the work in Leipzig and his letters are full of its excellence — " going for bacteria," he writes. But in the midst of this he received an unexpected call to Philadelphia and wrote to Dr. Ross in Montreal:

" Dear Ross:

Shepherd forwarded me a letter this week which played the deuce with my peace of mind. Tyson writes asking me if I would accept the Chair of Clinical Medicine in the University of Pennsylvania, if appointed. His letter is quite unofficial and nothing may come of it, but after much meditation I decided to reply in the affirmative. The temptation is too great, but the prospect of severing my connection with McGill and Montreal gives me no end of worry. However, it may come to naught; but, of course, I wrote to H at once. Now I think, so I told him, it had better be kept quiet — not let a rumour get about if possible. It would stir up another Hospital agitation. Shepherd may possibly have twigged it from the opening sentence of the letter. I sometimes think it may be a hoax but the matter-of-fact communication — which Howard has — does not look like it. 'My heart within me is even like melting wax' at the thought of the possibility of leaving you all."

Another note on the same subject to H. V. Ogden is interesting:

"I have been in England about three weeks and am enjoying London again. It is the world. How I should like to live here! Perhaps you have heard that by October first I may have changed my allegiance and joined you as a citizen of the Great Republic. I have been asked by some of my Philadelphia friends to be a candidate for the Chair of Clinical Medicine, vacant by the transference of Pepper to the Chair of Medicine. I have consented and from what Pepper writes me I think they mean to elect me. At any rate, I have the strong professional backing of the electionary board. The salary is about what I get at McGill and of course the temptations are the larger centre and the prospects of consulting work. I am grieved at the thought of leaving McGill and Dr. Howard, but they will get along quite well without me — any one man is never essential. . . . I leave on the 7th and take out with me an Aunt — a young girl of 84."

Dr. Howard did all in his power to persuade him to remain in Montreal, and every effort was made by the McGill faculty to keep what Dr. Howard called their " potent ferment," but his decision was made for the reason he gave — the opportunity of a broader field. And a similar reason controlled his later move from Philadelphia to Baltimore.

Thus came to an end his official connection with Montreal. His work there cannot be summed up better than in the words of Dr. Cushing:

" During the short span of years since his McGill appointment he had stirred into activity the slumbering Medico
Chirurgical Society; he had founded and supported a students' medical club; he had brought the Medical School
into relation with the University; he had introduced the
modern methods of teaching physiology; he had edited
the first clinical and pathological reports of a Canadian
hospital; he had recorded nearly a thousand autopsies and
made innumerable museum preparations of the most important specimens; he had written countless papers; many
of them ephemeral, it is true, but most of them on topics
of live interest for the time, and a few of them epoch-making; he had worked at biology and pathology both human
and comparative, as well as at the bedside; he had shown
courage in taking the smallpox wards, charity in dealing
with his fellow physicians, in and out of his own school,
generosity to his students and fidelity to his tasks; and his
many uncommon qualities had earned him popularity unsought and of a most unusual degree."

The genuine esteem of his world — and it came close
to adoration — merely made him forget himself. He only
took the honours that were thrust upon him as a sign of the
affection of his friends. " How my friends have pushed me
forward! " he would laughingly say.

Philadelphia

Personal, first hand intercourse with men of different lands, when the mind is young and plastic, is the best vaccination against the disease [*Chauvinism*].

Wm. Osler — *Chauvinism in Medicine.*

CHAPTER IV

PHILADELPHIA

IT was a marked epoch in William Osler's life when, in 1884, he left Canada for the United States. He was, as he once said, " British to the core." Nevertheless in whatever direction his steps were turned they were turned towards home, he so completely identified himself with the community in which he happened to be living. The life in 1884 was not as standardized as it is to-day; there was a stronger individual flavour in the cities and the sections of the country. Philadelphia and Baltimore were both very individual and provincial; Montreal and Toronto were also individual and provincial. In Canada the attitude of the people might be likened somewhat to a family which recognized the control of a parent. In the States it would seem that the family were more completely in the hands of the children. The United States covers so large an area that the interests and traditions of the different sections are not the same.

At the time of Dr. Osler's coming to the States the aftermath of the Civil War had still left traces of bitterness and it might appear that the outlook for a country with so much sectional prejudice would be a little dubious. North, South, East, West, each thought itself the most important. The wounds of the South were raw and the North was inclined to put salt and not salve upon them. The South felt the North incapable of understanding a Southern Cavalier, and the North knew the South could not understand a Northern Puritan. The Middle West was quite certain that the East constituted a set of snobs, and the far West thought itself too far from the central government to have its needs appreciated. A stranger might justifiably look upon the country as a house divided against itself! Suddenly some years later came the Spanish war and the country sprang to arms with a single purpose.

The Massachusetts regiment marched through the streets of Baltimore — the very regiment that in 1861 was stoned and hissed as they passed through the angry crowds in a city draped in black! and now the flag of the Union floated from every house. Shouts of welcome greeted the troops and they were showered with flowers and gifts, meeting at every turn the splendid gesture of a country in a national crisis.

Dr. Osler said: " I shall never forget the impression made upon me — a nation that could do a thing like that belongs to the great of the earth." But his interests lay almost entirely in the medical world. When Minerva Medica arose, she alone was to be considered and he did his part in reconciling differences. Wherever he found a faithful servant of the guild, he brought him forward, wrote about him, gave him honour; where he came from was of no consequence. The boundaries of his profession swept the horizon of our globe and he swung along with his brothers everywhere. He saw only the man under the veneer of traditions and prejudices, and to the man he gave his hand.

> " But there is neither East nor West
>   Border nor Breed nor Birth
>   When two strong men stand face to face
>   Tho' they come from the ends of the earth."

There had been a storm of protest in Philadelphia over his election, and though such men as Weir Mitchell and

Samuel Gross were responsible for him, and his fame was well known, it would have been difficult for him to make an easy entrance into Philadelphia had he been other than he was. A graduate of that period wrote: " The remarkable part of Osler's entrance was, that while the report of his election raised waves of regret and indignation, his actual plunge in the pond at once had the effect of making its surface placid and this without any manifest effort on his part to ingratiate himself with any one of all the factions. He entered so gracefully and ably, and so naturally, that he seemed almost at once to be one of us, young and old. He was gracious to his elders, cordial to his contemporaries, encouraging to his juniors, and jovial almost to the point of frivolity with all — but the dominant factor that made his way successful with all hands was, to use a student's phrase, ' he was up ' — that is, he knew his subject and how to teach what he knew. His first class was an eye-opener. In it he fairly frolicked in enthusiastic delight and in a few moments had every man interested and avid for more. Every new specimen that he came to at autopsy, and every interesting manifestation of disease in the living was to him a treasure, and just as Leidy saw in every flower and stone and bone, and worm, and rhizopod, an inner beauty, so Osler, to change my metaphor, was as the light-hearted child who, finding a field of daisies, shouts his delight so exultingly that all of the other children become interested and gleeful and shout with him. Osler did more than any other man of his day in this city to teach all men that the study and pursuit of disease is a pursuit which a properly trained mind can follow with as keen enjoyment and uplift as an artist can study great pictures or a musician can hear great Masters."

We have a still clearer picture from Dr. Howard A. Kelly: " I was living in the big mill district of Kensington, culling a surgical out of a large general practice, and at the same time keeping in close touch with things at the University of Pennsylvania, for eight years my College, when it became manifest that some fresh and stirring blood had entered the college life. The University with so many eminent men camping on her very doorstep in Philadelphia, and with a tendency to nepotism — a form of paternal pride seen in all successful institutions — had, as we young men thought, driven John Guitéras, of brilliant promise in general medicine, away from her doors in order to protect Pepper from rivalry, and now without great hesitation as we understood, she had actually shaken her shackles, thrown tradition to the wind and pulled William Osler down from McGill. Fresh invigorating currents of life and new activities in our stereotyped medical teachings began at once to manifest themselves, and every sturdy expectant youngster in short order lined himself up as a satellite to the new star. Osler breezes were felt everywhere in the old conservative medical centre and yet it was not without some difficulties that he securely established himself." That a man in a frock coat, a flowing red necktie, low shoes and heavy worsted socks, who rode in a street car and carried his lunch in a black satchel, could by any chance have been urged upon their community by Dr. Weir Mitchell and Dr. Pepper was as great a wonder as anything in William Osler's life or in the lives of those exquisite, fastidious physicians. For, without in the least suggesting that they were snobs, they did not make mistakes in a social world any more than in an intellectual one; and for them to recognize a potential Sir William in the young Canadian was indeed a miracle on both sides.

We have Dr. Osler's own story of his inspection by Dr. Mitchell: " Dr. Mitchell cabled me to meet him in London, as he and his good wife were commissioned ' to look me over,' particularly with reference to personal habits.

Dr. Mitchell said there was only one way in which the breeding of a man suitable for such a position in such a city as Philadelphia could be tested: ' Give him cherry-pie and see how he disposes of the stones.' I had read of this trick before, and disposed of them genteelly in my spoon — and got the Chair."

After looking him over and seeing him properly dispose of the cherry stones, Dr. Mitchell wrote: " He (Osler) has every social need; his age is 35. He has won distinction as an investigator and writer and will therefore add to our illustriousness, and as to competence as a teacher, if anyone can be believed, he must be a really unusual instructor." And again, " Osler is socially a man for the Biological Club." Nothing more need be said. This club was a source of great pleasure to Dr. Osler. A group of congenial men met and dined together the second and fourth Fridays of every month, for no special reason except that they might keep in touch with each other in the midst of rather strenuous lives. Dr. Leidy was Dr. Osler's particular delight at the Club meetings. A copy of Leidy's *Monograph on Rhizopoda,* illustrated by his own wonderful drawings, was a treasured book in Dr. Osler's library and in addresses and letters in after years he constantly refers to the author. After Leidy's death he wrote: " But what shall I say of Leidy the man in whom the leaven of science wrought with labor and travail for so many years? The written record survives, scarcely equalled in variety and extent by any naturalist, but how meagre is the picture of the man as known to his friends! The traits that made his life of such value — the patient spirit, the kindly disposition, the sustained zeal — we shall not see again incarnate. . . . When I think of Leidy's simple life, of his devotion to the study of nature, of the closeness of his communion with her for so many years there recur to my mind time and again the lines:

'He is made one with Nature; there is heard
His voice in all her music, from the moan
Of thunder, to the song of night's sweet bird;
He is a presence to be felt and known
In darkness and in light, from herb and stone,
Spreading itself where'er that Power may move
Which has withdrawn his being to its own!' "

There was necessarily much uphill work for Dr. Osler when he first went to Philadelphia but he steadily carried things before him and his friendships grew apace. Dr. S. W. Gross, who had early recognized his quality, had become a close friend. Pepper had yielded to his fascination and Weir Mitchell gave him entire approbation and something, too, like affection. The list of those who held him in their hearts would be a long one.

With Dr. Osler the rational and emotional life were both convincing, both genuine — it was impossible for him to be either sentimental or irrational. His intellect was entirely truthful and he found truth often in the most unpromising places; but he left a broad margin for the opinion of others and to rectify mistakes. There were several disputes in the medical world that tried him, particularly a very serious altercation that had taken place among the physicians of the United States. The Ninth International Medical Congress was to be held in Washington in 1887, and Dr. Billings as Chairman of the committee of organisation had formed a program which would have made the success of the Congress certain; but sectional prejudices entered in; exception was taken by the controlling element of the American Medical Association to Billings' list of professional officers, and great injustice done them. Dr. Osler took a spirited part in the controversy, but after saying what he had to say in no uncertain words and feeling keenly the injustice done some worthy physicians and hating the pettiness of it all, he nevertheless would not allow his personal feelings to break his relations with the American Medical Association. He did his part to clear out the dead wood, but he had no desire to destroy the ship; it would come out of the storm in time, he thought, and the ignorant would become in the end a negligible minority. He loved peace; but when he fought, it was an invigorating sight — a clean fight, leaving in the aftermath not a trace of bitterness where he was personally involved; but there was much bitterness and strain for many years to come between other eminent physicians and the Association. It was partly due to this that the Association of American Physicians had its birth October 10, 1885.

The contrast between Pepper and Osler must have been striking to the students. Pepper, the perfect gentleman, gracious, if a little ornamental, in manner; fastidiously dressed, with a fine eye for effect and a brilliant style of address; and the young Canadian with his indifference to effect, his unconquerable youthful spirits, his progressive and very simple and direct mind, and above all his love for scientific truth that could only be found through the microscope and laboratory, and at the bedside. Dr. Pepper and Dr. Osler were friends, though the way of tweedledum was not the way of tweedledee. But they were united in one purpose: to raise the standard of medical education and each respected the other's power to attain their common object.

Like the majority of physicians connected with the Philadelphia Medical Schools, Dr. Pepper had a large private practice. He was provost and head of the medical department of the University of Pennsylvania and was actively at work adding to its resources; so that he rarely came to the wards, and Dr. Osler had them almost to himself. The greater part of each morning found him in the wards with an enthusiastic group of students about him. Research work — original work of any kind — had been unknown to the clinical students. There were no facilities for laboratory work; but Dr. Osler soon after his arrival rigged up a small laboratory under part of the hospital amphitheatre, and developed there the same enthusiasm he had in the students' cloak room at McGill. The students flocked to the laboratory, a new experience for those who had heretofore only heard generalizations from the platform, and one of them said: " It was like a breath of fresh air let in a stifling room."

The old order was changing, and, as in other cases, the tide of the new era was almost unnoticed in its approach. Dr. Osler was a leader in the new era but was not so far in advance of his generation to be out of touch with it. During his entire life his arm was about the youth of the world, gaily a little in the lead. This in part accounts for the fact that he had so little opposition. The young were with him and the old, though at times they looked askance, were drawn by his full appreciation of what they stood for, what they had done, their contributions to knowledge, and his gratitude for what he had learnt from them. His eyes twinkled at American values, but they were equally alive to whatever was worth while.

Coming from Montreal where so able an executive as Dr. Palmer Howard had, to a great extent, controlled affairs, Dr. Osler must have felt shut in by the over-conservative walls that enclosed the oldest medical school in the States. The United States, he thought, was behind Montreal in medical conditions. He is quoted as saying: " How it is that such a shrewd, practical people as those in the United States should have drifted into such a loose, slipshod way of conducting medical schools, is unintelligible." In reality both Canada and the United States were far behind Germany, Austria, France and England.

The new buildings of the McGill Medical Faculty were opened in the autumn of 1885 and Dr. Osler as President of the Canadian Medical Association chose Dr. Pepper to make the opening address. This was a brilliant plea for better endowments of the Medical School. Eminent men in Canada and the States were pressing on the note of higher standards and better equipments, longer apprenticeship. In the States President Eliot of Harvard was the first to sound the note; and it was next taken up by the University of Pennsylvania.

The times were ripe for reform and advance, and " Osler breezes " were being felt. The ideals of what a hospital should be were quickly developed in America; its genius for making things comfortable and efficient rushed ahead, soon putting its hospitals in the front rank — more than that, they became models. But the new standards of medical education were not readily appreciated. An American of a very usual order, when told the story of the obscure Dutchman Leeuwenhoek, the pioneer microbe hunter of two hundred and fifty years ago, whose education after sixteen was gained in a dry goods shop, said: " There now, you see if a man's got it in him he'll get there. I don't believe in all this elaborate education; it wastes a lot of time." To get somewhere and to get there quickly was the American spirit. Nearly to the end of the nineteenth century nine people out of ten felt that way; and the achievement of men who changed this national point of view was remarkable.

It is difficult to find any part of the medical life in Philadelphia in which Dr. Osler did not take an active part, except that of general practitioner; and as all physicians at the hospital were engaged in as large and lucrative practice as they could command — they thought him on that question quixotic. Within a few months after he was settled at his work as Professor of Clinical Medicine at the

University of Pennsylvania he became an active member
of the Philadelphia Neurological Society. Dr. Weir Mitchell was President and from the beginning it included an
extraordinarily able set of men. Dr. Osler at once took an
important part and aroused the greatest enthusiasm among
the students and his colleagues. He wrote two monu-
graphs on the nervous diseases of children from the material he gained in the Philadelphia Hospital. Dr. Dercum,
who was chief of the clinic under Dr. Wood (Clinical
Professor of Nervous Diseases) writes: " At this time
Eadweard Muybridge, the distinguished student of animal
locomotion, was conducting a remarkable series of investigations in an enclosure on the hospital grounds. Instan-
taneous photographs of men and animals in motion were
made with an apparatus consisting of twenty-four cameras
arranged in a series — the exposure taking place succes-
sively at definite intervals of time. I induced Mr. Muybridge to photograph some of the patients from the great
nervous wards of the Philadelphia General Hospital.
While Dr. Osler was not directly concerned in these investigations he evinced the liveliest interest in them, and
was frequently present, and when opportunity offered,
sent patients from his own service. The Muybridge results
were subsequently published in a very elaborate series of
photographic plates and are especially memorable because
they constituted the forerunners of the modern moving
pictures."

It was in the Dead House at Blockley, with a crowd
of students about him, that he was most constantly to be
found. The Blockley Hospital, originally the Philadelphia
Alms House, is the oldest hospital in the United States.
It was twice moved as the city grew and it finally settled in
the township of Blockley on the west side of the Schuylkill.
Creeping their way to the big Poor House came the
sorry procession of the wrecks of humanity. The Poor

House, the Dead House, the Potter's Field — a sad picture upon which religion and science have pondered and worked.

In 1870 the University of Pennsylvania moved from the city of Philadelphia to property adjoining the Blockley Hospital, and a few years later erected there a hospital of its own. You could leave the University Hospital by the rear and enter the Blockley enclosure by a postern gate in the old wall. Near this gate stood a little red building, a half-way house to the Potter's Field. Blockley had then over two thousand patients, with all manner of maladies, and the opportunity for post mortem studies was unusually good. The old servant in the Dead House soon saw Dr. Osler's enthusiasm and whenever an examination was waived, he would at once inform Dr. Osler who, at the earliest possible moment, collected a crowd of his students and carried them off to make an autopsy. At first he was not specially connected with Blockley and that being the case, it was against the regulations for him to conduct a post mortem there. But later he was given an appointment, and his post mortems became regular. At this time there was nothing but a storage vault and a stone table on which the examinations were made; but in spite of every possible inconvenience the chance of performing an autopsy was never lost and his books show no less than 162. This method of teaching pathology was an innovation which was enthusiastically received by the students. The post mortems supplied him with specimens of diseased tissues which, when properly prepared, were carefully studied under the microscope.

While in Philadelphia he published thirty-nine papers covering nearly every phase of clinical medicine. The three greatest clinicians in America, Austin Flint, Edward G. Janeway, and William Osler, felt their success was due to their groundings in pathology. Dr. Osler, the greatest of the three, kept up his pathological work during the en-tire Philadelphia period.

We know that even in the early days of his career, he was skeptical of the constant use of drugs. An interne of that time writes: " Dr. Osler's rational use of drugs was too much for staid Philadelphia. Can't you imagine a naturally conservative city to whom the eloquent Wood was extolling the value of drugs, and the equally eloquent Pepper recommending a dozen different drugs in the treatment of individual disease, shocked into insensibility by having a young professor of medicine, recently come into their midst, go through the wards with his internes and finding nothing definite the matter with a patient, say: ' Did we give the last fellow compound tincture of chinchona or compound tincture of gentian? ' . . . But in reality Osler was a very good therapeutist as we internes realized and used drugs not empirically but scientifically, and in his teaching laid great stress upon the general management of the disease."

When talking of Dr. Osler with nurse, or student, or colleague or patient, invariably comes some story of his humanity, like the following from one of the old Blockley nurses. Knowing Dr. Osler it seems credible. An old man, a pauper, was being rolled into the operating room when Dr. Osler came whistling from the corridor. One of the stu-dents said, " Oh, Dr. Osler, look at this," and showed the old man's foot with an ingrowing nail that they were going to cut out. To their immense amazement Dr. Osler turned into a white rage and said, " Don't you dare, you . . . touch that old man. You can do him no good, and you know it. Take him back to the ward." The old man, with tears streaming down his face said, " O God bless you Sir! " Whereat Dr. Osler patted him on the shoulder saying, " Why, you dear old chap, I am coming to see you this afternoon," and turning to the aghast internes, said: " Do you hear what I say? I'm going to see this man this afternoon, so leave him alone," and off he went. The nurse told the story with emotion. She may have added some picturesque language but it is the order of story one constantly hears of him — even to the language.

This recalls an incident in his Montreal days told by his cousin, Marian Osborne; " On one occasion I was trotting with him through a ward in the Montreal General Hospital. There was an old Scotch woman there making ' a devil of a row,' as one of the doctors expressed it, because she had to go under an operation. She was rocking to and fro in an agony of grief and lifting her hands and voice in despair to Heaven. Dr. Osler went to her kindly and patted her shoulder. ' Poor old Scotch body,' he said kindly. ' Thole it a bit, thole it a bit.' She turned and clasped his hands in hers, smiling through her tears. ' O, Sir,' she cried, ' I haven't heard sic a talk since I parted frae Edinboro — Bless you, I maun try to stop frae greeting and grizzling.' He talked to her for a few moments and left her calm and resigned. He used to say to his students, ' Never forget the rights of patients.' " He was, at the time of this story, twenty-three.

Dr. Osler's admiration for Dr. Weir Mitchell began when they first met. He was deeply interested in the rest cure for nervous patients. But in spite of his approval of Dr. Mitchell's methods any person who had gone to Dr. Osler for his or her nerves, unless there was genuine trouble, must have realized that the malarial parasites would have been for him a simple relaxation compared with seeing a lady through a rest cure. A woman went to him once (she told this tale herself), " I just can't sleep. I keep twitching and jerking my feet, and my hands fly out of the cover and all the fingers go like spiders; and my toes curl up." Dr. Osler: " I hope your good man has another bed." The woman indignantly: " Dr. Osler, I am old-fashioned. I shall not discuss that with you. My husband loves me." Dr. Osler, *sotto voce,* but not so *sotto voce* that she doesn't hear him: " Poor devil! " " Dr. Osler," she went on, " I came here to ask you to help me to get some sleep, some rest, and you treat it like a jest." He made a careful physical examination, asked a few questions, then went to the door and with his hand on the knob, said firmly: " I know your husband, Mrs. ——, a fine chap, with a small income. There's nothing whatever the matter with you. Go home and do your own housework and see how much you can save your husband." The woman furiously: " Do you mean to insult me? I see I have been foolish to come to you." " Not if you do what I tell you," and he opened the door for her to go. She told the story, ending it with " The idea of calling him a saint! He looks like a Mephistopheles and I think he is terribly overestimated. He didn't know what was the matter with me and just bluffed."

Few of the anecdotes that reach us ever come from Dr. Osler, but patients will talk even if their physician refrains; and his colleagues and students all made up a good score against his reticence. The function of a biographer is much that of cross questioning the witness and in the end, if your subject never acts out of character, you get a pretty good idea of what is probably true and what is certainly not. Of Dr. Osler one can say confidently that anything or any person that was genuine would get his sympathy, and with what was not genuine he would have nothing to do.

When there was real nervous trouble he was all consideration, as the following very typical letter shows: —

" Dear Miss ——:

I have heard from Dr. Keyser, and he quite confirms my idea that these sensations are manifestations simply of a slightly used-up nervous system. I think in the first place you should not allow yourself to be worried by them or regard them as specially serious. Then for the next three or four months take good care of yourself and avoid all sources of worry and irritation, anything that you know is apt to exhaust or worry you. I do not think you need take any medicine at present. I have told the doctor when you go to the country if you still have those feelings what I think you might take, possibly with benefit.

Very truly yours,

Wm. Osler.

P.S. Notify any bores of the troublesome variety to keep away this summer."

The boy that survives to the end in many men was in full force with him to the last days of his life. But he was not gay. Ariel and Puck kept up a constant ripple on the surface but the depth of his nature was serious. A certain whimsical humour was his, but that, too, was near the surface. George Eliot has said: " If we had a keen vision and feeling of all underlying life it would be like hearing the grass grow and the squirrel's heart beat and we should die of the roar which lies on the other side of silence." He ever saw the underlying tragedy of life; and to save himself from tears he whistled and played for a moment — and worked. Open his books; read his essays — his words reach you like the sound of an organ interpreting the lives of the long dead; his spirit brings back to us their thoughts and loves and the wisdom of the far past, the truths that have not been invented but have always existed. The charming whimsical touch which entered into what he wrote would not have struck a discordant note with the saddest of themes. He was not a teller of good stories; he rarely told an anecdote; he was not overinterested in hearing one, and never in hearing three or four. His jest was a quick rapier thrust — with the button on — at your frailties, or else an out-and-out practical joke. We always have to keep in mind what he said: " If I laugh at any human thing, it is that I may not weep." A man who at 21 took for his life's most intimate companions Sir Thomas Browne, the Bible, Milton, saturating his mind nightly with their spirit, could not be called a humorist. There was a certain enchantment about the man not easily accounted for. He did not appeal to sex or to pleasure but to something very definite as to duty, and very indefinite as to the result of doing that duty. One wonders why many left him with any comfort whatever unless an increased self respect was comforting and the realization of something that swept pettiness out of existence.

He was under discussion by a group of people one afternoon when one of them said: " You say that he only sees the essential and yet it seems to me that he was constantly attending to the trivial. Imagine, for instance, his running back squares out of his way just to tell a deaf woman that his wife had not noticed that she was deaf." That was exactly the order of thing he would do over and over again. And Dr. Weir Mitchell had seen that quality in his candidate as well as the nice disposal of cherry stones.

If, as a boy, he cared for games and pleased his mother by being " Osler first " on the playgrounds, all interest in games ceased when his work as a physician began. When he wished to clear the cobwebs out of his mind, he would dash into the nursery of some friend and have an out-and-out romp with the babies; or he would shock a sedate matron, or put a Martha's well-ordered scheme awry and leave a protesting, but never really angry, household — that was his sport.

He did not want private patients and could not be induced to take a practice; yet he was constantly at some bedside, in the wards of the hospital or as a consultant;

and wherever he went he followed his cases with an amazing thoughtfulness. Everybody wondered at the rapidity with which he accomplished his work; over and over again a physician has asked, " How does he do it? " The following anecdote answers this question:

Mrs. ——, an old lady of the smart world whose once fine house was gradually growing shabbier, who seemed to be wearing fewer and fewer diamonds and whose friends were outdone with her because they felt sure that her unspeakable scamp of a son was draining her of all her means, and whose pride was in the dust because these so-called friends would offer advice, unsympathetically sympathizing, wandered one afternoon into Dr. Osler's consulting room. He was very busy but he knew her and the stories about her. He jumped up as she came into the room, put her gently into a comfortable chair, sat on the table with his legs swinging and looked at her. She said: " I can't sleep. I am growing old. No beauty parlor will help me now." And the feathers in her hat did seem to be shaking over the made-up face beneath them. " Oh, come now," he answered, his eyes twinkling, " people of your courage don't give up. I want you to take a strong toddy every night for a week at 9. P.M. and at the end of that time, come — no, I'll run in to see you. Tell me, is Tommy (her son) in Paris? " She shuddered fearing some slam at Tommy and advice as to how she should steel her heart against helping him. " Yes," she said, " he is there now. He's leaving soon for the south of France " — and firmly and defiantly — " he has a weak chest." Dr. Osler: " Handsome young scamp. What's his address? I am going to send him a letter of introduction to some nice people. They have two delightful daughters. It's a gay house, but not so gay that *our* boy will get into trouble." That was all, but she went out of the room with a few years thrown off and having contracted an irritating habit of telling her friends casually to their great disgust, " Dr. Osler has given Tommy a letter of introduction to the ——'s in Paris" and the feathers in her hat would assume a triumphant wave — for were not the ——'s among the most important and exclusive people in that city?

The story just told was often heard in detail from the old lady, and when she told of his saying *our* boy she surreptitiously wiped her eyes, though she wanted to give you the impression that he might have been honoured to have a son like her Tommy. The whole of such an interview with Dr. Osler would consume not more than fifteen minutes; not so amazing really, for when a physician can, without a moment's waste of time, put his finger on the right spot, the remedy (in a psychological case) may be quickly applied — and a life reinstated even in fifteen minutes. One thing is absolutely certain: no human being ever left him disheartened. Those who entered his door in despair left it in hope.

"There are people in life," Dr. Osler once said, "and there are many of them, whom you will have to help as long as they live. They will never be able to stand alone." Those without a word of advice he helped.

Dr. Cushing has rescued from an unpublished manuscript an account of Dr. Osler's first meeting with Walt Whitman. "Not long after removing to Philadelphia," Dr. Osler wrote: "a telegram came from my friend Dr. Maurice Bucke of London, Ontario: 'Please see Walt and let me know how he is' — to which I had to answer: 'Who is Walt and where does he live?' It was very stupid of me as I should have remembered that a few years before when Dr. Bucke had been a guest at one of our club dinners in Montreal, he had startled us into doubts of his sanity by extravagant praises of one Walt Whitman, a new seer of a new era, whom he classed with our Saviour, Buddha and Mahomet. Then, I remembered, too, to have

seen notices of a book he had written about Whitman;
but I had no idea where the prophet lived. The next morning I had the answer: ' Mr. Walter Whitman, 328 Mickle
Street, Camden.' In the afternoon I crossed the Delaware
ferry and in a clean, quiet, democratic street I found the
little old-fashioned two-story frame house. A pleasant,
middle-aged woman answered the door, to whom I showed
Dr. Bucke's telegram. ' He will be glad to see you — to
see anyone from Dr. Bucke. Mr. Whitman is better to-day
and downstairs.' The door opened into what appeared to
be a room, but I had no little difficulty at first in getting
my bearings. I have seen what a tidy housewife calls a
' clutter ' but nothing to compare with the front room,
ground floor of No. 328 Mickle Street. At the corner, near
the window, the head and upper part of a man were
visible — everywhere else, covering the floor, the chairs
and the table, were, to use his own description, ' heaps of
books, manuscripts, memoranda, scissorings, proof-sheets,
pamphlets, newspapers, old and new magazines, mysteri-
ous-looking literary bundles tied up with stout strings.'
The magazines and newspapers, piled higher than the desk,
covered the floor so completely that I had to pick my way
by the side of the wall of the room to get to the desk. I
thought of Professor Teufel's room in *Sartor Resartus*.
After a hearty greeting I had some difficulty in explaining
that I did not come directly from Dr. Bucke, but that he
had sent me over from Philadelphia to find out how he
was. There was nothing serious the matter — a transient
indisposition which had passed away. With a large frame,
and well shaped, well-poised head, covered with a pro-
fusion of snow-white hair, which mingled on the cheeks
with a heavy long beard and moustache, Walt Whitman in
his 65th year was a fine figure of a man who had aged
beautifully, or more properly speaking, majestically. The
eyebrows were thick and shaggy, and the man seemed lost

in a hirsute canopy. . . . My visit was made without any of that preparation — that expectation, upon which Gideon Harvey dwells as influencing so profoundly our feelings. I knew nothing of Walt Whitman, and had never read a line of his poems — a Scythian visitor at Delphi! . . . That evening at the Club after dinner I opened the volume of *Leaves of Grass* for the first time. Whether the meat was too strong, or whether it was the style of the cooking — 'twas not for my pampered palate, accustomed to Plato and Shakespeare and Shelley and Keats. This has been a common experience; even Dr. Bucke acknowledging that ' for many months I could see absolutely nothing in the book, and would even throw it down in a sort of rage.' Whitman himself has expressed this feeling better than anyone else, speaking of his ' strange voice,' and acknowledging that critics and lovers of poetry may well be excused the ' chilly and unpleasant shudders which will assuredly run through them, to their very blood and bones,' when they first read him, and exclaim: ' If this is poetry, where must its foregoers stand? ' . . . At this time, of the two men Bucke interested me more. Though a hero-worshipper, it was a new experience in my life to witness such an absolute idolatry. Where my blurred vision saw only a fine old man, full of common sense and kindly feelings, Bucke felt himself in the presence of one of the world's great prophets. One evening after dinner at the Rittenhouse Club with Dr. Chapin, Dr. Tyson, Dr. J. K. Mitchell, and a few others who I knew would appreciate him, I drew Bucke on to tell the story of Whitman's influence. The perfervid disciple, who talks like Chaerephon in the *Apology*, is not often met with in these matter-of-fact days. It was an experience to hear an elderly man — looking like a venerable seer — with absolute abandonment tell how *Leaves of Grass* had meant for him spiritual enlightenment, a new power in life, new joys in a new existence on a plane higher than he had ever hoped to reach. All this with the accompanying physical exaltation expressed by dilated pupils and intensity of utterance that were embarrassing to uninitiated friends. This incident illustrates a type of influence exercised by Whitman on his disciples — a cult of a type such as no other literary man of our generation has been the object."

Whitman created in his followers a fanatical adoration. Dr. Osler created an enthusiasm that led to a rational way of life. He was so objective that the egocentric type must have seemed to him abnormal. He recognized after a time Whitman's creative genius and what he meant to many men, but they were not his kind. Dr. Osler's adoring disciples must turn their thoughts to God and their fellow men with a humility that would make them forget their own ego. Living more completely in the hearts of his students than he could possibly conceive, he was a vital incentive to do and be in a simple, matter-of-fact way.

A patient of his at that time, a young man with tuberculosis, gives a characteristic account of his method: " He talked to me a few moments very ardently about a book he had been reading; then he stopped abruptly, stood up, and putting his hands in his pockets, looked at me intently, and said: ' You could, of course, dear boy, have an easier time if you went to the Adirondacks but you could get as much good here if you actually live out-of-doors and your heart will be easier about your wife and the kiddies — it will mean a great deal of self-discipline. Try for a month and then come back and we will see if we are playing a winning game without too high stakes.' There was not a week during that trial month that some little gift or note of encouragement from him failed to reach me — and that's thirty years ago."

Any one following where his finger pointed would take the right road — that he could inspire them to do it when it often meant hard, dull work and no flags flying, was his unique genius.

Probably his most important contribution to clinical medicine and clinical pathology from the Philadelphia Hospital was his study of malaria. No matter how familiar the pathological picture was likely to be, he apparently felt that there was always something to learn. A paper on Pasteur's work on rabies shows that he recognized that the talk of germs in 1881 had been a little in advance of his appreciation but now he had caught up with the wonder of it. He writes of Koch and says: " Though there are protests in Germany and France and a remnant still in this country who stand out against the germ theory, the younger generation to a man have stained fingers."

In the spring of 1885 he delivered the Goulstonian lectures in London. These lectures were given from time to time by one of the latest elected fellows in physic at the Royal College of Physicians. He had been asked to give these lectures before he left Montreal — and they were based on work done at the Montreal General. The work he had done when a young man in Canada was so fundamental that it remained always as a reference-book. His most valuable work on endocarditis was described in these lectures. They were based on over 200 reported cases and on much of his own experience at the Montreal General. Physicians have said that these lectures gave such a wonderful exposition of the pathology, clinical picture and diagnosis of endocarditis that they were unequalled in medical literature. They contained the complete history of the subject written in a matchless style. Dr. Allbutt, a few years his senior, had delivered the lectures the previous year. Dr. Osler came in curious contact with leaders making unconsciously for the same goal in their profession. Sir Clifford Allbutt later became Regius Professor of Medicine at Cambridge, and Dr. Osler was to hold a similar position at Oxford; and he had earlier crossed the path of Burdon-Sanderson whom he succeeded as Regius Professor at Oxford.

His four years in Philadelphia had made him seem essentially a part of the place, and when there were rumours that a call to Baltimore was forthcoming, though many of his friends were undoubtedly anxious, they could not believe that he would leave them. Such a catastrophe was not to be borne. So that the following note to Dr. Pepper came as a shock even to the few who knew that it was to be:

" To William Pepper, M.D.   Oct. 3, 1888.

I have received a definite offer from the Johns Hopkins authorities and have determined to accept it. I shall leave with great regret. You have been like a good kind brother. There need be no hurry about any official action."

The months between the Baltimore call and his leaving Philadelphia were filled with strain. During these days came to him the heavy sorrow of the death of his beloved friend and preceptor, Dr. Palmer Howard of Montreal; and also the death of a later friend, Dr. Samuel Gross, Jr., whose home during the Philadelphia years had been as his own. The " potent ferment " he had been in Montreal was just as vital in Philadelphia and the feeling for leaving his friends, colleagues and students was just as deep; but the Baltimore call offered him the opportunity of his life. Some years later he wrote: " The opening of the Johns Hopkins hospital in 1889 marked a new departure in medical education in the United States. It was not the hospital itself, as there were many larger and just as good; it was not the men appointed, as there were others quite as well qualified; it was the organization. For the first time in an English-speaking country, a hospital was organized in units — each one in charge of a head or chief. The day after my appointment I had a telegram from Dr. Gilman, President of the University, who had been asked to open the hospital, to meet him at the Fifth Avenue Hotel, New York. He said to Dr. Welch and me: ' I have asked you to come here as the manager is an old friend of mine. And we will spend a couple of days. There is no difference really between a hospital and a hotel.' We saw everything arranged in departments with responsible heads, and over all a director. ' This,' he said, ' is really the hospital and we shall model ours upon it. The clinical unit of a hospital is the exact counterpart of any great hotel or department store.' "

In Philadelphia and Montreal the Universities were part of the community and had developed in the course of years strong traditions of their own. They were also to some extent under political control. In Baltimore the new University was entirely independent, and was able to break new ground; in it Dr. Osler could realize his own ideals of what a medical school should be. The years spent in Philadelphia deepened his understanding of the science and even of the art of Medicine. To have worked with such men as Keen and Samuel Gross in Surgery, Weir Mitchell, Pepper and Leidy in Medicine, was an enriching and broadening experience, and perfected his fitness for the great position he was to fill.

A Child with Children

Thus Rafael once venturing to show God in Man
gave a child's eyes of wonder to his baby Christ.

  .   .   .   .

Yet for the gift of his virgin intelligence
a child is ever our pictur of happiness:
'tis a delight to look on him in tireless play
attentively occupied with a world of wonders.

          Robert Bridges — *The Testament of Beauty.*

CHAPTER V

A CHILD WITH CHILDREN

WHEN the great Dr. Johnson was bored he diverted himself by thinking of Tom Thumb. Dr. Osler's thoughts turned to little children in all moods. No one can appreciate his psychology unless they know him with children. They trooped after him in ever-growing numbers from the time of his young manhood, when he was Prince of Fairyland to them, to those last years when it was their hands that best piloted him through rough waters into the harbour. In the last days of his life, when he was slowly sinking, he asked for the miniature of a child he loved and kept it by him.

Five years is a long time in the life of a child; and it was during his five years in Philadelphia that most of his letters to children were written. After that, though his army of innocents steadily increased, they were generally in the same city with him. He was, what few grown people are to children — of their own age; only he was their chosen Captain. The lithe form full of vitality, the beautiful dark face so vivid, and the radiant eyes, were all sympathy for them; their pleasures, their woes, were his pleasures, his woes; everything in their lives was a part of him. Often he would tell them the most realistic tales, such as the story of the wicked little boy who crept out of bed on a black, howling, stormy night and cut out the tummy of his sister's precious doll and how, when he was wiping his gory knife on his little shirt and licking his lips in fearsome glee, his father, armed with a cane, crept up behind him; and then, at the most exciting moment, the children thrilled, he would say there was a dear old lady with a pain in her pansy, and he must go at once, which he would proceed to do with the howling children in full pursuit.

In the midst of his strenuous life in Philadelphia, young, with not much surplus in his bank account, adventuring into a new country, many eyes watching how he would acquit himself, with very vital interests, his life with the children in Canada was almost as complete as when he lived there. There was no radio in those days but the nine little Francis children felt the air full of communications from him. To Willie Francis, " Willum," his " little Doctur "; " Did I just hear your voice in the choir (I was about to spell choir, quire) singing ' Days and moments quickly flying? ' It is only 650 miles to Philadelphia and the ducks and other birds are flying South. Let me know what I shall bring you for Christmas."

And to Beatrice:

" Dear little Trixie Girl: You can I always remember. Did you get my 10000000000 blessings on Dr. Osler's card? Whisper! good Trixie girl! do you want anything, sweetheart? The doctor is a bad old man. He went to Mr. Wanamaker's yesterday and bought you three dresses and a lovely spring coat. I hope you found your watch; it was very sad to lose it. The old doctor can stand another one. Bill to Dr. Osler. . . . Are you better? My heart bleeds for you in seven places. I think you will love the rings I have bought you — such beauties! There are one or two other things which I have got. Sweeties, too, beauty chocolate. So you shall have a nice Xmas."

" Dear Willum:

Its myself that's longing to see you old boy! Why do you not come down some night in your sleep — *you could* come; perhaps your skinny little body could not as it could not fly through the air but your *spirit* could. What if it did not get back in time for your body to wake up in the morning? I think you had better stay at home until you can come, body and all. . . . Write me a letter soon. Xmas seems very far away. I wish it came every month. . . ."

" Dear old Willum: It is a long time since I heard from you. *A'SLEEP!* Wake up! Do you hear me shaking you? How your poor bones rattle! Get fatter. How glad you must be to get to the Island again; but it's cold, my Willum, and your poor bones have not much to cover them."

" My dear little Missus: You can I never forget! Perhaps in your sleep about 12 o'clock you sometimes hear me say ' Good night Missus! Good night Bea! Perhaps you hear me in your sleep." The children, with their little heads on the pillows in the darkened nursery, listening hard to catch his " Whisper! blessings on you, don't be afraid. Your own doctor loves and all will be well," almost certainly they held tight in their fists under their pillows a very solid quarter of a dollar from him to bring dreams to reality — and the Sweetie shop.

After a visit to the Zoo in Philadelphia, a colleague, imagining that he was writing up something learned about animal motions or habits, would have had a surprise had he looked over his shoulder. How it would have puzzled Dr. Mitchell and Dr. Pepper to read:

" Dear Willum: Do you know what happened to that tiger — the one with the lady inside? Well! Just listen! He fell asleep after that heavy dinner and her clothes were hard to digest which made him snore. Three East Indians in Bengal, where the Tigers live, heard the noise; and, said the biggest one called Gwynjosepher to Jackalaph, ' Send Willumjumbee for the big net and we will throw it over the Tiger while he is asleep.' So little Willumjumbee brought the strong wire net and they crept up and pulled the end tight. He did not even wake but slept on for 2 days, 6 hours, 4 minutes and 10 seconds. And then wasn't there a row! but no good! he could not break or get out of the net. They kept him there for 10 days until the lady was all digested. And poor Mr. Tiger was so weak from the want of food that even little Willumjumbee could knock him over. They took him to Calcutta and sold him for $500. And where do you think he came? but here to Philadelphia, the Zoological Gardens; and when you come down you shall see him. Said he to me the other day as I stood by his cage, ' Lady taste good. Wish I was out again. This beefsteak which we get here is not so nice.' And when I told him that *you* knew about his tricks he looked pretty blue; and when I showed him your letter he growled and raged and said: ' It is Willumjumbee. I know his writing and if I could get to 126 Wilton Avenue he should take a ride inside me and I would not ask for his school ticket.' I am very sorry I gave him your address, but if he came he would prefer, I know, Mrs. Francis or the cook.

Goodbye, write soon.

Your loving old Doctor? "

The unprepossessing little Tommie cat that his colleagues were accustomed to see ruminating in his room was in reality a creature of imagination, tenderness and philanthropy; he was Katamont — King of Kats, doing missionary work through the mail in numerous letters to the kittens of the Francis children.

" Dear Miss Pussie: It is a long time since I left you at the Island in the tender care of your dear little Mistress, Miss Gwendolyn Francis. You were very young then and I think your manners were not very good. You will pardon my referring to the fact but I know you will not mind very much and I feel sure that now you are a model little kitten, just as good as your mistress, I hope everybody is kind to you, and please, if Miss Beatrice or Master Jimmie should tease you do not scratch them very hard. Be careful of Miss Gwendolyn and touch her very softly *with your claws in*. If you see her sad-looking or unhappy go and purr to her and if you can, get on her shoulder and whisper in her ear — ' *Cheer up, your uncle Doctor loves and all will be well.*' You will see the sweetest smile break over her face and you will mew for very joy.

" Now Miss Pussie you are growing big and fat and you will soon be getting very tired of milk and of cooked meat and you will feel *compelled* to go hunting mice and rats. I have a great favor to ask — please like a good little Cattie when you catch a mouse, if you *must* kill it, do so quickly and do not torture it. I would love you much more if you would just take it up gently with your *lips*, not your *teeth* and carry it to Miss Gwendolyn. She has such a kind heart that I am sure she will be able to per- suade you to let it go. If you only knew what nice people Mr. and Mrs. Mouse and the little Mouseses are you would ask them to tea and be very kind. They talk so prettily and dress in such nice brown clothes. Do try to be friendly with them. I know it is hard as your family and the Mouses have been bitter enemies for hundreds of years, but try just once and you will never regret it and I know your little Mistress will love you ever so much more if you are kind. Good bye.

Katamont
King of Kats."

" My dear Miss Pussie:
    The nice kind man called Dr. Osler was at breakfast the other morning when the girl brought in a letter from your little Mistress. You should have seen just how glad

he was and he read aloud that nice piece of poetry and if I am not mistaken I saw a tear glisten in his eye. He told me how good his little missus — for so he calls your mistress — was and how kind and he said he hoped some day that she would come and live with him. He talks too of a little girl called Bee — says she is his sweetheart. He is a very funny man but I like him as he gives me meat and milk and never drives me away. I hope you are growing fat and strong. I feel my skin too tight for me very often. I am just three months old and I have not yet got my second teeth. Goodbye.

Your distant friend
Tommie Catte."

The anti-vivisectionists in Philadelphia would have found this attitude in their arch enemy most irritating; and would have referred those who thought it lovely to the story of the Walrus and the Carpenter.

We know them, these benign wizards of the nursery; but there was never one just like him. Harlequin came with him, and the Brownies, and the Fairies. And when tired of the dream there came reality in dollars, and pretty dresses, and books, and skates.

With his little cousins, the Francis children and the children of his sister, Mrs. Gwyn, and the Palmer Howard children, he was perhaps in closest relationship. But no house was ever entered by him, if it contained a nursery, that he failed to make that his first objective. To steal the children's cat, hide it (and anyone trying quickly to catch and hide a cat knows it to be no light feat) and then start on a hunt with them until it was triumphantly recovered with shrieks and war whoops, was pure refreshment for his soul. He knew how children loved the same words — and myriads of notes begin with " You do I never forget," or " You do I always remember "; and when they

are ill his heart is always " bleeding in seven places," or
" It's a sad day for this Israel."

On every birthday — and there seemed to be one at least
for every month in the calendar — a Mr. Webb was called
upon to supply cakes and candies, ice cream, or jelly.
There would certainly have been a slump in the house
of Webb had an overworked young physician in Philadelphia put away childish things.

" Dear Willum: I hope mammy arranged for your birthday Kake. Do not let her forget; we should have ordered it
ourselves. You shall have buns, I shriek — dozens not near
one — if you'll be bad yea, tons and tons of buns. This
day two weeks I shall be on the briny. Ugh! Ugh! throwing up the whole thing perhaps."

Dr. Francis explains that " Our parson in a sermon had
said that if anyone could disprove the Resurrection ' I will
throw up the whole thing, collects, epistles and gospels,
right here in this place.' "

" My dear Willum: ' A lion emerged from his lair, for a
short summer cut to his hair, But the barber he wept,
While his customers slept, As they waited their turn in
the chair.' Did you ever see anything to beat it? the face
of the lion! the hair! and the tears of the poor barber. The
yawn of the kitten in the chair — never saw anything better in my life! and the old sheep. How I laughed over it!
The little pussy asleep in the other one's hat. And then the
old bald eagle coming to get a lotion. Oh! it is just *awful
good.* I hope you saw it in November number of St.
Nicholas. Has Mama got it yet? I told her to. The breeches
on the small kitten and the buttons. I wonder are they
sewed on his skin."

How old was he, we wonder? Ages young! But we old

boys and girls, many of us, remember that picture in St. Nicholas and how we too laughed at it.

"You are a gay old codger," he writes Jack Francis. "I wish I were near enough to pounce on you. Do you see this $1.00 bill? That's a fine old lady, is she not? She is fat, fatter than grandmother and can stand the cold; so I do not mind sending her north."

In another letter:

"I am sorry you have had such a bad attack of the jolly-go-nimbles . . . I enclose $2. I say, Jack, these are pretty clean bills. The old lady is Mrs. Washington. Say 'how-do-you-do' to her; she was a fine woman."

Never before had Mrs. Washington caused a laugh; but you can hear Dr. Osler shouting as he romped away with those children. "Stop that laughing; she was a fine woman."

But it was not all laughter by any means — education and religion, the props needed to keep the little trees straight as they grew in his sunlight, were seriously considered; but he broached these problems from the child's level.

To the little girls when he feared they were trying too hard to please him: "Let me know how you get on with your exams. *Two* or *three* would be first-rate — better than one. The other poor girl needs that first prize. Do not try too hard for the medal; have you not got me? Am I not worth many medals and perhaps the other girl who wouldn't have it has not an Uncle doctor."

"My dear Willum: I wish you and Jack to have some lessons through the summer which will prepare you for Port Hope when you go in September. You will not mind, old fellow, will you? . . . It will only be about three hours a week and it will be such an advantage to you to go there knowing a little Latin."

And then when the little doctor does go, he writes:

" Dear old William:

. . . I envy you. I had such a happy life at school. May you have the same. You are such a little schooner *sailing with* a gaff that the light is too strong for my eyes, when I think of you away from home, but you are a plucky little laddie; so keep cheerful and write soon to your loving old
Doctor."

And again:

" I think of you very often but it would be nicer to see your cheerful little face, my friend. I have ordered your cake from Mr. Webb and ice or jelly — whichever you like best. I have sent Palmer Cox's Brownies. Such a lovely book. You will love it. Sarah Crew I have sent to the little girlies . . . Poor Sarah, I am glad she was happy at last. The light was rather strong, my Willum, as I read that story."

" My dear little Willum

I am sad all over at the thought of your ear being so bad. I hope it is much better today. It must have been very painful but you are a good little codger. I wish I had been with you to help nurse you. The beating on your drum must have been very loud but that it should have *burst* is very sad. A person feels the loss of one drum when he wishes to make a noise."

On a postcard he wrote:

> I will to you speed
> If you truly me need
> But meanwhile apply
> Three or four crumbs of bread
> To the edge of your head
> If relief does not come
> While you spell the word thumb

Take a hair of your mother
Or sister or brother
Cut it up very fine
And take it in wine
No head can withstand
A medicine so bland
The ache will just fly
Like the glance of an eye.
For advice thus by post
My charges at most
Are a dollar a word.
                    Mailliw Relso, D.M.

Dr. Francis is inclined to think this is his only venture in verse. When the " little doctur " was older, in a big school, ill with typhoid his playmate was Physician-in-chief in the Johns Hopkins Hospital — and the following letter shows he had not changed:

" Dear Willie: —

I was so distressed to hear that you had the jim-jams, and had been laid up in the sick room at school. That was a very sad day for Israel, but I hope your pansy is better, and your tongue clean, and your diaphragm working all right, and your pansy all right, and your liver not swollen, and your spleen not tender, and your temperature down, and your pulse not more than 120, and your head clear. I think whenever you feel very badly you should send me a postal card, and say so, because it is very shocking for me to hear that you have been ill and not to have sent you a line and said that the light was too strong for my eyes, but I expect by this time that you are doing well, but please do not work hard, and don't mind about old general proficiency. Let some other fellow have it this year. Don't be a hog. You have got enough of those things, and had better stop it."

Grant, the oldest of the Francis children, died in the winter of 1888, and he wrote:

" My sweet little Missus:

I am just longing to see you. It seems years since I kissed you good bye in February. I have just been as sad as sad can be about poor dear Grantie's death but God knows what is best and when we are sent for we must go. I shall be home in a few weeks now — about the 10th of July and I shall just eat you and Bea. We shall have such a good time together. Write to me soon and tell me what I shall bring you, any nice little things you would like. I shall buy nice summer dresses. Good bye darling, Your loving old   Doctor."

The wisdom of his way with the children was shown by their love for, and confidence in, him. No child would ever have told him a lie — why should they? He understood. The little money boxes he gave them were to be filled for purposes they approved of — no " Waste not, want not " pasted on their lids.

Dr. Francis writes: " You can imagine our adoration of him, the days were always marked off by us on the calendars he gave us, towards his next promised visit; and tears when he couldn't fulfil the promise."

The writers of the children's great classics cannot equal him in love; they wrote for children; he was one of them. Some unmarried women have almost equalled him, but not quite; they had no other vocation and, being women, were too seriously minded; wonderful nurses and comforters, but not so good as playmates.

Robert Louis Stevenson knew one child — himself — so perfectly that all children know themselves through him. Though Lewis Carroll only knew a few children intimately, he did give the world *Alice* and other priceless nonsense. Dr. John Brown has given us *Marjorie Fleming* and very few children like her at all; his knowledge of children was almost limited to her alone; and she was brought into his life only at auspicious moments. And though Wordsworth could write *Lucy Gray* and *We are Seven,* you cannot imagine his enjoying any but a most melancholy child — and the thought of a group of children prancing about Grasmere is terrifying. Of the modern writers Milne has made a delightful contribution to children's classics; and Walter de la Mare has given us charming poems. The world should rise up and call such writers " blessed." But they are very busy writing and the number of children they know personally is very limited and authors must not be interrupted too often. Some of the most beautiful poems about children were written by a man who kept his own children in a state of subordination, and his wife harassed almost to death keeping things right for the birth of his mental infants.

Dr. Osler knew hundreds of children; hardly a day passed that he did not enter some child's life. As you look over the piles of notes and cards and letters he wrote to them the impression they make is hard to explain, difficult to analyse. You feel like saying, " What a heavenly person "; and " the light is too strong for your eyes."

Who among the writers of fiction could have drawn him? Only Dickens. Not that Dickens could have painted Osler, the man of culture; Osler, as he haunted the Bodleian, and followed the trail of his profession down the echoing aisles of the past; nor yet Osler, the great physician. But only Dickens could have been one with him with children or in the wards of the poorhouse, sitting beside the down-trodden, the lowly and the suffering. Only Dickens could have measured comprehendingly the sweetness and tenderness of the great heart of a child in the brilliant man, making all his rich endowment merely a setting for his humanity.

Baltimore

For countless generations the prophets and kings of humanity have desired to see the things which men have seen, and to hear the things which men have heard in the course of the wonderful nineteenth century. . . . To us whose work is with the sick and suffering, the great boon of this wonderful century, with which no other can be compared, is the fact that the leaves of the tree of Science have been for the healing of the nations. . . . There is no one measure which can compare with the decrease of physical suffering in man, woman, and child when stricken by disease or accident. This is the one fact of supreme personal import to every one of us. This is the Promethean gift of the century to man.

Wm. Osler — *Medicine in the Nineteenth Century.*

CHAPTER VI

BALTIMORE

First Years at Hopkins — Marriage

JOHNS HOPKINS, on his death, left seven million dollars for a university to foster higher education, and a hospital to relieve suffering — both in the city of Baltimore to perpetuate his name. A part of the community was unimpressed. The Old Baltimore had an ingrained aversion to change of any kind but the community at large felt a little thrill at the thought of a big college in its midst and was greatly disappointed when the College emerged into the University. It was opened in 1876 (without prayer and without buildings). Johns Hopkins had selected an extraordinarily clear-headed board of trustees, and after two years of deliberation they brought from California, Daniel Coit Gilman, installed him as President, and were guided by him in developing the policies of the new university, and the selection of the staff. It was Mr. Gilman's influence that put the idea of a university, other than a college, into being; and in doing so raised the whole standard of education in the United States. It was men and not buildings that he emphasized; and nothing, and no one could influence him in the choice of his professors other than what he felt was in them to make them men of destiny. How he succeeded is history. " Where is the Johns Hopkins? " a stranger asked an old darkey. " It ain't anywheres, sah! " was the reply. " Just a lot of queer gentlemen going about; but they won't do nobody no harm, tho' some of them are ijuts with long hair." It was after this manner that Baltimore met fame in a modern dress.

When Mr. Gilman came to Baltimore the pressure put on him to select Maryland men for high places left him unmoved; with an unwearied smile ever on his face he insisted that sectional considerations were not to be entertained — the right man, wherever he was, East or West, North or South — and somehow there did not seem many right men South. It was incredible! Still President Gilman smiled, and the trustees backed him and the University became even in its infancy a beacon. Baltimoreans, when they left their city, were much surprised to find that the Hopkins was well known; and when they went abroad were horrified to realize that it was the only thing known about their State. Oysters, canvasback ducks, terrapins, beautiful women — some of the *élite* had heard of these, but not many; and all had heard of the Johns Hopkins. It was astonishing! President and Mrs. Gilman were delightful, but most of the professors — no, they seemed to be thinking of something else and no one knew what it was. Then the University had been opened without prayer! And no explanation could make that right to the majority of Baltimoreans.

Dr. John S. Billings was appointed medical adviser to the Hospital. It was he who planned the buildings and for twelve years, while they were in progress of building, he went over the country lecturing, showing his plans, and advertising the Hospital and the future Medical School. And Mr. Gilman was consulting all over the world men of the highest medical and intellectual standing.

The Hospital and the University were independent foundations with independent funds; but it was planned that the University should develop a medical school which would function in close coöperation with the Hospital. Though the Philosophical Department of the University was opened in 1876, the Medical School was long delayed. The nucleus of the medical faculty was developed in 1883 with Ira Remsen in chemistry, Newell Martin in biology and William H. Welch in pathology. To have a chair of pathology on a full university basis was a new departure in this country. A number of young medical men assembled at the Hospital and engaged in advanced studies. By 1886 this had developed into something like an institute of experimental medicine, with Dr. Welch as the leader of a group of enthusiastic workers.

On May 6th, 1889 the Hospital was opened — with all flags flying — and prayer! Mr. Gilman smiled, and he had a right to smile, for had he not made a medical nucleus out of men, where only men and not bricks and mortar were needed? And now when buildings were needed, here was the very last word in a Hotel Dieu — and with it he was presenting two guaranteed immortals, Drs. Welch and Osler, and around them a group of luminaries. Surely it was a cloudless sky! Far from it. If the community in 1876 felt keenly that no Maryland men were on its faculty, it felt even more deeply the fact that none of their able physicians were to find a berth in the new hospital.

The University of Maryland had important and able men on its faculty and the discontent over a rival school was intense. It was the day of family doctors, many of them admirable masters of the art of medicine, much cared for by their patients, with whom they were autocrats. You did not decide upon your ailments and go off, on a friend's advice, to a specialist; your family physician settled that. He was often wrong but more often right — not from scientific knowledge but from knowledge of his patient from birth, and of his forbears. The physician was one of the family and the family budget was well known to him and always considered; such a state of things was not to be easily overturned. Every house had its old people very personally cared for by its young people. "My grand-father," said an old Baltimorean to a new-comer, "is in his 85th year. He walks about two miles every good day and never fails to take a strong toddy before going to bed. My great-grandfather was a hundred when he died — and so I think we can get along very well without looking up germs." Baltimore was not a wealthy city; there was no lavish expenditure except upon food and wine and servants. The Baltimorean had much the English feeling — a comfortable home first, family portraits and a coat-of-arms in the dining room, beautiful women in the drawing room, and the men taken very much into account. Germs, hygiene — it was hardly proper to discuss such things, and Science was a dangerous, ill-mannered cub barking at their reverend parsons. There were open gutters in the city that were only cleansed by the rains of heaven. In the alleys where the colored population swarmed, the odors in a dry season had better not be described. And what was true of Baltimore would have been true of all cities South, and of many North and West! But Baltimore was entirely satisfied; the houses were kept clean by many servants; the red brick pavements and great trees, and even the gutters with their stepping stones, were picturesque. Into this paradise first entered Johns Hopkins with his money and his nose for reform, and following him the Johns Hopkins University with Mr. Gilman in control, having drawn about him from all parts of the country and from across the water a group of keen-eyed scientists. Science and Art are irreconcilable step-sisters. The candle or the electric light; the wood fire or the steam radiator; the old horse pulling the plow with the strong man dreaming as he guides or the steam cultivator; the one-horse buggy with the doctor driving — his darkey boy slouched by his side or the jolly little Ford. The former was deep in the hearts of the people. But the old order was changing

— had changed — and the old horse went to the bone yard and the old doctor thought he saw his own grave in the near future.

Dr. Welch had been five years at the Hospital and was more than any other person responsible for Dr. Osler's coming. He had made his place with the medical world in Baltimore from the beginning. That was not only due to his extraordinary personality but also to the fact that his line of work offered no competition with the practising physicians. With Dr. Osler it was different. He was entering their field, especially in consultations, but there was not a physician in the city who did not soon feel him his friend though with ungloved hands he attacked the condition of things that made " the American system of medical education a byword among the nations." There were five medical schools in Baltimore: the best granted diplomas, with the right to practise, after two years' instruction; and most of the candidates had ended their general education with the high school. The rivalry between the homeopaths and regular practitioners was very strong. Feeling, as Dr. Osler did, the necessity for a thorough training for physicians, he strongly advocated the reservation to the State of the power to grant the right to practise. It is to be noticed that a Bill advocating the creation of a State Board of Medical Examiners had been rejected by the Legislature a few years earlier.

On his arrival in Baltimore Dr. Osler was asked to give the annual address at the meeting of the Medical and Chirurgical Society of Maryland. He chose for his subject *The Licence to Practise;* this is in part what he said: " It makes one's blood boil to think there are sent out year by year scores of men called doctors who have never attended a case of labour, and who are utterly ignorant of the ordinary every-day diseases which they may be called upon to treat; men who have never seen the inside of a hospital ward and who would not know Scarpa's space from the sole of a foot. Yet, gentlemen, this is the disgraceful condition which some school men have the audacity to ask you to perpetuate; to continue to entrust interests so sacred to hands so unworthy. Is it to be wondered, considering this shocking laxity that there is a widespread distrust in the public of professional education, and that quacks, charlatans and impostors possess the land? "

He showed his magnanimity and practical grasp of the situation, and recognized that the legislature could not differentiate between different sects in medicine, when he added: " We cannot, however, escape from the important fact that in the eyes of the law we all stand equal, and if we wish legislation for the protection of the public we have got to ask for it together, not singly. I know that this is gall and wormwood to many — at the bitterness of it the gorge rises but it is a question that has to be met fairly and squarely. When we think of the nine or ten subjects which we have in common, we may surely in the interests of the public, bury animosities and agree to differ on the question of Therapeutics! " He pointed out the way he thought they should go to work and in a comparatively short time he won the confidence and love and coöperation of the Baltimoreans. He made it clear that unless they awoke to the situation their medical diplomas would, in a few years, be useless scraps of paper. The United States by and large was awakening, Harvard had started; the University of Pennsylvania followed; and in Baltimore the new university was about to spring into leadership. Its ideals were not to please Baltimore but to lead the country. For the University of Maryland, the Johns Hopkins, the Medical Colleges here and there, all Dr. Osler wanted was their good, and they knew him sincere. The Johns Hopkins was starting a big experiment; all would share in it; and soon they all did. No one could possibly have accomplished this but Dr. Osler. Without the least touch of diplomacy but with great sympathy, he drew all into the general advance. The country physicians were poor and many of them very ignorant. Dr. Osler got hold of them, brought them together, lifted their positions. He was a great believer in frequent medical meetings bringing men from all parts of the community together; and the clasp of his hand was rarely forgotten and the word he said was always remembered.

When this quickening power is in the personality of some human being it is the most powerful alchemy for good or evil in the world. It is not merely love; it is inspiration; undying life touches us. Dr. Osler had this power. Women who knew him were not silly about him. They did not imagine themselves in love with him. Men were not his slaves, but they were suddenly alive; saw beauty, forgot themselves.

When Dr. Osler took the chair of medicine at the Johns Hopkins Hospital the opportunity to establish a clinic such as he had long conceived was open to him. Dr. Welch occupied the chair of Pathology and Dr. Osler gave up his work along this line and devoted himself to clinics; and he created what Dr. Welch calls " the first medical clinic in any English-speaking country worthy of the name." At a dinner given by the profession in the United States and Canada in 1905 Dr. Osler spoke of his ambition " to build up a great clinic on Teutonic lines, not on those previously followed here and in England, but on lines which have placed the scientific medicine of Germany in the forefront of the world." And he writes: " If I have done anything to promote the growth of clinical medicine, it has been in this direction, in the formation of a large clinic with well organized series of assistants and house physicians and with proper laboratories in which to work at the intricate problems that confront us in internal medicine. For the opportunities which I have had at Johns Hopkins Hospital to carry out these ideas I am truly thankful."

To the German method he added the English system of clinical clerkships. He was especially interested in teaching undergraduate students of medicine; but the Johns Hopkins Medical School was not opened until five years after he came to Baltimore; and during this period he was engaged in " the dry husks of graduate teachings " at the Hospital, and in developing the plans of the Medical School. Nevertheless the teaching at the Johns Hopkins even before the Medical School was opened was an inspiration and a model for the entire medical world. Following the methods of German clinics long term residents took the place of the usual short term interneship. His first Resident Physician had under him three assistant residents, forming a nucleus, and the vitality and enthusiasm which emanated from it steadily increased.

Mr. Gilman had undertaken to be acting director of the hospital, making his home there until a Superintendent could be found. There is something rather fine in the way in which, after securing his marionettes, he gave them the stage; backing, encouraging them; giving himself, but refraining from any attempt at control. In 1889, Dr. Howard A. Kelly, the gynecologist, and his assistant, Dr. Hunter Robb were brought down from Philadelphia and in August of that year Dr. Henry M. Hurd became Superintendent of the Hospital and Mr. Gilman was relieved. The little group lived together like one family; there were no disputes. They were all young; Dr. Osler under 40; Dr. Welch a year younger; Dr. Halsted 37; Dr. Hurd 36; and Dr. Kelly only 31. Dr. Welch, of whom Dr. Osler said: " He has the greatest mind, the greatest soul, and the greatest heart of any man I know "; and lately, on his eightieth birthday, others increased the echo of those words into a mighty sound; Dr. Kelly, a terrifically rapid worker, a wizard of a surgeon and a perfectly orthodox Christian; Dr. Halsted, the surgeon — the Professor, so called; not so willing as the others to communicate his ideas. They all worked together, admiring each other, and all his colleagues loved the dark-eyed Canadian in a way few men have been loved. To them belongs the credit of organizing the professional staff of the Hospital and it was the first time in America that young resident physicians and surgeons had a chance for prolonged clinical training equal to those already existing for assistants in the preclinical laboratories.

Many accounts come down to us of the delightful life the first young doctors had together — eager work, congeniality, high spirits, a common purpose and an uncommon opportunity. The air was kept lively by each playing some hoax on the other, their chief the greatest sinner of them all. Not a high order of wit, but it served to refresh them, and their work was of a very high order; no letting down on that. You feel like crying with Miranda, " O brave young world that has such people in it! " Dr. Osler writes of this time: " The men of the first few years of the existence of this hospital formed a very happy band — young and eager, with a great problem before them, too great, indeed, to be fully appreciated by us. It was a motley group that the gift of a new foundation in medicine had brought together, strangers to each other, strangers in a strange city; yet there was something in the spirit of the place, that quickly ripened a mutual trust into good fellowship. The ' lead ' already given by the great Triumvirate, Remsen and Welch, with Mr. Gilman's strong personality and intense interest in the Hospital, made the running comparatively easy. It has often been remarked that the reputation at the Johns Hopkins Medical School has been made by its young men, to which I may note incidentally my shelves bear weighty testimony in the twelve volumes with the 500 papers of the graduates of the school during the first eight years."

He was ever active in organizing societies, encouraging his associates and assistants to work together for the common good and for their individual advancement. The most important of their societies was the " Monday Evening." Dr. Cushing records that " the first meeting was held on October 22nd, 1889, with Welch presiding and Hunter Robb acting as secretary; and before this group of enthusiastic young people, eager to acquire knowledge and to control opinions by experimental tests, hardly a subject could be mentioned that did not lead to further work in view of the free and suggestive exchange of ideas. In the history of medicine there has never been anything quite like it. There was no need to drum up an audience for these meetings, and it is recalled that Reginald H. Fitz, who had about this time come down from Boston to learn something of the spirit of that new place which already was being so much talked about, likened the life to that of a monastery, with the unusual feature that the monks did not appear to bother their minds about the future."

A week later the Journal Club, similar to the foreign periodical clubs that Dr. Osler had organized in Montreal and Philadelphia, was started. The purpose was to keep the staff informed of the work being done in every branch of medical science throughout the world. Current literature was reviewed, book notices written and many subjects were enthusiastically discussed. President Gilman would not let all this go unrecognized. The seal of the Hopkins must be upon it; and in December the first number of the *Johns Hopkins Hospital Bulletin* came into being. It was most important in bringing the work of the Hospital before the medical world. The staff, and now the people in the city, had been disappointed at the delay in opening a Medical School. The Hopkins Bulletin gave an announcement of courses to be offered to graduates. Teaching was, they felt, essential even for men engaged in research.

The Historical Club was also established at this time. Dr. Billings, Dr. Osler and Dr. Welch were responsible. It met one Monday every month and Dr. Osler for fifteen years never failed to attend unless he was ill or out of town. This Club started interest in the bibliography and history of the profession.

Only those who knew Dr. Osler well, could imagine how he missed his intimate relation with the College of Physicians in Philadelphia and its fine library. In Baltimore the library of the Medical and Chirurgical Faculty was crumbling into disuse. It possessed a few hundred volumes kept in the basement of the Maryland Historical Society. The very mention of them made one think of mould and dust. Dr. Osler volunteered to go on the Library Committee and he served on it devotedly until he left the city in 1905. He brought the library into life, secured for it good quarters, increased it from a few hundred volumes to 15,000, helped to support it, both morally and financially, until it was on its feet, succeeded in getting a trained librarian; and his interest remained with it as long as he lived. This is typical. His interest in any library once begun never ended — the library at McGill, the Surgeon General's in Washington, the College of Physicians in Philadelphia, the Johns Hopkins Hospital, the Maryland Faculty, and many others. This was one of the great absorptions of his life. Dr. Welch has written: " It may, I think, be safely predicted that history will preserve Osler's fame as a serious and scholarly student of medical history and as a bibliographer as only second to his repute as a great clinical teacher. Possibly being based more upon written records than upon tradition, it may be more enduring. But his interest in this matter arose not only from the mind but from the heart. He was a passionate lover of books: ' It is hard for me,' he writes, ' to speak of the value of libraries in terms which would not seem exaggerated. Books have been my delight these thirty years and from them I have received incalculable benefits. To study the phenomena of disease without books is to sail an uncharted sea; while to study books without patients is not to go to sea at all. . . . There should be in connection with every library a corps of instructors in the art of reading who would, as a labor of love, teach the young idea how to read. An old writer says there are four sorts of readers: " Sponges which attract all without distinguishing; Howre-glasses which receive and powre out as fast. Bagges which only retain the dregges of the spices and let the wine escape, and Sives which retaine the best onely." A man wastes a great many years before he reaches the " Sive " stage. . . . For the general practitioner a well-used library is one of the few correctives of the premature senility which is so apt to overtake him. . . . It is astonishing with how little reading a doctor can practise medicine, but it is not astonishing how badly he may do it. . . . I should like to see in each library a select company of the immortals set apart for special adoration. Each country might have its representatives in a sort of alcove of Fame in which the great medical classics were gathered. Not necessarily books — more often the epoch-making contributions to be found in ephemeral journals.' "

And in another address: " What should attract us all is the study of the growth of the American mind in medicine since the starting of the colonies. As in a mirror this story is reflected in the literature of which you are guardians and collectors, in letters, in manuscripts, in pamphlets, in books, and in journals. In the eight generations which have passed, the men who have striven and struggled — men whose lives are best described in the words of St. Paul,

' in journeyings often, in perils of water, in perils of the city, in perils in the wilderness, in perils in the sea, in weariness and painfulness, in watchings often, in hunger and thirst and in fastings ' — these men, of some of whom I have told you somewhat, have made us what we are. With the irrevocable past into which they have gone lies our future, since our condition is the resultant of forces which, in three generations, have moulded the profession of a new and mighty empire. From the vantage ground of a young country we can trace in the literature how three great streams of influence — English, French and German — have blended into the broad current of American medicine on which we are afloat. Adaptiveness, lucidity and thoroughness may be said to be the characteristics of these Anglican, Gallic and Teutonic influences, and it is no small part of your study to see that these influences, the combination of which gives to medicine on this continent its distinctly eclectic quality, are maintained and extended." And again in another place: " An evolutionist cannot neglect sources, the original texts. You cannot ignore or be ungrateful for the work of the past. The new order issues from the old. And a physician who does not need a library sinks to the level of a cross-counter prescriber."

On October 9th, 1889, the Nurses' home was opened; and the Training School for Nurses, under Miss Isabel Hampton, inaugurated. It rapidly took a high rank and it was the first time such a school had been recognized to be an essential part of a hospital. Dr. Osler always had a good deal of sympathy for the nurses; perhaps he thought their lives a little drab. Fortunately for the discipline of the School there was a woman at its head to whom a joke had its serious side and whose subordinates could leave no work neglected because they were women. Dr. Osler's gay banter, however, lightened many a grey life and freshened the atmosphere of a place where human wrecks were always being swept into sight.

In the Spring of 1890 he went abroad — going first to England, then spending the months of May and June making careful inspections of the leading German and French clinics. July found him in London again — and then home. He sent a series of " Letters to My House Physicians " and these were published serially in the New York and Montreal Medical journals. In one from Strasburg he wrote: " The universities of Germany are her chief glory, and the greatest boon she can give to us in the New World is to return our young men infected with the spirit of earnestness and with the love of thoroughness which characterizes the work done in them."

He spent three weeks in Paris where he attended Pasteur's hydrophobia inoculations. In Berlin he heard Koch's famous address on " Bacterial Investigations," in which the latter announced the discovery of tuberculin as a cure for tuberculosis. The medical world went wild over this, but it was premature. Dr. Osler was keenly interested and on his return home made his students thoroughly familiar with the subject. He gave the tuberculin exhaustive trial in the hospital and reported: " The extraordinary enthusiasm which has been aroused by the announcement is a just tribute to the character of Robert Koch who is a model worker of unequalled thoroughness, whose ways and methods have always been those of the patient investigator, well worthy of the confidence which other experts in pathology place in his statements. The cold test of time can alone determine how far the claims which he has advanced will be justified, and meanwhile the question has been transferred as far as human medicine is concerned, from the laboratory to the clinical ward, in which the careful observations of the next months will furnish the necessary data."

Dr. Osler formed a society for the purpose of studying tuberculosis in all its phases, and he named it *The Laennec* after the famous Frenchman, the inventor of the stethoscope, who had done so much work in the study of that disease. With his interest thoroughly aroused he became the prime mover in the crusade against tuberculosis in Maryland. And this subject held his interest unflaggingly throughout his life.

As late as 1902 Baltimore, in many respects, was an overgrown village. The streets, in general, were paved with cobble-stones; and, as has been said, the drainage was carried off by surface gutters, which were so irregular that little puddles of stagnant water were common. And in the streets, here and there, were public pumps which drew from the contaminated subsoil, and supplied many people with their drinking water. No wonder that typhoid fever was rife! Such a condition, and the need of an infectious disease hospital, and the general apathy of the community and of the city authorities with regard to the public health, naturally aroused Dr. Osler's ire; and at a public meeting he actually shook his finger in the Mayor's face. Those who recall the Mayor of that time would agree that it would have required an earthquake to arouse him; but Dr. Osler's finger did it. Dr. Cushing tells us that " Dr. Bowditch of Boston, the guest of the evening, recalls that this unlooked-for tirade made his hair stand on end, and he fully expected that a Southern duel would be precipitated, but to his surprise, later in the evening, he saw the Mayor with his arm over Osler's shoulder talking to him in a most affectionate manner." And it may be opportune to mention at this point one characteristic of Dr. Osler's — his disregard for professional etiquette at any moment where a patient's good was concerned. Just as frankly as he had disregarded the Mayor and the whole corporation where the health of the city was concerned, so in consultation he saw only the patient's need, and wasted not one second in correcting an erroneous diagnosis; and like the Mayor, to the surprise of all, his corrected colleague would, as a rule, walk off with his arm around Dr. Osler's neck, or *vice versa*. The reason for this is perfectly evident; every physician felt himself safe in Dr. Osler's hands; he knew that he could, by no possibility, have a better friend in the profession; that if, with the tip of his finger, he gaily knocked down his house of cards, he would see to it that the foundation was left solid; and no one would contribute so many bricks to the new edifice.

Dr. Osler's work as a propagandist of public health measures was so far-reaching that many thought it his greatest service to his generation; but though he was often the match that lit the fire his work was essentially that of the great humanist clinical physician. An idealist is more often than not neither a propagandist nor a promoter. Dr. Osler did not destroy, but illuminated his sound common sense with his idealism making him that unusual combination, an inspiration and a guide.

In 1890 the Hospital staff was greatly increased and a large number of post graduate students were coming for the winter course. Everything was in full swing and if Dr. Osler's master word was " work " he was showing a discouraging example, for his average speed was beyond most men's. There were, however, those among his colleagues at this early period of the Hospital's life who were also making world records and he had the stimulus of his intellectual peers.

The need of a text-book of medicine for students was being felt and all eyes naturally turned to Dr. Osler as the inevitable man to write it. He had already contributed chapters to several large systems of medicine; his pathological knowledge was unusual in a clinician; he had a far-reaching and intensive knowledge of medicine and a felicitous pen. He was, however, most unwilling to undertake the work. His own words give us the story:

" On several occasions in Philadelphia I was asked by Lee Brothers to prepare a work on Diagnosis and half-promised one. Indeed I had prepared a couple of chapters but continually procrastinated on the plea that up to the fortieth year a man was fit for better things than textbooks. Time went on and as I crossed this date I began to feel that the energy and persistence necessary for the task were lacking. In September 1890 I returned from a four months' trip in Europe, shook myself, and towards the end of the month began a work on Practice. I had nearly finished the chapter on Typhoid Fever when Dr. Granger, Messrs. Appleton's agent, came from New York to ask me to prepare a text-book on Medicine. We haggled for a few weeks about terms and finally, selling my brains to the devil, I signed the contract. My intention had been to publish the book myself and have Lippincott or Blakiston (both of whom offered) handle the book, but the bait of a guaranteed circulation of 10,000 copies in two years and $1500 on the date of publication was too glittering and I was hooked. October, November, December were not very satisfactory months and January first, 1891, saw the Infectious Diseases scarcely completed. I then got well into harness. Three mornings of each week I stayed at home and dictated from 8 A.M. to 1 P.M. On the alternate days I dictated after the morning Hospital visit, beginning about 11:30 A.M. The spare hours of the afternoon were devoted to reference work. Early in May I gave up the house at 209 West Monument Street and went to my rooms at the Hospital. The routine there was: 8 A.M. to 1 P.M. dictation. 2 P.M. visits to the private patients and special cases in the wards, after which revision, *etc.* After 5 P.M. I saw my outside cases; dinner at the Club about 6:30. Loafed until 9:30; bed at 10 P.M. Up at 7 A.M. I had arranged to send manuscripts by first of July and on that date I forwarded five sections but the publishers did not begin to print until the middle of August. The first two weeks of August I spent in Toronto and then with the same routine I practically finished the manuscript by about October the 15th. During the summer the entire manuscript was carefully revised for the press by Mr. Powell of the English department at the University. The last three months of 1891 were devoted to proof reading. In January I made out the Index, and in the entire work nothing so wearied me as the verifying of every reference. Without the help of Lafleur and Thayer, who took the ward work off my hands, I never could have finished in so short a time. My other assistants also rendered much aid in looking up references and special points. During the writing of the work I lost only one afternoon through transient indisposition and never a night's rest. Between September 1890 and January 1892, I gained nearly eight pounds in weight." The last item must have been mentioned to encourage the young.

It seems worth while to be present at the birth of a book that had such a vital life and such vitalizing effect. To some the weak spot in his book was his distrust of drugs; to others that was where it was most in advance of its age. A wonderful book! Indirectly it created the Rockefeller Institute, for it caught Mr. Rockefeller by its lucidity, and sent Mr. Hanna off with a copy under his arm to minister to the sick in Florida. Indirectly it rescued the Hopkins Hospital from its financial troubles after the Baltimore fire: " and, finally," as Dr. Cushing tells us, it contributed " to the incalculable benefit of humanity which the General Education Board has rendered with Mr. Rockefeller's money, owing to its interest in the prevention and cure of disease. Indeed the present position of his colleague Welch as Director of the Institute of Hygiene is remotely due to the fact that Osler set himself thirty years before to write a text-book of medicine and as Falconer Madan said years later, ' succeeded in making a scientific treatise literature.' " The wonderful thing about the book was that specialists agreed that in their specialties he was accurate and illuminating. It has gone through edition after edition and has been translated into French, German, Spanish and Chinese.

The Practice of Medicine was practically finished by the end of December 1891. The dedication to his three teachers, William Arthur Johnson, James Bovell and Robert Palmer Howard starts one thinking of the wonder of it all, of the undeviating strength of his affections. No one who showed him a kindness was ever forgotten. Even their children and grandchildren were befriended by him, not as a duty but as a pleasure and a matter of course.

There is no doubt that the magnetic Canadian with his banter and his seriousness, accorded *Chief* by all, would seem providentially sent for some one's daughter, and some one's daughter, in a city of pretty girls, providentially made for him. He was firmly convinced that a man should be established in his work before he married. To the youth at the University of Toronto in 1903 he repeated what he had said very often in his earlier years: " The mistress of your studies should be the heavenly Aphrodite, the motherless daughter of Uranus. Give her your whole heart, and she will be your protectress and friend. A jealous creature, brooking no second, if she finds you trifling and coquetting with her rival, the younger, earthly Aphrodite, daughter of Zeus and Dione, she will whistle you off and let you down the wind to be a prey perhaps to the examiners, certainly to the worm regret. In plainer language, put your affections in cold storage for a few years, and you will take them out ripened — perhaps a bit mellow — but certainly less subject to those frequent changes which perplex so many young men. Only a grand passion, an all-absorbing devotion to the elder goddess can save the man of congenital tendency to philandering, the flighty Lydgate who sports with Celia and Dorothea, and upon whom the judgment ultimately falls in a basil-plant of a wife like Rosamond."

But now the time was ripe. He was 42 and the matrons were anxious. Baltimore was unfortunate! Philadelphia held the ace of hearts. The straight course of his abounding luck was unbroken. Exactly the right woman from every conceivable angle was there to marry him at exactly the right time. She was the widow of Dr. Samuel Gross, of Philadelphia, and before her first marriage was Grace Linzee Revere, of Boston, a descendant of Paul Revere. There had been some rumours about Dr. Osler and Mrs. Gross, but they were not taken seriously until one morning there broke upon his friends and colleagues the news that the Chief and Mrs. Gross had been married very quietly the previous day.

No announcement of his engagement had been made, except to two or three just before the marriage, and they were bound over to keep it secret for a few days. Mrs. Gilman was one, and when, with a beaming face, she came into her breakfast room saying, " I have a wonderful piece of news for you," Mr. Gilman answered, " Is it about Osler? He was married yesterday." One of Dr. Osler's confidantes was little Beatrice Francis:

Dearest Trixie:
Do not laugh but be very sober and quiet when I tell you — stop that laughing — that I am going to be married. It is Mrs. Gross this time — You will love her I am sure — for your old Doctor's sake as well as for your own. . . .
Your loving Uncle
Willie.

A little while before his marriage his text-book done, it is reported that he carried the first copy to Mrs. Gross and throwing it in her lap exclaimed: " There! Take the darn thing! Now what are you going to do with the man? "

The account of the wedding is entirely characteristic of both and is delightfully told by Dr. Cushing. " On a lovely Saturday morning in May Osler took an early train to Philadelphia. There was nothing unusual in this, nor in the fact that in the course of the morning he called at 1112 Walnut Street. Here ' unbeknownst ' even to the faithful colored servants, Morris and Margaret, some trunks had been packed and sent by an expressman to the station at an early hour in the morning. Shortly before lunch, James Wilson dropped in, and finding Mrs. Gross and his former colleague sitting under a tree in the garden, remarked: ' Hello, Osler, what are you doing over here? Won't you have lunch with me? ' ' No,' said Osler. ' I'll come in to tea. I'm lunching here. Why don't you stay? ' This he did and Wilson recalls that ' we talked lightly of Grand Manan which they knew; of St. Andrews and the salmon rivers, and moose hunting; of northern New Brunswick of which I had a knowledge; and of the charming Canadian doctors, Osler's friends, whom we had met.' This dragged on between the two men, until presently Mrs. Gross asked to be excused, with the statement that she was going out and a hansom was waiting at the door; whereupon Wilson made his manners, pleading an appointment, leaving Osler, who said that Mrs. Gross would give him a lift as she was going in his direction. It was not until then that the devoted Margaret was told by her mistress that she was to be married at 2:30, and, darky fashion, the faithful girl overcome by the informal ways of ' white folks,' exclaimed: ' My Gawd, Mam, only a hansom! Lemme go and fetch a hack! ' Leaving their bags at the station they drove to St. James Church where the ceremony was performed, and having walked back to take their train, Osler sent this telegram to Wilson:

> ' It was awfully kind of you to come
> to the wedding breakfast.' "

Before they were married and soon after the death of Dr. Gross, Dr. Osler had said of Mrs. Gross: " She is the noblest wife and bravest woman I have ever known " — at least it is said that he said that — perhaps he didn't, it doesn't sound like him. But the statement would have been true and would have continued to be true after her second marriage. She was a rather splendid creature, tall, with a proud, handsome, highbred face, large grey-blue eyes that were kind or quizzical, or indifferent; a beautiful short Roman nose and an attractive mouth. With great feminine efficiency there was something of the nice boy about her — brave and downright and such a ' good sport.' Dr. Osler's phenomenal luck reached its highest point when he married.

After their marriage they went at once to visit the Osler connection in Toronto and Montreal, then to Boston for the Revere relatives and friends; a few days followed in Philadelphia; a business trip to Baltimore and an address in Washington, and they were off for their trip abroad, having in ten days assured all relatives and friends that their marriage did not mean a single old tie weakened on either side. In fact the marriage was a shining example of what all marriages should be. Two people, sure of each other, a ceremony unobserved, followed by a quick series of receptions all over the country where the bride and bridegroom had to take all the trouble, show their credentials, and their unabated interest in others not themselves; after which a trip abroad — some relaxation on the ship going over and returning being permissible. Mrs. Osler's letters from abroad would be interesting to an outsider as she had an eye for the pageant and a light touch that brought it before you. Dr. Osler's thoughts are found in his addresses not in his letters — except a few written after coming in contact with some phase of his work — and these were generally precursors to an address. The hundreds of little notes from him to people were written out of the kindness of his heart, such as:

"I came upon your boy's tutor yesterday; he spoke so pleasantly of him." To another: "That is good work, write notes on the subject" — Important to the recipient but not of general interest. They were, however, his passport to humanity. Then there were hundreds of other short notes, such as:

"Dear H. V. O.:

So glad to have your address this A.M. from Batchelor. Mrs. O. (!!!) has often said to me, Where is Dr. Ogden? I should like to meet him and apologize for the theft of his friend. Our programme is as follows: to-morrow to Exeter and Dartmoor; Cornwall until the 25th." Then follows his time table.

There are many still duller than this — merely time tables without even the virtue of accuracy. Why were they kept? Only because *he* had written them. But in his addresses, we get below the surface and catch his deeper feeling.

Dr. Osler's reaction to something beautiful in Nature or in Art was always a spiritual reaction — something that went beyond the mere pleasure in sight or sound. Artist he could never have been except in his profession, and in that there was none greater. Art for Art's sake would have been jargon to him. When he saw a beautiful work of art it instinctively led him to other things, to the human being who had created it; for instance:

"Sitting in Lincoln Cathedral and gazing at one of the

loveliest of human works — for such the Angel Choir has been said to be — there arose within me, obliterating for the moment, the thousand heraldries and twilight saints and dim emblazonings, a strong sense of reverence for the minds which had conceived and the hands which had executed such things of beauty. What manner of men were they who could, in those, to us, dark days, build such transcendent monuments? What was the secret of their art? By what spirit were they moved? Absorbed in thought I did not hear the beginning of the music and then, as a response to my reverie and arousing me from it, rang out the clear voice of the boy leading the antiphon, ' That thy power, thy glory and mightiness of thy kingdom might be known unto men.' Here was the answer. Moving in a world not realized, these men sought, however feebly, to express in glorious structures their conceptions of the beauty of holiness and these works, our wonder, are but the outward and visible signs of the ideals which animated them. To us in very different days life offers nearly the same problem; but the conditions have changed and, as happened before in the world's history, great material prosperity has weakened the influence of ideals, and blurred the eternal difference between means and end. Still the ideal State, the ideal Life, the ideal Church — what they are and how best to realize them. Such dreams continue to haunt the minds of men, and who can doubt that their contemplation greatly assists the upward progress of our race? "

On their return from abroad Dr. Osler rushed down to Baltimore and bought the house at 1 West Franklin Street. It was as rapidly and independently done as most of his transactions — and as successful. Mrs. Osler at once took charge of affairs. " Smart people do everything smartly." Her house was beautiful to look at, her servants well ordered and personally devoted; her table always just what it should be; and all without any apparent effort on her part. It was an open house to his students and friends and Dr. Osler was left free to do as he pleased, the atmosphere about him just what he wanted. The tale is not all told, for Mrs. Osler laughed heartily over all his jokes even when she was the victim; and his jokes would have been trying to anyone less unselfconscious or less assured. She made his house almost a delightful Club for his friends and in it an inviolable peace and quiet for himself. Dr. Osler cared nothing at all for money but then she saw that he had no need to care. To the people she loved she was warmly affectionate, but to the majority she was coolly indifferent, a little abstracted indifference that quickly turned to action and interest if they were in need; a little impatient of stupidity or dowdiness, a little contemptuous of the advanced woman or the over-intellectual one — but that was merely a traditional mood against their kind, not a conviction against their causes. She thought them awful nuisances and that was all. Her tea room was, as Dr. Thayer has said, a " Mecca " full of gay talk and laughter and gossip. Into it would breeze Dr. Osler for a cup of tea, and all gossip ceased; harmless jokes took its place and his personality pervaded the room. A quarter of an hour would be a long stay for him and he was off. Most people with his hatred of gossip and his intrinsic spirituality might have thrown a wet blanket over a trivial group of not malicious mischief-makers; but he brought an atmosphere rippling with clean fun and human sympathy. When he left the room you perhaps realized he had put a lid on, for many would sink back into the self he would not see, and which it was easier for them to maintain.

No priest could have kept more rigidly to himself the lives of his patients, or any life into which he had an insight. Mrs. Osler had no confidences from him about

them. " Willie, why didn't you tell me," she once said,
" that Mrs. —— had cancer? But " — with a laugh — " of
course you wouldn't! If you keep on the way you are doing people will say we don't get on." " Too bad," he answered, " but here *is* something I will tell you. Mrs. ——
is expecting." " No! why Willie, she's over fifty, oh, the
poor dear! " " I wouldn't mention it," he said gravely.
" I certainly shall. I intend to see her at once, poor dear!
I hadn't an idea why you were going there so often —
oh, the poor dear! " Mrs. Osler went off to condole with
her friend and found it all a hoax. This is the right version of the story but it has been told in many forms, some
of them rather lurid. Mrs. Osler told this with much
laughter at herself for being taken in. Another story she
was fond of telling was that he had invited a distinguished
physician to lunch and he told her that the man was almost hopelessly deaf and that she would have to shout to
him. He then told the physician that Mrs. Osler was aw-
fully deaf and the worst of it was she wanted to hear everything that was said. The consequence was they shouted
at each other through the entire meal and only learned a
few days later that neither was in the least deaf. Most
women would not have thought that amusing. She thought
it very amusing.

Within the circle of his profession he was an incessant,
almost miraculous, worker. Outside of it he was sought
and admired but he was not to be obtained. For Medical
Social Clubs, yes. For just Social Clubs, no. For a meeting
or reception to honour a colleague, yes. Otherwise, no.

Dining with the Oslers meant almost dining with a
fraternity, Dr. Osler Chairman. As the dinner progressed,
he would jump up, run off to his library and come back
with a book from his treasured collection. " Listen to
this ": and he would read a line or two, and then — " Wait
a minute. Old Burton has something to say on that," and

he was off, and in a moment back again with Burton. By the time dinner was over a pile of books would be on the floor by his side. Mrs. Osler, who was not especially intellectual, put her intelligence, which was of a high order, upon his hobbies and became deeply interested in them.

He was talking eagerly about *Amiel's Journal* one afternoon at the tea table when in a pause some one said: " Dr. Osler, isn't it amazing that the ——'s are getting a divorce? " He had his finger in the book searching for the line he wanted, and he looked up with such withering scorn that the offender almost burst into tears, and though the words were not audible, his lips seemed saying something like " go to H . . . ! " After the offending gossip left everyone laughed and Mrs. Osler said: " I see nothing to laugh at — horrid manners — you were hateful to ——." Dr. Osler: " She's a venomous little beast! " Mrs. Osler: " It's not morals with you, Willie. You are just put out because she interrupted you when you were explaining your anaemic Monsieur Amiel." Everyone laughed, Dr. Osler joining. " I'll send her a box of chocolates," he said. " Oh, will you? " Mrs. Osler replied. " You mean I'll send her a box of chocolates and all the work you will do will be to write: ' Nasty temper, forgive, read something in the Bible about Charity! ' I know you, Dr. Osler." " You do! here's my card," and he scribbled a text from the Bible, tossed it on the tray in front of her and seizing one of his young students who was present dragged him off with him to his study. Mrs. Osler looked at the card and after reading it aloud, said: " Poor ——, I am certain that she hasn't a Bible. She only subscribes to *Town Topics,* and I adore hearing all she has to say. I do wish Willie had let us hear about the ——'s. Never mind, we'll find out." Mrs. Osler was herself far too big-hearted and too busy to be a gossip but many of her friends, like most of us, were inclined that way. She enjoyed them, laughed, but gave her life to making things go Dr. Osler's way — and succeeded. The house carried, without conflict, the stamp of both personalities. How delightful it was, how inspiring to young men, would be attested by hundreds.

Neither Dr. nor Mrs. Osler were in the least difficult to understand; their characters were obvious and would have worried psychologists exceedingly because of there being nothing to worry about.

"Did you know Dr. Osler?" some one asked another. "Yes," was the answer, "intimately, but I only saw him once. It was late twilight; the city square was almost deserted when a woman carrying a heavy child came slowly up the center of the square and sat down to rest on the coping that separated the pavement from the grass. The child's heavy head was pressed against her bosom and she seemed *all in*. I started to speak to her when up the square came jauntily along a man in full evening dress, in top coat, silk hat, flower in his button hole, light gloves in one hand and his cane deftly swinging in the other, evidently singing. In an instant he saw the woman and her burden. He stopped, made a playful drive with his cane at the child, then throwing cane and gloves on the grass, he gently lifted the child into his arms holding its head against his own breast as he talked to the mother, then whistling to a little boy who chanced in sight he said: ' Get a cab as quick as you can and if you are back in five minutes, riches! for you! ' and he patted his breast pocket. The boy flew off and was back in record time with the cab. The Good Samaritan put the woman in the cab, carefully placed the child on her lap — then he wrote on a card, ' This is Mrs. Osler's youngest. See that he is well taken care of until I come to-morrow night.' He read what he had written aloud to the woman, winked his eye at me, gave the driver his fare, told him to drive at once to the

Hopkins Hospital, see that the woman and boy were safely attended to — then pressing a five dollar bill in the woman's hand, said: ' Your laddie will be well looked after at the hospital. I will see him to-morrow. You go to your home and get drunk,' slammed to the door of the cab and was off. All done while I was trying to say, ' Can I help you? ' "

The Medical School at Baltimore

Hence cometh all the need and fame of teachers, men of inborn nobility, call'd prophets of God,

.   .   .   .

the loved and lovable whose names live evermore.
Robert Bridges — *The Testament of Beauty.*

CHAPTER VII

BALTIMORE

The Medical School

THE Graduate Course at the Hospital was carried on by every member of the staff, but the delay in opening the medical school for undergraduates was beginning to bring serious discontent. The cause of the delay was the financial difficulty that had been steadily accumulating. The Philosophical Department of the University and the Hospital had so far weathered the storm; but the Medical School which was included in the hospital plan had to wait. The situation was becoming critical. Dr. Welch had a call to Harvard and McGill was using every inducement to get Dr. Osler. These were anxious days for Mr. Gilman. More money was needed. The campaign to secure $500,-000 began. A Baltimore woman generously gave a sum sufficient to put up one of the buildings; but things were going very slowly. Mr. Gilman watched the small amounts coming in with, no doubt, a great deal of fear and with, no doubt, a great deal of exasperation at the way so many harped on Johns Hopkins, the man, and forgot Johns Hopkins, the University. Was he to lose his immortals because of local prejudice?

Then, at a critical moment, Miss Mary Garrett wrote saying that she would make up the sum needed to open the Medical School provided women could come in on the same basis as men. There were other points trying to the masculine mind of that period; but the trustees met and accepted the offer. And on Christmas Day, 1892, the first Christmas the Oslers spent at 1 West Franklin Street, the house officers met there at dinner and Mr. Gilman himself handed in the letter and there was rejoicing in that house of Good Fortune.

Perhaps the following from Dr. Osler's address at the Harvard Medical Alumni Association in 1894, when the Johns Hopkins Medical School had completed its first year, may give an idea of some of the talk at that jolly Christmas dinner in 1892. After referring to the very high requirements for entrance to the Hopkins Medical School he turned to co-education. " It has wrung your withers here to some slight extent. When I parted from my pre-ceptor he gave me a copy of the *Apocrypha,* on the title page of which he wrote: ' When a woman woos what woman's son will sourly leave her till she hath prevailed? ' Now while on principle I am opposed to co-education, guided as I have always been by the *Apocrypha* and my preceptor, I was warmly in favor of it, particularly when the ladies came forward with half a million dollars. You know, of course, that this was offered to Harvard Medical School and that President Eliot and the late Dean strug-gled over the offer a good deal. We had but one serious opponent in Johns Hopkins — Dr. Councilman, who, brought up in the theological schools, and with a strong theological bias (!) was opposed most thoroughly to co-education, and would have nothing to do with it. Accord-ingly we made a bargain with President Eliot and Dr. Bowditch. We took the money and you took the man. We have co-education without Councilman, and you get Councilman without co-education. All our plans succeeded and everything went smoothly and quietly. The board of lady supervisors arranged with President Gilman and Dr. Welch, the Dean, that Minerva Medica should not be the presiding goddess — she was not good enough — but that elder Aphrodite, the motherless daughter of Uranus, should be installed as the presiding genius of the school. Under her there would be loyal devotion to truth, to science, and to work. The younger Aphrodite, the daughter of Dione and Jupiter, was banished, and ordered not to be seen within the walls. When you go against Nature, you utterly fail. I am here to-day with sorrow in my heart to tell you that co-education has proved an absolute failure from the elder Aphrodite's standpoint. When I tell you that $33\frac{1}{3}\%$ of the lady students admitted the first year of the Medical Faculty of the Johns Hopkins University, are at the end of one short session, to be married, then you will understand why I say co-education is a failure. If we lose $33\frac{1}{3}\%$ at the end of the first session, where will the class of lady students be at the end of the fourth? In all other respects co-education is a great success." It is to be noted that just three women students were enrolled at the first session.

The opening of the Medical School seemed now assured, and the tempting offers to Montreal were put aside. Dr. Osler was to have the undergraduate work he so wanted. There are hundreds of letters kept by his pupils showing how intensely he cared for their work and for them.

Along with his active hospital work and his ardent co-operation with all city and civic health propaganda, he was having a stream of visitors at 1 West Franklin Street; not only the innumerable *habitués,* for no physician ever came to the city who failed to find his way to Dr. Osler's home, and who would not, after being refreshed with his hospitality, be carried off to the hospital and first of all be shown the Pathological Department. Dr. Welch's laboratory had been in operation for some years, and had developed men who were sent out all over the country to teach advanced methods. It was here that Walter Reed gained his knowledge of bacteriology, which led to his work on yellow fever and, later, in Cuba, to his discovery of the part played by the mosquito in the transmission of that disease. Dr. Osler's popularity was so great that it was far from an unmixed blessing; little could be done without his signature, or a word from him — a word as a rule so brief that the effect seemed quite out of proportion. As Dr. Thayer said, " No one talks to Dr. Osler consecutively against his will "; and yet everyone seemed to have had the word they most wanted from him.

The first year of the Medical School closed in June 1894 and in July he was off for England where he attended the British Medical Association meeting in Bristol. The Marquis of Salisbury presided and in his address was a little supercilious and condescending about the Darwinian School. Huxley was engaged to offer the vote of thanks for the address and suppressing his contempt at the inanities of the Marquis, he, as he afterwards wrote, " conveyed criticism in the form of thanks."

It was a busy time for Dr. Osler in England, attending meetings, reading in the British Museum, preparing a paper on chorea, and getting some sea air at Langland; for though supposed to be on pleasure bent he had an insatiable mind. The autumn found him back at his post in Baltimore for the opening of the School session, and to take up the routine of his quickly moving life.

In the autumn of the following year there was a wave of excitement from reports that he might accept the place of Principal Dawson, who was about to resign from McGill; but he did not want executive work, and the position at the Johns Hopkins was satisfying to him in every way. His pen was busy revising his text-book and writing numerous biographical essays, among them *Alabama Student,* which was the one he liked most of all. His essays are not characterizations; they are idealizations of what was best in his subject, of what the man might be, not exactly what he was. Perhaps in *Alabama Student* he came more nearly to a characterization than in any other of his writings. When you put down the volume of biographical sketches which contains this essay you are left with a somewhat exaggerated idea of the virtues of his subjects.

Dr. Osler's work as a consultant was rapidly increasing. In one of his short notes for the Montreal Medical Journal he writes: " A consultant's life is not without unpleasant features, chief among which is the passing of judgment on the unhappy incurables, on the cancerous, ataxics, and paralytics, who wander from one city to another. Few are able to receive the balm of truth, but now and again one meets with a cheery, brave fellow who insists upon a plain, unvarnished statement of his prospects. Still more distressing are the instances of hopeless illness in which, usually for his friends' sake, the entire ' faculty ' is summoned. Can anything be more doleful than a procession of four or five doctors into the sick man's room? Who does not appreciate Matthew Arnold's wish? —

> Nor bring to see me cease to live
> Some doctor full of phrase and fame,
> To shake his sapient head, and give
> The ill he cannot cure, a name.

How often under sad circumstances has the bitterness of the last line occurred to me? "

On December 28, 1895, his son Revere was born. (In 1893 a boy had been born but, to Dr. and Mrs. Osler's great sorrow, he lived only a week.) After Revere's birth no one could think of the father without also thinking of the son. Mrs. Osler and the Chief were radiantly happy; the students adored and the colleagues admired. The halo about the parents now extended to the nursery. An old black mammy informed all that after nursing innumerable babies, all in the best families, there had never been one like this baby; and everyone agreed that must certainly be true. The old darkies of those days are no more, and babies now are less glorified. Some one laughingly said to the old mammy: " Mammy, I do believe you nursed Moses and took him out of those nasty wet bulrushes." " Dat's true; dat Mars Moses wasn't going to take no colds when I was dar." After this fashion Revere's mammy reminisced to the delight of his New England mother and his Canadian father. So serious, however, was Dr. Osler's attitude towards education that when Revere was old enough to talk, it was no longer a joke. He heard Revere say with a full darky accent, " Hist dat window," and at once a good Scotch governess was secured.

Dr. Osler had never become a naturalized American citizen and soon after Revere's birth he had him registered a British subject. Perhaps he was led to do this so quickly as our politicians had been stirring up embers of trouble by the dispute over the Venezuela-Guiana boundary; the newspapers were having a delightful time headlining rumours of war.

Dr. Osler wrote to one of his friends: " It would be an awkward business for me, as I am British to the core," and to another: " Damn those politicians; if they raise a war, it will play the devil with me. I should go back and stand by the boys."

In 1896, the third year of the Medical School, clinical teaching was well under way. Dr. Osler's seven years in Baltimore and his work in Philadelphia and Montreal had shown his powers as a teacher, but now that he had the control of his own clinic his success was astonishing even to those who thought they knew him. In selecting men he was more fortunate than discriminating. Unlike Mr. Gilman, who felt that character was desirable but brains imperative, Dr. Osler put the man, his personality and character first; and he felt sure that given the power to work and the desire, sufficient brains were probably there. The requirements for a student coming to the Hopkins were such that he had to have some ability — and Dr. Osler's inspiring qualities would certainly get a response if there was anything in a boy that could respond. Some one has said that a great teacher is not one from whom you learn mere facts but one who is able to communicate his enthusiasms. Dr. Osler had the faculty of bringing to life latent abilities and of inspiring ideals. To take a student, urge him to stand on his feet, arouse his interest, give him praise and encouragement, help him in every direction, was all in the day's work. His feelings towards his students had much of the element of an ambitious and devoted father, who longs to give his best to his sons and is happy in seeing them honoured, thinking nothing of honour for himself. He would urge his students to achievement — work. He would advise: " Take notes; publish; make yourself known." And at the same time he would be a little fearful lest they might fail in the most important part of all — being just good men. He was a very great teacher, which is almost the opposite thing to being a pedagogue. As with children, so with youth, he met them on their own level — which a pedagogue never does.

His Saturday evenings were devoted to his fourth year students — and would always find him at the head of the table at his home, 1 West Franklin Street, and around him a group eagerly listening to his talk. On the table there would be books and beer and tobacco — and any recounting of these evenings by his pupils has almost the touch of idolatry. Next to his house lived a few of the young associates who were called the " latch keyers "; they kept the hated telephone which he would not have in his house; and there was an opening in the wall between the two gardens giving them even a more informal way of en-

trance than by the latch key. Ask them in a busy moment
to tell you of that time and hear how they warm to their
reminiscences; and you will also learn of the wonder of
Mrs. Osler — for she made much of it possible — certainly the comfort. In this perfectly ordered home the
spirit of freedom and kindness was all-pervading. The
students caught the atmosphere and old Morris, the butler,
felt a distinct pride when sixteen unexpected guests arrived. Small wonder that the students felt, and often unfortunately said to other women: " Why can't all women
do that way? " But really it was hardly fair to the future
wives of those youths to set up such a standard. She was
not, however, the right woman for every man; a dull one
would not have caught her attention and a lazy one would
have had a most unrestful life. All that is said of a virtuous
woman in the Bible was certainly true of Mrs. Osler but
one can't put her into old literature — she was too thoroughly modern — except in the virtues. In spite of her
assured manner, her quiet executive ability and the unstinted admiration she received, she was at heart sweet —
and very humble. He talked most beautifully of humility
but it was not his outstanding quality. Generosity, however, loomed large among his virtues. His purse was always
at the top of his pocket; he never had to rummage for it,
as the Baltimore beggars knew; no one who came for aid
was turned away from his door without money. " There
was no discrimination," he said, " in the charity of the
Good Samaritan who stopped not to ask the stripped and
wounded man whether it was by his own fault the ill had
come; nor of his religion, nor had he the wherewithal to
pay his board." It was the early days of the Charity Organization, and Dr. Osler was a sore trial to their agents.
Mrs. Osler laughed, adored, but secretly kept an eye on
the bank account; and gave, when he was not looking, to
the Organized Charities. It would do her an injustice not

to add that she never interfered with the distribution of the pennies at the door. Indeed there would have been no one brave enough to try that.

Dr. Osler added to his extravagance in giving, one other extravagance as we know, the buying of books, old books. It was becoming more and more a passion with him. Medical libraries had for him the most tyrannical of appeals; he must add to their treasures; they would provide material for the history of medicine; and time and thought spent on them would be returned in purest gold to the students. Little did Father Johnson think when he awakened in the boy at Weston the appreciation of the beauty of the *Religio,* that he was also laying the foundation of his passion as a bibliophile. The little library of two books, the *Religio* and the *Globe Shakespeare,* was the beginning of the great collection the *Bibliotheca Osleriana* now at McGill University. Libraries and medical museums were his adopted children; he must provide for them. He could talk of a rare old volume in a way that would almost reduce you to tears, and even though you did not care at all for the thing, you felt that you too, must possess it. He aroused your interest very often to your great cost. An adoring medical student, who had never read any poetry more subtle than Longfellow in his most obvious flights, spent all his monthly allowance on an old edition of Chaucer; and nothing he possessed was as valued by him though he could not read it. Because when, with beating heart, he showed it to the chief he had said, " Why, that's a find! the . . . edition! " and clapping him on the back, " Good! " and the infatuated boy filled with pride said: " He talked to me longer than he ever had before." And the strange part of it was that by degrees this same boy grew wonderfully at home and happy in a library.

Dr. Maude E. Abbott, Curator of the Pathological

Museum of McGill University, gives an account of one of those Saturday evenings. " Dinner over, the great experience of the evening came, for this was one of Dr. Osler's students' nights, in which I had been invited to participate. Seated at the head of the long dining table, now covered with a dark cloth, with nine young men and three young women ranged around it and me beside him at the end, and with a little pile of books before him, he began by introducing four rare editions from the Classics of Medicine to his hearers, with a few wise words of appreciation on each. Then followed a delightful talk upon points of interest or difficulty in the week's work, for these were all his clinical clerks, the reporters of cases in his hospital service. ' Well, Miss, what is your trouble this week? ' he began. ' And yours? ' turning to another. And then, as I sat there with heart beating at the wonderful new world that had opened so unexpectedly before me, he turned suddenly upon me. ' I wonder, now, if you realize what an opportunity *you* have? That McGill Museum is a great place. As soon as you go home look up the *British Medical Journal* for 1893, and read the article by Mr. Jonathan Hutchinson on " A Clinical Museum." That is what he calls his Museum in London and it is the greatest place I know for teaching students in. Pictures of life and death together. Wonderful. You read it and see what *you* can do.' And so he gently dropped a seed that dominated all my future work. This is but an illustration of how his influence worked in many lives." Reminiscences like this, coming to us of Dr. Osler's influence, are among the most irritating in all biographical literature — why a word or two, that seem very ordinary, thrown off in the most casual way, should start into life incipient secretaries or editors, or heads of hospitals, is hard to be borne by those of us who have toiled in vain to persuade someone to take even one step in the right direction. To be sure Dr.

Osler gave himself with his word, and in an extraordinary degree he continued throwing fertilizer upon the seed he had sown — nevertheless the effect was that of magic. In these informal meetings he came to know his own students intimately — and his influence upon them could be accounted for, but it is hard to account for it with the passing stranger. Time has shown what his pupils could accomplish. Work and method and a great example have brought many up to a high standard and to efficient lives — and the few who were born physicians and could add to their training Charity are to-day having their own disciples.

In the year 1896 the fourth year students, including the undergraduates and graduates, came into the wards for the first time as clinical clerks. He regularly visited the wards with them three mornings in the week from nine to eleven. And it was here at the bedside that all felt he was at his best.

That Dr. Osler could hold the attention of the medical world in a day when Science was in the saddle came not only from his compelling personality but quite as much from his first-hand knowledge of most things relating to the human body. As Dr. Cushing writes: " The paragraphs of his text-book, which deal with Therapeutics, critics had regarded as the weakest feature of the volume, and his courageously expressed views upon the futility of many of the drugs in common usage had been deemed nihilistic. Perhaps because of this, perhaps because of his unusual powers of visualizing disease, gained in the postmortem room, he was far more tolerant than most of his contemporaries with the so-called surgical invasion of the traditional province of internal medicine which took place during the next twenty years. He knew surgeons well, and their particular point of view; and it has been said of him that few physicians have ever shown better surgical judgment or had a more instinctive and certain knowledge of the proper moment for surgical intervention."

It was during his visit South in 1896 that he gave the address on " The Study of Fevers in the South." He began by saying, " Humanity has but three great enemies: fever, famine and war; of these by far the greatest, by far the most terrible, is fever. Gad, the seer of David, estimated aright the relative intensity of these afflictions when he made the three days' pestilence the equivalent of three months' flight before the enemy, and of three (seven) years of famine. As far back as history will carry us, in ancient Greece, in ancient Rome, throughout the Middle Ages, down to our own day, the noisome pestilence, in whatever form it assumed, has been dreaded justly as the greatest of evils." He goes on to say that typhoid was, " in the United States *the fever,* just as it was when the old New England physicians recognized its recurrence year after year with the fall of the leaves. Of no disease is the history better known; the measures of its prevention are everywhere recognized; the minimization of its occurrence is an unfailing index of the sanitary intelligence of a community. With good drainage, pure water, and pure milk, typhoid fever goes the way of typhus and cholera. The greatest sanitary triumphs of the century have been in reducing to a minimum the mortality from this disease in the great centres of population in Europe. The mortality returns of Washington and of Baltimore, and of many smaller cities demonstrate that we are culpably negligent in allowing this most easily preventable disease to continue its ravages. I estimate that in the latter city there were during the year 1895 not less than 2,500 cases."

At the end of his lecture he speaks of the third great enemy of humanity: " For one only of the three great curses the close of the century brings no gleam of hope. It will be in another democracy, in another century, perhaps far distant, that the race will realize the earnest long-ing of the son of Amos, that 'nation shall not lift up sword against nation, neither shall they learn war any more.' The gradual growth of a deep sense of the broth-erhood of man, such an abiding sense as pervades our own profession in its relation to the suffering, which recog-nizes the one blood of all the nations, may perhaps do it. In some development of socialism, something that will widen patriotism beyond the bounds of nationalism, may rest the desire of the race in this matter; but the evil is rooted and grounded in the abyss of human passion, and war with all its horrors is likely to burden the earth."

In *Aequanimitas,* his volume of addresses, covering the period from 1889 to 1903, his ideals for himself, his stu-dents and colleagues are given in beautiful but no uncer-tain terms and his deep reverence for his profession per-meates the book. The students who heard him must have seen that most wonderful of all things, a speaker uncon-sciously illustrating by himself the worth of what he says. A stranger listening to his address, " The Master Word in Medicine," might have exclaimed: " Who could live up to that standard? " And instantly the answer would have come: " The Chief does! " He gave them as the mas-ter word 'work' and then went deeper into the matter: "A conscientious pursuit of Plato's ideal of perfection may teach you the three great lessons of life. *You may learn to consume your own smoke.* The atmosphere is darkened by the murmurings and whimperings of men and women over the non-essentials, the trifles that are in-evitably incident to the hurly burly of the day's routine. Things cannot always go your way. Learn to accept in silence the minor aggravations, cultivate the gift of taci-turnity and consume your own smoke with an extra draught of hard work, so that those about you may not be annoyed with the dust and dirt of your complaints.

More than any other the practitioner of medicine may illustrate the second great lesson that *we are not here to get all we can out of life for ourselves; but to try to make the lives of others happier*. This is the essence of that oft-repeated admonition of Christ: ' He that findeth his life shall lose it, and he that loseth his life for my sake shall find it,' on which hard saying if the children of this generation would only lay hold, there would be less misery and discontent in the world. . . . The practice of medicine is an art, not a trade; a calling, not a business; a calling in which your heart will be used equally with your head. . . . And the third lesson you may find the hardest of all — that *the law of the higher life is only fulfilled by love, i.e., Charity!*"

A thrilling teacher! And much of the seed he sowed fell upon good ground; but he was prodigal in the sowing of seed and never a very good judge of the depth or quality of the soil. And after all those are the wonder-workers — those whose storehouses are so full that they have no need to economize.

The medical social functions grew apace; and the teaching and the health measures and addresses and investigations grew apace. And more than all, the practice he did not want became steadily more and more importunate. Frequent consultations were urged upon him which he felt should not be refused; and there were always the little people with no bank accounts whom he would not refuse. So the bow was becoming too taut. An urgent call came to him from his old College at Montreal and was refused. Then came a tempting call to Edinburgh; this he wavered over. The chair of medicine at Edinburgh was perhaps the most important position in British medicine, and Revere was growing into childhood and he wanted him brought up on the other side with traditions more like his own; but a storm of protest bore down upon him and he gave it up; since he was in poor health at the time. The letter of President Gilman shows how he felt about the matter:

"Baltimore, March 24, 1900.

My dear Dr. Osler:

I have just heard through Dr. Welch you have declined an extraordinarily attractive overture from Edinburgh. You may be sure that every one of your associates, Trustees, Professors and students, would have grieved deeply if your decision had been different. In the short period of your residence in Baltimore, you have won such a position as no one else has had, and as no one can fill, if you give it up. In the Hospital, in the Medical School, you have the utmost influence while your love of letters and your skill as a writer would give you the same influence among our literary co-workers if they could only see and hear you more frequently. Now I hope that nothing more attractive than a call to Edinburgh may ever reach you, and that through a long life you will continue to add to the distinction of the Johns Hopkins foundation.

Ever your sincere and grateful friend,

D. C. Gilman."

All this was no doubt gratifying; the world seemed suddenly bent on reforms and on progress and his voice was needed; nothing could be done in Baltimore without an Osler inspiration. The Anti-Vivisection controversy was started up again. Dr. Welch had, in 1898, prevented the enactment of a regulatory law by the State Legislature. Now again Dr. Welch made the chief argument against a new bill of the same kind and Dr. Osler backed him heart and soul. Faster and faster life was moving for Dr. Osler. His quick trips to Europe were far from restful; calls came from home for consultations or addresses; and the constant revision of his text-book, which had now reached the 4th edition, called for much work. Then came the

death of his brother, Britton Bath Osler (February 1901).
As Crown Counsel in Canada he was famous throughout
that Commonwealth. A man of compelling personality, a
great orator, a great lawyer, a very unforgettable person.
He was the first to die in a family which, as the Canadian
papers said, " had produced more distinguished men than
any other contemporary family in the Commonwealth."
To pass over Britton Bath Osler with only a line is hardly
possible, he marches so visibly into the foreground of remembrance. A sombre figure, heavier and squarer than
his brother William, with the same dark colouring; and
the look of an Indian ancestry, which did not exist, was
very striking. The high cheek bone, deep dark eyes, and the
tightly-drawn skin gave the square face an almost fleshless
appearance that is rarely seen except in an Indian face.
When he talked all listened — there were flashes of wit,
great humour, and a penetrating, balanced wisdom. An
orator, but also an absorbed listener. When he spoke of
his younger brother his face softened as though seeing in
imagination something very wonderful and beautiful. His
expression then would have amazed the criminals of
Canada.

The two brothers, singularly alike in appearance and in
brilliancy of intellect and in integrity of character, looked
at life from different angles. Had William Osler taken to
the law he would, as counsel for the defense, have given
his brother Britton Bath Osler, Counsel for the Queen,
a stiff fight. In the scales of one was justice with a predilection against the criminal; in the scales of the other, mercy
with a predilection for the criminal. Quickly, if one spoke
of a sinner, would come from Dr. Osler the answer of the
Master: " He that is without sin among you, let him cast
a stone." One certain conviction he had: that good was
stronger than evil.

There were some who resented Dr. Osler's practical

jokes, harmless though they were. He excused them by claiming to have a troublesome double. As Sir James Barrie once said: " It is M'Connachie who has brought me to this pass. M'Connachie, I should explain, as I have undertaken to open the innermost doors, is the name I give to the unruly half of myself; the writing half. We are complement and supplement. I am the half that is dour and practical and canny, he is my fanciful half . . . who prefers to fly around on one wing. I should not mind his doing that but he drags me with him." To his M'Connachie he gave the name of Egerton Y. Davis, and under this name perpetrated jokes which sometimes reached the height of audacity. On one occasion he followed Mrs. Osler to Atlantic City and registered at the hotel under the name of Davis. Some one who came to Atlantic City to consult him, and was unable to locate him, wondered who this man Davis could be who was always with Mrs. Osler. When, after losing much time, he discovered what Dr. Osler had done, he didn't think the joke in the least amusing. Many people, as we know, have been fearfully bored hearing his tales told second-hand with shouts of laughter from the narrator, who felt that, as Osler jokes, they must be amusing. The really trying thing was the way his internes and students imitated his gestures, his manner. He was *Chief;* what he did was right and they could not see why they couldn't jauntily put an arm about some woman's shoulder with " How's the good man and the chicks? " when she was probably an old maid of fifty. The reception they received was a shock to them and some never did learn that you can't act another's part unless the likeness is more than skin-deep.

The movement of these Baltimore years is so incessant that you hold your head in despair that anything human could keep such a pace — and Dr. Osler quotes " es bildet ein Talent sich in der Stille"; the miracle was that he could be aloof and actively present almost at the same moment, so rapid were his spiritual reactions. Grasp the flying moment and "a man's reach should exceed his grasp or what's heaven for?" Mind, heart and soul kept even pace; but the active power was charity. The years of 1890–1896 might be called the full noonday of his life. His clinic was formed; his text-book written; his marriage had taken place, the Medical School came into full blast and his son Revere was born — unstinted good fortune, as a superlative could be written after each high light. His life proved the fallacy that it takes poverty and adversity to make a saint. Dr. Welch, referring to these years, writes: " Osler's great opportunity came with his call to the Chair of Medicine in the Johns Hopkins Hospital in 1889. Here were spent the sixteen golden, most productive years of his life, and here he made his two greatest contributions to medicine, the most important being the creation of the first medical clinic worthy of the name in any English-speaking country, and the other the publication in 1892 of his text-book presenting with rare literary skill and unexampled success the principles and practice of medicine adequately and completely for the first time in English after the great revolutionary changes brought about by modern bacteriology."

In March 1902 J. Pierpont Morgan and John D. Rockefeller gave large sums to the Harvard Medical School. Mr. Rockefeller stipulated that a sum equal to his own should be raised by the community. Mr. Gates, Mr. Rockefeller's agent in charitable investigation, had read Dr. Osler's text-book and he became so impressed that he communicated his enthusiasm to Mr. Rockefeller; and in time, because of this, the Rockefeller Institute was established. The following is from a letter of Mr. Gates to Dr. Osler: " In the course of our study of the subject we became acquainted with the very excellent work being done at

Harvard and while it was not thought best to connect the Institute with the Harvard Medical School, we were profoundly impressed with the very superior work done at that Institution. Accordingly, after the establishment of the Institute in the tentative way above described, Mr. Rockefeller contributed a million dollars to the Harvard School. Both of these gifts grew directly out of your book. The first while not, as yet, large in money, has in it possibilities by no means circumscribed by the present gift. It has occurred to me that possibly you might be gratified to know of an incidental and perhaps to you quite unexpected good which your valuable book has wrought." Osler thought very little of this at the time but later he recalled the note and used what influence he had for the Hopkins in its need.

On February 22, 1902 — an ominous day for the Johns Hopkins University — President Gilman retired. He was seventy and he had placed the Johns Hopkins University and the Hospital on a firm foundation, and had developed the lines on which they were to grow. Now he wished to devote his time entirely to developing the Carnegie Institution. It was the 25th anniversary of the opening of the University, and representative men from all over the country surrounded Mr. Gilman to do him honour; and in the minds of all was the memory of a time when people came to Baltimore to see a University that, within a few years of its birth, had become world-famous; and they could not find it because it consisted of men and not of buildings. Some of these men were dead on the 25th anniversary but their pupils could be found in almost every institute of learning in the States and Canada. There were, however, still men of destiny, on the platform around Mr. Gilman; noticeably in the Medical School, Dr. Welch and Dr. Osler; and, delivering the address for the alumni to the retiring President, Woodrow Wilson of Princeton, of whom Mr. Gilman said: " His vision is so broad that it includes both North and South; a master of the principles which underlie a free government." Behind the suave Professor from Princeton stalked grim tragedy; it seemed to those listening to him, that his was to be a peaceful academic career, and instead he was to be a Peace President of the United States in a ghastly war. Dr. Osler sat twirling his pencil, probably scarcely listening to the eulogies (he was a very poor listener), but he recalled years later Mr. Wilson's face at that time with a whimsical comment on the ironical in life. Dr. Osler, no doubt, was feeling " It is good for Mr. Gilman to get his rest — and I am 52 and soon I shall be off for a nice eventide with my books and my boy! " But behind him brooded the Good Samaritan, and for those he has marked for his own there is never any rest. To fill in the pictures of the past from to-day's knowledge is a little like renovating an old portrait; one has to be very careful indeed. Certain it is that no one in the audience at that function thought other than that the affairs of the University would go the right way; and that Mr. Gilman was merely handing the reins to another expert driver, and that the horses were as fresh as ever. But the Hopkins had suffered many financial disasters. Other universities had caught fire from Mr. Gilman and of the important ones the alumni were many and rich whereas the Hopkins alumni were few and poor; and among the Trustees and Faculty there was anxiety. When money difficulties creep in, vision droops for a while; the two rarely go together and never successfully except in the state before the vision materializes. Mr. Gilman, at first, had the means and the courage to put into effect his conception of what was essential. The result was instant, but as time passed the unessential began to be felt necessary, or advisable, or delightful; and Pandora's lid was off. Mr. Gilman had given to America a torch with a single light: Truth as seen through great intellects. No other hand has since held that torch as steadily. But the Hospital and the Medical School were not losing their leaders and undeviatingly pursued their upward course.

The Hopkins suffered another financial loss. On February 7, 1904, a great fire broke out in the business section of the city destroying a great part of it and causing the Hospital to lose at least $400,000. It was then that Dr. Osler recalled the letter from Mr. Gates telling him of Mr. Rockefeller's gift to medical research which had been induced after reading his text-book; so he wrote to Mr. Gates asking if he thought the dire condition of the Hopkins might induce him to come to its aid. Mr. Rockefeller sent his personal representative in benefactions to look into the matter and make an estimate of the Hospital's losses. There was a period of anxious waiting, and Dr. Osler wrote the following letter to Judge Harlan, president of the Hospital Board:

" Dear Judge Harlan:
     In case we do not get a supplementary endowment for the Hospital, I shall be very glad to place my salary ($5,000) for ten years at the disposal of the Trustees to be used in maintaining our publications. Please say nothing of it outside the Committee.
                         Sincerely yours,
                                   William Osler "

Fortunately this sacrifice was not necessary. Early in April John D. Rockefeller Jr. wrote to Dr. Osler that " in view of the high work which the Hospital and Medical School are doing in medical instruction and research including the training of nurses, which work he understands will otherwise be materially curtailed because of losses, my father will give $500,000 to Johns Hopkins Hospital."

The joy over this was naturally great and once again the Hospital was on its feet.

Before the fire Dr. Osler had been occupied preparing for the Tuberculosis Exhibition in Baltimore, he acting as chairman of the Committee on Organization. The public was aroused to a great deal of enthusiasm when they saw what had been, and what could be, done. Belief in Doctors Welch and Osler was now absolute in the city; but this was far more than a local affair; it led to the International Organization for the study of the disease, and secured the interest and coöperation of the leading physicians throughout the world. He had also undertaken a piece of work that was to follow him for the greater part of his life — the editing of a *System of Medicine,* to comprise seven volumes, with Dr. Thomas McCrae as assistant editor; it was his idea to have only younger men as contributors. Added to this, he was revising his text-book for a 6th edition. " I am sweating away at a new edition," he writes, " am almost rewriting the infectious disease and knocking many of the other sections into splinters." Many other matters were demanding his time, among them the Ingersoll Lecture on Immortality, which he had agreed to give. This lectureship was founded by Miss Caroline Haskell Ingersoll in memory of her father. There had been previously a number of notable lecturers on this foundation, but judging from their lectures, the subject had been beyond their grasp. When Dr. Osler was asked in 1904, to give the lecture he was under no illusion as to his power to explain the inexplicable. At first he refused, but was overpersuaded, and the result is one of his few addresses that leave one cold. He divided humanity into three groups: The Laodiceans, who believe in immortality but are not influenced in their lives by their belief; the Gallionians, who were unconcerned about it; and the Teresians, whose faith is their controlling motive. Among the final words of his lecture are these: " Some of you will wander through all phases, to come at last to the opinion of Cicero who had rather be mistaken with Plato than be right with those who deny altogether the life after death, and this is my *confessio fidei*." The scientists would consider this intellectual dishonesty and the Teresians would think it far too much of a compromise. When Mr. Wells wrote his story, " Mr. Britling Sees It Through," something very deep was stirred in the human heart; but when he gives us " God the Invisible King," we are left unconcerned. And so it is with Dr. Osler. Every act of his life was steeped in Christian faith illuminating a character that was profoundly religious. His theories do not bring much light to the subject but his philosophy of living points the way.

Last Days in Baltimore

I am a part of all that I have met;
Yet all experience is an arch wherethro'
Gleams that untravell'd world, whose margin
fades
For ever and for ever when I move.
                          Tennyson — *Ulysses.*

CHAPTER VIII

LAST DAYS IN BALTIMORE

THE strain of his life was telling on him. In letters to his colleagues he shows that he was going beyond his power of endurance. To one he writes: " I am on the down grade, the pace of the last three winters has been such that I knew I was riding for a fall." At this juncture Sir John Burdon-Sanderson, Regius Professor of Medicine at Oxford, made known his intention of resigning. He had held the chair for twenty years and there was great anxiety and much discussion over his possible successor. In the midst of the conflict of opinion in Oxford some one mentioned Dr. Osler's name to Sanderson, and immediately he said, " That is it — the very man," and at once wrote to Dr. Osler:

Oxford, June 8, 1904.

" Dear Professor

You are doubtless aware that I am on the point of vacating the Regius Professorship of Medicine here. The appointment of my successor is in the hands of the Prime Minister (Mr. Balfour) who in this matter acts independently of the University. He appears at present to be unable to decide on the proper course to be taken. My colleagues and I have placed before him our opinion in favour of appointing our ' Reader in Pathology ' who is also our Director of the Pathological Laboratory, he being in our judgment a man of higher scientific position than any one *to be had in the United Kingdom* at present. It appears, however, that certain objections have been suggested to Mr. Balfour, which from a statesman's point of view have value, however groundless they may seem to us.

This being the position of matters, it has seemed desirable to communicate to the Minister our hope that if, for the reasons referred to, he is unable to take the course we suggested several months ago, he should as the next best course ask some distinguished representative of the science of Medicine, outside of this University, to occupy the position. I now write to ask you whether we may venture to entertain the hope that you might be induced to accept the position if it were offered to you. . . . The work is very light. The Regius Professor need not reside more than one-third of the year, so that he can, if he likes, avail himself of the proximity of London for any work or purpose that may require his presence.

I understand that you are to be in Oxford at the meeting of the B. M. Association. Will you and Mrs. Osler be our guests? You would find my house conveniently situated for the business of the meeting. I would have written sooner but I have been ill and have only lately found myself in a position to make any arrangement."

Dr. Osler handed this letter to Mrs. Osler. She had been so uneasy about the pressure he was under in Baltimore (his consultations there almost amounted to a private practice) that she would not let him wait a moment before telegraphing he would consider the place. It was very like her; she was exceedingly clear-sighted where his good was concerned; and when any action seemed right the deed followed close on the thought. And so spurred on, he telegraphed and wrote to Burdon-Sanderson:

1 West Franklin Street
(Tuesday June 21st)

" Dear Sir John: —

I feel highly flattered that my name should be mentioned in connection with the Chair. I am sorry that so good a man as Ritchie should be passed over. There are so many things to be considered that I cabled you asking if an immediate decision was wanted or whether I could confer with you upon the question in Oxford. In many ways I should like to be considered a candidate. While very happy here and with splendid facilities, probably unequalled in English-speaking countries, I am over-worked and find it increasingly hard to serve the public and carry on my teaching. I have been in harness actively for thirty years and have been looking forward to the time when I could ease myself of some of the burdens I carry at present. With the income from my book we have a comfortable competency, so that I am in a measure independent. My only doubt relates to the somewhat relative duties of the Chair. I am interested in clinical teaching, am fond of it and have acquired some aptitude for bedside work which gives me a certain value in the profession. I should miss sadly the daily contact with the students unless I could arrange for clinical work in London. On the other hand, I have a mass of unfinished literary material on hand which the academic leisure of the new place would enable me to complete. Thanks for your kind invitation. Mrs. Osler does not accompany me. I have already accepted an offer from the Dean of Christ Church."

His visit to Europe brought the affair to a climax. He wrote to Mrs. Osler that he was still a trifle doubtful. As soon as she received the letter she cabled: " Do not procrastinate — accept at once." Which he did as soon as he received Balfour's official offer.

The news fell heavily in Baltimore. Those were sad days. There seemed no compensation for his loss.

In answer to a letter from one of Dr. Osler's colleagues Mrs. Osler wrote: " All that you and the others express for Dr. Osler — all that you say of his influence, *etc.,* touches me deeply, and during these days of diversified feelings, I hardly know how to express my appreciation and sympathy, and you can well know what a struggle it has been and such hard work for me to encourage Dr. Osler to do what I knew was really best for him. I am sure he can never regret this, but we both anticipate woeful days."

Mrs. Osler's quick eagerness for him to accept the offer almost deceived him and quite bewildered many of her friends. In a letter to her sister we find her reasons: " Thanks for your dear kind letter. Now that the deed is done I am filled with fear and anxiety; but I have quite made up my mind that I will only look forward to the pleasant things — and not anticipate the unpleasant and worrying things. . . . But when I think of the strain of the increasing work of the last three years I cannot but be glad to think a chance has come to make a break and put a comparatively restful life into Willie's way. I am grieved for Mother more than anything else — and feel that it is awful to worry her so much — but she will learn, I suppose, to enjoy the niceness of it. What could I do? Reverse the circumstances and one must agree that an American would be glad to come back to American traditions, *etc.,* having been brought up in them." She seems entirely to have forgotten that she, an American, was giving up her natural home, she was so entirely and unconsciously only thinking of him. One feels like saying what he said to his little nephew when he introduced Mrs. Washington on a dollar bill: " Say how-do-you-do to her. She is a fine woman."

Dr. Weir Mitchell struck the note that expressed the feelings of hundreds of his friends:

" I received your letter with mingled feelings — pained because your great example — so various in its values, is to be lost to the profession — pleased in what Oxford will gain in an untrammelled, clear-headed American physician. Yes, American. You will let me insist on that. I think you are wisely counselled to go. Twice in the last year I was on the point of writing to ask you to consider whether you were not being worked beyond your strength. Selfishly speaking, I am filled with the most honest regret. One by one the older men who shared with me the fates of the war and the contests of peace have died. I have picked up new friends — the younger ones — men and women — and among the best, you. And is it twenty years indeed? When I read your letter to my wife she said: " Isn't it splendid? " and I, " Isn't it sorrowful? " for, of course, this does take you out of my life, and at 74 the arithmetic of opportunity is easily summed up and made out. We shall see you, I fear, but rarely and very soon you will be saying raily for really and H's will be lost over the house, and you will say Gawd for God as is Oxford as she is spoke — Do be careful of your English. I am chaffing you to keep from saying more of the personal loss to me. As for the Johns Hopkins, perhaps you do not know that the Medical School at J. H. is or was William Osler. Are we not to see you before you go? I have a novel done and am made an Honorary Something of the French Academy."

During Dr. Osler's life in Baltimore his contemporaries realized more and more that he had sown seed in places where nothing had ever grown before. But anyone pondering over his life will acquire a deeper insight — not only of the miracle of his life-giving powers, but also of his greater care of the down-trodden, the lowly — those men and women whose paths were, through adversity, uncomplainingly travelled to unknown graves. From these, in his passion of pity and understanding, his own soul acquired strength — they, naked of all but their courage — and he, with so much. Dr. Walsh tells of a visit to the wards with him in 1894. Stopping by the bedside of an old woman whose case he wanted to show, " Mother," he said, " I would like you to tell Dr. Walsh something of your past life. When were you first in the hospital? " " At twenty-seven." " What was the matter? " " I had sarcoma of the right knee." " What did they do for you? " " They cut off the right leg at the hip." " Did you get entirely well? " " Yes, entirely well." " When were you in again? " " At forty-two." " What was the matter? " " I had cancer of the left breast." " What did they do for it? " " They cut off the left breast and the left arm." " Did you get entirely well? " " Yes, entirely well." " What are you in the hospital for now? " " For rheumatism; and Doctor," she said, with tears in her voice, and catching his hand, " I hope you will make me well in a hurry, because I have to go home to take care of my grandchildren." When the laurel wreaths were placed on his head, he bowed it humbly, remembering, " Naked of all but their courage."

Dr. Osler's final constructive task for America before he left was to found the Interurban Medical Clinical Club. His own intimate knowledge of young men, and his desire to advance medicine in America through them, led to the founding of the Club. It was particularly to be of benefit to young men who were engaged in original work. On April 28, 1905, he gathered together a number of men, six from each of the leading cities in the East — Boston, New York, Philadelphia, and Baltimore — for the initial meeting. The Club was patterned on the Surgical Club formed in 1903. All its members were medical clinical teachers and their meetings were to interchange their various methods of teaching and to hear reports on the latest scientific results in research. In the evening at their dinner the matters described in the day's morning and afternoon sessions were discussed. No one could go away from these meetings without having added to his store of knowledge and made friendships that would certainly enrich his life and outlook, and send him back to his home more valuable to his community. The initial meeting of the Club was held in an amphitheatre crowded with physicians and students and members of the Club — he in the pit standing by his patient, one of the sick poor, and on the other side of the patient, a student. That was all. But the atmosphere was charged with emotion — the great clinician was holding his last public clinic.

After this the banquets and eulogies might seem too commonplace to mention except that his heart warmed to the love shown him. Generally when a great man is fêted there comes a curious impression that the man is lost sight of in the hubbub and hurrahing, and that he, too, has lost sight of his ideals in a flurry of accredited achievements. But Dr. Osler — at the great banquets in his honour, when the laughter and gay talk are over, the last toast drunk, — suddenly rises and turns the whole assembly into a Cathedral of Souls. His after-dinner acknowledgments become lay sermons, something from the very warmest depths of his heart appealing to yours. He made three valedictory addresses. That at the Hopkins brought him the first and only disagreeable result of his jests. The address was twisted and gave him a good deal of annoyance and pain. The reporters were out for a sensation and for a time he was the prey of yellow journalism. He affirmed that the great majority of men do their best work before forty, and he quoted airily from Trollope's *Fixed Period,* " that it might be a good thing if all were peacefully chloroformed at sixty." But subtle jokes don't go in a mixed audience. The fact that Dr. Osler was himself fifty-five, was about to take a distinguished position, and that he had spent his own life prolonging the lives of others and bringing latent talents to life, counted for nothing at all. He was head-lined as an enemy of old age. He really cared a good deal though he jestingly remarked to a friend: " It's not pleasant to wake in the morning and find yourself, not famous but infamous," and he never liked to hear the joke mentioned. On the platform, much amused, with a twinkle in his eye sat Basil Gildersleeve, 73. It was so obvious to him that Dr. Osler was merely making a jest with a sentimental coloring, that he was greatly surprised at the concern of his own friends, who feared he might be hurt. " Nonsense! " he said to some one, " the boy Osler's best work has been done after forty. And he had the impudence after that age to secure one of the handsomest women in America for his wife "; and Professor Gildersleeve shook with laughter and prophesied Osler would regret the jest — which, as we saw, he did.

Fourteen years later when the night had nearly come for both, Professor Gildersleeve, 87, dean of the classical world, wrote for Sir William Osler's seventieth birthday this sonnet:

William the Fowler, Guillaume l'Oiseleur!
I love to call him thus and when I scan
The counterfeit presentment of the man,
I feel his net, I hear his arrows whir.
Make at the homely surname no demur,
Nor on a nomination lay a ban
With which a line of sovran lords began, —
Henry the Fowler was first Emperor.

Asclepius was Apollo's chosen son,
But to that son he never lent his bow,
Nor did Hephaestus teach to forge his net;

Both secrets hath Imperial Osler won.
His winged words straight to their quarry go,
All hearts are holden by his meshes yet.

Dr. Osler's very early maturity in character, mind and purpose, led him to underestimate the powers of the later-maturing man. He took his own life as the rule whereas it was the exception. How much a man's creative powers are used up before the age of forty is certainly a debatable question; but that a man should have developed, as he did, at a very early age, into the complete synthesis of great manhood, puts him into an unusual class. Col. Fielding H. Garrison, with his usual clear-sightedness, goes to the root of the matter when he writes: " But Osler's reasoning about the comparative uselessness of men at sixty, in the face of the imposing exceptions in Longfellow's ' Morituri Salutamus,' was obviously an expression of his essential preference for and innate sympathy with the oncoming race of younger people, whose worth he had sensed many times over in his beloved pupils."

The address before the Medical and Chirurgical Faculty shows his reaction to the yellow journalism — not bitter, not petty — just a little sad.

" It may be that in the hurry and bustle of a busy life I have given offense to some. Who can avoid it? Unwittingly I may have shot an arrow o'er the house and hurt a brother — if so, I am sorry and ask his pardon. So far as I can read my heart I leave you in charity with all. I have striven with none. Not as Walter Savage Landor says, " because none was worth the strife " but because I have a deep conviction of the hatefulness of strife, of its uselessness, of its disastrous effects, and a still deeper conviction of the blessings that come with unity, peace and concord. And I would give to each of you, my brothers — you who hear me now and who may elsewhere read my

words — to you who do our greatest work laboring incessantly for small rewards in towns and country places —
to you the more favored ones who have special fields of
work — to you teachers and professors and scientific workers — to one and all throughout the length and breadth
of the land — I give a single word as my parting com-
mandment: ' It is not hidden from thee; neither is it far
off. It is not in heaven, that thou shouldst say, Who shall
go up to heaven, and bring it unto us, that we may hear
it, and do it? Neither is it beyond the sea, that thou
shouldst say, Who shall go over the sea for us and bring it
unto us, that we may hear it, and do it? But the word is
very nigh unto thee, in thy mouth, and in thy heart, that
thou mayest do it ' — CHARITY! "

In the Farewell Address at the dinner given him at the
Waldorf-Astoria, in New York, this, in part, is what he
said:

" I have three personal ideals. One, to do the day's work
well and not to bother about the morrow. It has been urged
that this is not a satisfactory ideal. It is; and there is not
one which the student can carry with him into practice
with greater effect. To it, more than anything else, I owe
whatever success I have had — to this power of settling
down to the day's work and trying to do it well to the
best of one's ability, and letting the future take care of
itself.

" The second ideal has been to act the Golden Rule, as
far as in me lay, towards my professional brethren and
towards the patients committed to my care.

" And the third has been to cultivate such measure of
equanimity as would enable me to bear success with
humility, the affection of my friends without pride, and
to be ready when the day of sorrow and grief came, to
meet it with courage befitting a man.

" What the future has in store for me, I cannot tell —

you cannot tell. Nor do I much care, as long as I carry
with me, as I shall, the memory of the past you have given
me. Nothing can take that away.

"I have made mistakes but they have been mistakes of
the head, not of the heart. I can truly say, and I take upon
myself to witness, that in my sojourn with you

> I have loved no darkness,
> Sophisticated no truth,
> Nursed no delusion,
> Allowed no fear."

And then he repeated the line from Tennyson's *Ulysses:*
"I am a part of all that I have met."

The words "irreparable loss" do not fit him, for he was
never lost. As a matter of fact his gain was our gain. Who
would have had him miss his Oxford life, for their own
sakes as well as his? He belonged to us, and has enriched the
American and the Canadian medical world. It would have
been to hundreds an "irreparable loss" not to have known
the "Open Arms"; and to England he brought something
of America it could ill afford to miss.

First Years at Oxford

The mighty ocean rolls and raves,
To part us with its angry waves;
But arch on arch from shore to shore,
In a vast fabric reaching o'er,

With careful labours daily wrought,
By steady hope and tender thought,
The wild and weltering waste above —
Our hearts have bridged it with their love.

Clough.

CHAPTER IX

FIRST YEARS AT OXFORD

IN America life is like reading a rapidly written book without margins; in England the margins are broad. Dr. Osler's fifty-five years of life had been spent at full speed; the contemplation of slowing down must have been a curious sensation for him. The Max Müller house, which was his first home in England, literally breathed leisure for thought; the great trees, the river, the birds and the flowers in the garden — and more than all the beauty of the ancient colleges — were enchanting to the tired man; but leisure was never possible to him for any length of time. Teas, dinners, lunches, poured in upon them, and were at first interesting; the cordiality of their reception meant a great deal to both; but his eye was out for professional work and almost immediately he was back in harness.

Even before he landed in England his tentacles were stretching out to the friends he had left behind, suggesting improvements in their work, encouraging those who needed encouragement, writing obituaries for those who had fallen out of line, sending checks large and small to the needy, carrying, as was his custom, all his past with him as he stepped into a new environment.

It was " Eights " week in Oxford and everybody indoors and out was given over to a holiday spirit. On June 19th Mrs. Osler wrote: " I have 113 visits to pay "; and as the receptions and dinners kept on increasing it is not surprising that after two months of it they felt the need of a change. He had been duly matriculated as an undergraduate of

Christ Church — the ceremony quickly followed by another, conferring upon him the degree of M.D., and giving him a seat with the Dons. And as Regius Professor he had become a Curator of the Bodleian.

They had hunted for a house unsuccessfully, and had finally given it up, and decided to keep the Max Müller house for a year; which would give them time to look about. So, having taken all these steps to establish themselves, they went for a holiday in Scotland. One thing caused great jubilation to their American friends. During the early days of May the American yacht won the international race, and was so far ahead at the finish that they thought her an auxiliary vessel. One American said in glee, " It's just a tap from us to remind you that you haven't burned your boats."

The outing was delightful but, somehow, we lose sight of him in the Highland scenery; and though he fishes with Revere, it's Revere, not he, who is the fisherman. After a week with the Henry Phipps at Beaufort Castle, Dr. Osler was looking brown and robust. It was a delightful outing for him, but he doesn't seem quite in focus; and after a month you may be sure he was glad to be back in Oxford again.

The Oxford poise did not get into his blood; but the charm of the place entered his heart and the Bodleian was his inevitable love. His deep-seated passion for books, especially relating to his profession, increased and was only second to him to his love of humanity. The latter could not be diminished, but for it to increase would have been to reach the breaking point, as was proven when the War came. He fitted naturally and happily into his new surroundings for the customs of England were his inheritance by birth.

Nevertheless, though appreciative of old customs, as a rule their place was for him in appropriately bound volumes in his treasured library, where they could be taken down and studied in a comfortable chair before the fire when the day's work was done; but the day's work must be done with all the efficiency the present could command. His sense of continuity was always marked; the evolution from the rich sources of the past to the young world of the present was a stream he loved to follow; but no matter how far back he wandered he always returned a youth with youths. He could never have been a lonely thinker; his nature was too fresh and vigorous for that. He must share every thought with his students and, what made them adore him, he wanted to hear their ideas as much as he wanted to tell them his own.

As in Canada and the States so it was in Oxford, his coming brought new life and light. The changes in Oxford had this difference: there it was grafting new buds on the old trees; in the Dominion and in the States the young buds sprang from the ground. His predecessors in the chair of medicine at Oxford had been men of great scientific distinction but with little practical experience as physicians in the broad sense of the word. The new Regius Professor had covered the whole field; he knew medical schools as a musician knows the keys of his piano; and his many years of clinical teaching, with its foundation of scientific knowledge, his humanity and magnetic personality, made him an ideal physician. All doors were opened to him. Everyone recognized in him a leader whose judgment was as sound as his personality was charming. His efforts from the very first were to bring the academic and practical side of medicine into harmony. He would, of course, at once start his clinics; and they were eagerly attended by medical practitioners and medical students. He was a constant visitor to the wards, and he made a very special effort to help the divisional and branch meetings of the British Medical Association; he felt it most important to bring the country and city practitioner into contact. It is all so very reminiscent of his early Baltimore days.

The Radcliffe Infirmary stands in the centre of Oxford. It is a small hospital; its old buildings are fairly covered with vines and it has most lovely and generous gardens. The foundation dated from the seventeenth century, and it was by way of sleeping on its traditions, Dr. Osler awakened it into life; every ward was quickened through his influence, and in time the laboratory and pathological building were modernized. It became the heart of the medical life in Oxford. The Radcliffe Scientific Library, like every library he ever touched, expanded and grew in every direction under his hands.

Among the many new duties that were his was the mastership of the Old Alms-house at Ewelme. The house with its adjoining chapel is five hundred years old. It was built and endowed by Alice of Suffolk in the fifteenth century. In the ancient church adjoining the Alms-house is her beautiful alabaster tomb. The inscription on the tomb reads: " Pray for the soul of the Most Serene Princess Alice, Duchess of Suffolk, Patron of this Church and First Foundress of this Alms-house, who died on the 20th of May in the year 1475." And time paused. Thirteen old men live in the Alms-house; they are each allowed two rooms; and should any possess a wife or daughter, one or the other may live there and look after her husband or father. There is a surgeon to attend to their wants, and the Regius Professor at Oxford becomes *ex officio* Master. The preceding Regius Professors did not concern themselves overmuch with the Alms-house. A visit now and then in years sufficed them; but Dr. Osler entered seriously into his duties; it would have been impossible for him to be merely a figure head. Every week saw him at Ewelme. This particular duty was delightful to him — the Ancient Alms-house

— the old men — how clearly you see him in these surroundings!

A physician from the Middle West of the States was
visiting Oxford and asked to be taken to Ewelme, expecting to see something curious and unique. A chapel, a surgeon, two rooms apiece for thirteen old men, was not a
Westerner's idea of efficiency; and in telling the story he
said: " I went intending to say to the Regius ' In America,
you know, we would call all this stuff and nonsense. We
would look out for a hundred old duffers for what is being
done here for thirteen; picturesque but not practical, and
it's sentimental.' These were the very words I had in my
mind; but after my visit I didn't say them for I saw something so living and human that I found myself wiping
my eyes to make sure there was any other life. Dr. Osler
went from one to the other of the old men, playfully pulling the toe of one, or seriously sitting down by the side
of another, and talking their language. You felt that they
must all have come from the same childhood home; the
atmosphere he brought to each was so real and individual
that all the rest of the world seemed a long way off. I shall
never forget it, the ancient house, the contented old men
and Dr. Osler! Well, I've never tried to picture Christ but
he must have looked something like him, and do you know
what I did say to Dr. Osler when I went out? I said ' Damn
it! What's the sense in progress anyhow, and mind you, I
come from the Middle West! ' He took me all over Oxford,
showed me everything; and what he had done for the Radcliffe Infirmary even in a few years was something to
brag of. I didn't tell him so but I thought ' That's the
American in you '; and he made a perfect image of an
English doctor actually laugh — and before my visit was
over I was friends with a man that if Dr. Osler hadn't
been there, I would have cut a corner to get away from —
he didn't seem natural. I told Dr. Osler this and he put his

hands in his pockets, looked me up and down, laughed and then said: ' Do you know he spoke after that fashion about you? Said he liked you so much, but he did wish you would not talk in that extraordinary way through your nose.' Then he put his arm about my neck " — and the doctor from the West looked a little silly and laughed apologetically — " Do you know it's queer, but I always feel his arm there? — But to go on with my story: He said ' I wish you two would work together. He is doing splendid work in tuberculosis and that was a first-rate paper you wrote. He knows more about the subject than you do, but you will make others understand it better than he will; now see if you can't get something done.' And I date the success of my work from that talk."

From a very different person to the western physician we get another impression of Osler at Ewelme: Dr. Arthur T. Hadley writes his recollection: " One of the most delightful days of my life was spent with the Oslers in a visit to the Alms-house at the ancient village of Ewelme. . . . Previous incumbents of the office had been content to take the stipend without going near the Alms-house more than once or twice a year. Osler addressed himself seriously to the duties of the place, perhaps one day each week; and by so doing, won not only great credit at Oxford but what was more desirable, great affection from the old men after whose welfare he looked. Many of the duties were of a mixed kind particularly congenial to Osler's mind and tastes. The fifteenth century cloister round which the dwellings grouped themselves; the charming little church with the rooms and yards adjoining it; and above all, the old books, long neglected, with their ancient manuscripts and bindings and royal seals; — all these afforded Osler never-ending delight and gave his friends who visited the place with him a wonderful background against which his face and figure stand out as clear as that of St. Jerome."

And again comes the picture from quite another type — a disillusioned, tired man who felt the greatest misfortune of all was to have been born; a man with many millions and a hideous life. A light came into the man's dreary eyes as he spoke of Dr. Osler: " No," he said, " I do not believe in your charity benefiting yourself. It is bread cast upon the waters and it never does return so much as a crumb to the giver; but after seeing William Osler at the Alms-house at Ewelme, I felt that perhaps it did pay humanity for a rich man to forget himself. It certainly would pay if there were more William Oslers; but I have, however, never seen another. The promoters of the world are the harpies on the rich man's pockets and the philanthropists are as a rule hypocrites; and that ancient dame, Alice of Suffolk, who founded the Alms-house, had to wait five hundred years before a Master came along with a heart like her own for the old men. After seeing William Osler with them I thought I would be willing to wait five hundred years for something of mine to become part of one like him. He sat by one of the old men's beds, his elbow resting on the pillow, his beautiful dark face silhouetted against the dull old man's; and as he sat there telling me of Alice of Suffolk, the old pauper smiling and nodding his head, I thought a few such would redeem mankind; and I had a strange feeling that time was not — Alice of Suffolk — the God who inspired her, and William Osler — they were all of the same date."

And years later from the old pensioners comes the priceless tribute of " not the great nor well bespoke, but the mere uncounted folk." One of them *sans* almost everything, said with dim eyes the night the Master lay under his purple pall alone in the watching chamber, " I'll see him soon; he'd know me in a hundred, he would. God bless him."

And so we have pictures of Dr. Osler at Ewelme drawn by many different personalities, and as they all show the same motif, the picture is a very convincing one.

Now and then an anecdote illuminates a life more completely than pages of careful study. The story of the woman who, when told her son had been sent into slavery tied to two other victims, exclaimed: " God help the bairn who's tied to our Jamie! " gives us a life picture of Jamie. And the old pensioner's comment " He'd know me in a hundred, he would, God bless him! " gives a very clear picture of William Osler. He almost invariably held those he came in contact with by only a word, or a look; but, as with the western physician, that word or look stayed always with them.

Few events have given him so much delight as when, one July day in 1906, he and his cousin, Dr. Francis, found in one of the rooms of the Alms-house an old safe that evidently had not been opened for many years. It was rusted and after trying every way they could to open it they gave up the attempt and sent to London for an expert. When the safe was opened they found it full of documents covered with mould and reeking with damp. They spread them out in the sun to dry and then took them to the Bodleian where they were put in order and bound. Such a find! A wonderful collection of documents of the fourteenth to the sixteenth centuries — one as early as 1359! There were ancient title deeds, indentures, audit accounts, conveyances, court rolls — some of them in Norman French. There was the original charter with the seal of Henry VI endowing the Alms-house at Ewelme with the manors of Marsh Connock, and Ramridge; and one of the earliest was a parchment roll of recipes for making gunpowder, which at that time had not been applied to warfare. And there were letters on parchment of Alice of Suffolk. They are all collected now in a great folio entitled, *Ewelme Muniments* and are shown with pride to visitors to the Alms-house.

· As soon as he took possession of the Max Müller House guests began to arrive, and the idea of a quiet academic life was quickly dissipated. Among the earliest guests from the States were his late colleagues Drs. Welch, Halsted and Kelly; and with Dr. Osler the four had their first sitting for Sargent who had been commissioned by Miss Garrett to paint the four doctors. Mrs. Osler wrote: " They all met me at lunch at the Carlton and reported it as intensely interesting. Sargent worried over posing them and evidently did not think them beauties. Dr. Osler tried to make Dr. Kelly drink whisky-and-soda, but he said he was just starting on a tour of temperance lectures."

There are many tales of Sargent's comments on his models; he delighted in Dr. Osler's olive-green complexion — and the group when finished was an immense success. You see Dr. Welch more certainly than in a long biography; and Dr. Osler's is a timeless picture. The spirit that animated the boy at Weston and, at seventy, threw broadcast the embers of his beautiful life, lives on the canvas. And Dr. Kelly and Dr. Halsted are as understandingly given. If, a stranger, you had not known who they were, you would have known what they were. If you did not know what they had done you would know what they would do. The events of a man's life may be dull or adventurous; the really great portrait painter is not concerned with them, only with the man as he would be in any circumstances. A written life is simply annals before such a portrait as Sargent's of the four physicians. There they are — you need no words — revealing themselves on the canvas, that now hangs in the Welch library in Baltimore.

The currents into which Dr. Osler's life gathered the greatest strength after going to England were history and collecting incunabula, with which he enriched his own library and made valuable additions to medical libraries throughout Great Britain, Canada and the States. His avocation had become a very important vocation; it had always run a very close second to his practical clinical work; but now he could indulge this taste to the full. When in November 1905 he was elected a delegate of the University Press he was put in touch with all current work; and the Bodleian was an inexhaustible storehouse for a bibliophile. The innumerable book sales never failed to catch his eye, and when on a journey he always had a catalogue in his pocket. His work as a health propagandist increased and the lessening of his consultations and the narrowing of his clinical work gave him less breathing time — perhaps — for the hundreds of people who never came in vain for cheer of one kind or another. There were great humanist clinical physicians in England. They with William Osler formed the last of the old guard who watched the approach of the specialists.

Late in September Dr. Osler was off to Paris to attend the Tuberculosis Congress, and very soon he did a characteristic thing — brought together about twenty American members to visit with him the tomb of Louis in the Cemetery of Mount Parnasse. He placed a wreath of autumn leaves on the steps of the mausoleum that held the remains of Louis and told the group gathered about him briefly and feelingly the story of Louis' life, and how he had created, through his pupils, the American School of Clinical Medicine. Naturally, this tribute to Louis was deeply felt by the French — and as usual the atmosphere where Osler was became warm with friendliness. Internationally-minded does not in the least describe him: to be that is merely to have a somewhat intelligent appreciation or indefinite sympathy with other nations than your own. He was at once the most local and least provincial of men. Wherever he touched he made quick and lasting contacts.

On his return to England after the few weeks in Paris a new edition of his text-book came out, and he gave his son Revere Number 100,000.

At this time fell the tercentenary of the birth of Sir Thomas Browne, October 19, 1905. The ceremonies were held in the local Museum at Norwich. Dr. Osler had given a casket and pedestal to hold the skull of Sir Thomas; and in response to a toast, he replied: " There are three lessons to be gathered from the life of Sir Thomas Browne, all of them of value to us to-day: First, we see in him a man who had an ideal education. He was thoroughly versed in the classics; he lived abroad for two years and thereby learned the hardest lesson in life, for he became denationalized as far as his intellect and human sympathies were concerned. All places made for him one country, and he was England everywhere. And the second important lesson we may gain is that he presents a remarkable example in the medical profession of a man who mingled the waters of science with the oil of faith. I know of no one in history who believed so implicitly and so simply in the Christian religion, and yet it is evident from his writings that he had moments of ardent scepticism. . . . The third lesson to be drawn is that the perfect life may be led in a very simple quiet way."

A few days before, he had given, at Guy's Hospital one of his most arresting addresses — its subject the *Religio*. He spoke of his own collection of the 55 editions being nearly completed. He gives his often reiterated appreciation of Sir Thomas, the naturalist, philosopher, scholar, physician and biologist — and closed his address with these words: " For the student of medicine the writings of Sir Thomas Browne have a very positive value. The charm of high thoughts clad in beautiful language may win some readers to a love of good literature; but beyond this there is a still greater advantage. Like the *Thoughts of Marcus Aurelius* and the *Enchiridion* of Epictetus, the *Religio* is full of counsels of perfection which appeal to the mind of youth, still plastic and unhardened by contact with the world. Carefully studied, from such books come subtle influences which give stability to character and help to give a man a sane outlook on the complex problems of life. Sealed early of this tribe of authors a student takes with him as *compagnons de voyage,* lifelong friends whose thoughts become his thoughts and whose ways become his ways. Mastery of self, conscientious devotion to duty, deep human interest in human beings — these best-of-all lessons you must learn now or never — and these are some of the lessons which may be gleaned from that life and from the writings of Sir Thomas Browne."

The young men who listened to him entirely believed in him — became enthusiasts; but they felt the last edition of the *Religio* incarnated in his warm, breezy, enchanting personality, as more attractive than the first edition of the seventeenth century. The true intellectual is too rare to have a large following in his tastes. The strange thing is that he did get his students to listen — and while he talked they felt they were enjoying themselves with old books; but it was Dr. Osler they were enjoying. Left alone in a library they would not have picked up the *Religio*. What he really succeeded in doing was not so much bringing his own tastes to life in his students as in stimulating their own. With his own son, who was not at first inclined to books, he seized upon his love for fishing to interest him in *Izaak Walton* and so enriched his knowledge. Later the taste for books did develop, but it was from careful nurture on his father's part of what was latent in his son.

It has been said that Dr. Osler was practically an ambassador to England from North America. No American from the medical world ever came to England but his first thought was: I must see the Regius Professor. No one knew better than Dr. Osler the fundamental likeness between England and America. Politicians may rave to the contrary but read the literature of yesterday and to-day and you cannot tell whether the puppets are English or American. Meet the creatures and you place them at once by some superficial trick of manner or accent of a vowel. This is true of no other nations. You could not in rhyme or story put a French man or French woman in any other country and not know them French. He was an unmixed blessing to mother and daughters as he felt England and Canada and the United States to be — only perhaps for his mother the reverence was deeper. Sir Clifford Allbutt, Regius Professor at Cambridge, in the preface to the memorial volume in honor of Sir William's seventieth birthday in 1919, seems to express, more clearly than any other, his unifying power. He writes: " Thus almost with the rapidity of thought, between Canada, the United States and Great Britain, an academic link threefold was forged. In no person as well as in your own could this unity have been so happily consummated. You arrived indeed from overseas but as a pilgrim child of Oxford. In you the literary and historic tradition of the beautiful city was united with the zeal and venture of the new world."

Young men literally flocked to the Osler house; and the Rhodes scholars felt it their home base. Curiously and unconsciously the interest centred in three people: Dr. Osler and the person to whom he was for the moment giving his attention, and Mrs. Osler who set the stage. Men and boys came and went from the Oslers and in their reminiscences you never hear: " I met such and such a distinguished man or woman there and heard them talk of ' shops, ships, sealing wax and cabbages and kings.' " You only hear very often of their, to you, extremely uninter-

esting selves — how they had obtained some new outlook
or virtue — how their lives had been guided or quickened
by a word from the Chief, or, in the older men — how
some advance had been made possible in the medical
world by suggestions from Dr. Osler.

Reminiscenses of habitués of other great men's homes
often picture a group of distinguished people, interesting
as well to outsiders. At the home of Sir James Paget, for
instance, the fortunate wayfarers may possibly have seen
Darwin, Huxley, Tyndall, Tennyson, Browning, Pasteur
— all quietly enjoying a little leisure for relaxed talk and
friendship — and he would have left with a pleasant
memory and a good story in which the insignificant visitor
did not figure. But at Norham Gardens the light of the
central figure somehow filled the scene — and you did not
resent, though you might be bored by the panegyric of
the multitude — for most probably, you would be one of
those whose road Dr. Osler had made more tolerable.

The first trip to America was made December 16th.
Seven months had passed since he had left and he was
longing to see his family and the boys. How he managed
to be eye to eye and hand to hand to all those who clam-
ored for him, cannot be accounted for. It is certain that
he was completely worn out. It is a glorious thing to be
' a part of all you have met,' but the process is a strenuous
one.

On his return to England he had still much work to do
for his *System of Medicine*. The Harveian oration was
also planned for the following autumn. The British Medical Association was to meet in Toronto in August and he
wanted to make it a success. He was elected to the Athe-
næum Club by way of serious amusement. The thing,
however, he cared most about was his election to the Bibliographical Society. It was a little on the down grade at
that time and he brought it into a fresh lease of life. Little

had been done for the Bodleian since 1860; but in 1906, with Dr. Osler as newly appointed Curator, a fresh enthusiasm developed. Many years before, the original copy of the first folio of *Shakespeare* had been parted with; and word came that it could be recovered. The London firm that had secured the folio was offered £3000 for it (they felt sure the offer had come from the U. S. A.) ; but it held back its answer hoping the Bodleian might be able to give the price offered. The Bodleian authorities were frantically anxious; they could neither borrow nor steal, and they had very little faith in the effect of their begging; and it seemed a hopeless situation. The new Curator subscribed largely himself and secured contributions from Lord Mount Stephen and from Mr. Henry Phipps; but that was not enough; and the time was growing short when Dr. Osler wrote to his old friend, Lord Strathcona, and a favourable telegram came which was promptly sent to the librarian, Mr. Nicholson. The latter, overcome with relief and gratitude, wrote: " My dear Osler, you deserve a statue in the Bodleian triangle." It is also reported that later when he met Dr. Osler, the librarian sat on the floor and wept. It's a delightful tale, not the least part of it being that when the man who had offered £3000 realized he could not buy the manuscript, he wrote imploring that they would let him have for his lifetime only, the Turbutt Folio, and he would give £1500 for the temporary loan. They wouldn't take the chance; which was cruel, but wise, as there is no subtler criminal mind than that of a collector when tempted. Dr. Osler had not only done this good deed for the Bodleian but he secured a seventeenth and eighteenth centuries medical library (The Warrington Collection) for the Johns Hopkins Medical School, where it now remains.

When news of the California earthquake and fire reached England he immediately thought of the loss the doctors of the Pacific coast would suffer by the destruction of their books. The Californians had declined outside assistance, but he thought something should be done and wrote J. H. Musser and John S. Billings urging them to organize a committee to collect books for the San Francisco library.

There was a movement in England to start a new Medical Journal of a type different to that of their customary publications. Dr. Osler suggested: " Why not form a National Association of Physicians first, and let the journal come to be its official organ? " The idea was at once adopted and thus came into being the Association of Physicians of Great Britain and Ireland with the *Quarterly Journal of Medicine* as its official organ; and the Oxford Press, for the first time, undertook medical publications. Again we see the effect of a casual word of Dr. Osler's.

In his very happy life the first years in England were perhaps the happiest. He had made the right move. Revere fitted into his surroundings and developed in a way that gladdened his heart; and Mrs. Osler was more than content. In January 1907 they took possession of their new home, No. 13 Norham Gardens which as " The Open Arms " was to be known throughout the medical world for its hospitality.

Mrs. Osler had not found it a hardship to move from one city to another when in America. Her friends often spoke of her lack of local feeling; wherever she was her house was her kingdom; but with Oxford it was different; her local attachment was instant and strong and enduring. All that was finest in her expanded in the English atmosphere. She insisted on having American ideals of heat, light and plumbing in her house; but what really meant more to her than such comfort was the prodigal wealth of flowers in the garden — home-made flowers, roses, lilies, laburnum, hawthorn. How she loved them!

After describing a dinner in the Common room of Corpus Christi, Mrs. Osler writes: "It was so mysterious and queer there. There was a dense fog and our coachman could hardly find his way. When we came out Willie and I walked about among the College buildings in the fog with the moon shining through. Willie's delight in the College life is a joy to see." You must have lived in England to understand evenings such as she describes: mysterious, beautiful, and to some unutterably sad — the shadow irresistibly overcoming the light. Mrs. Osler had an intense love of nature. It was all-sufficing to her, no leading on to other thoughts. She embraced its beauty, satisfied. He felt all beauty too, after a fashion, but with Nature as with Art it was merely an atmosphere where his thoughts were free to roam elsewhere. As he wandered about the old College in the moonlit fog, Burton was with him, and all his dear ghosts of the long past.

There is something in the English atmosphere which accounts for many national characteristics — belief in mystery, tolerance of ghosts, readiness to fight but slowness to wrath. Those who have walked in the fog step slowly and move with some common sense; and triviality avoids the Anglo-Saxon. He may often be a fool but he is rarely a flippant fool. The new Regius Professor was Anglo-Saxon and no one was deceived — only charmed — by his dancing step, flashing dark eyes, quick wit and romanticism. They were only flickers of light caught from his Celtic mother who was soon to celebrate her one-hundredth birthday. To be with her on this anniversary they both took a quick trip to Canada and the States in December 1906. The fine old woman who had, in her girlhood, elected as a duty and high privilege to suffer hardships, was now near the end of her long journey. Seated in her armchair in her room, surrounded by love and peace and honour, her bundle of sheaves marking only progress and conquest. The immense birthday cake with its hundred candles was made to represent the five rulers she had lived under: two Georges, William, Victoria and Edward. It was brought into her room and with it telegrams of congratulation from the Archbishop of Canterbury, the Governor-General, Earl Grey, the Canadian House of Commons and innumerable others. The chief glory of all for her was that these honours were in great part due to recognition of the services of her distinguished sons, men who, to her piety and integrity and energy, had added brilliant intellects, and so ranked among the most influential men in the Dominion. Britton Bath Osler, Queen's Counsel, considered the most brilliant of them all, had died in 1901, but near her were her other five sons, the Hon. Featherstone Osler, Justice of the Court of Appeals for Ontario; Sir Edmund Boyd Osler, a great financier, President of the Dominion Banks, Director of the Canadian Pacific Railway, and many other companies; and Sir William Osler, Regius Professor of Medicine at Oxford and about the best-loved man in the English-speaking medical world; Edward Lake Osler and Francis Osler; also her daughters, who entirely satisfied her ideas of what women should be. The two children who had died and her husband, were, she was confident, awaiting her when her pilgrimage was over. The certain faith which belonged to that age was hers to an extraordinary degree and descended to her children modified by their times, but automatically persisting in spite of the overthrow of dogmas and creeds. Her youngest son was singularly like his mother physically and morally but differed in temperament and turn of intellect. He said of his mother: " She had a fine outlook on life *ohne Hast ohne Rast*." A marvellous old figure she must have looked in her chair, one hundred years to the good, the face like clear-cut bronze, out of which the eyes looked straight ahead into the coming change, unafraid;

the mouth a little stern but contented and unperplexed. The cumulative effect of such a life as hers is like that of a great natural force, and it arouses the emotion felt when one sees a great mountain and recognizes the toil of the ages that raised it out of the plain. Her son's life took the same unswerving course; each day was lived simply at the level of his highest conscience; he was content to do his best, with great ambition for his profession and his friends — none for himself. He was happy in a simple unreasoning faith which was his as much as the colour of his eyes; but with his keen intellect, his inability for muddled thought, he knew it was inexplicable, though to himself it was sufficing. He was not to see his mother again for she survived her hundredth birthday by scarcely three months.

During the visit to America he was offered the Presidency of the University of Toronto. Indeed calls urging him to return to Canada came continually from one source or another; but Oxford was satisfying.

They sailed from New York early in January planning to return again to America for a medical congress the following April. On February seventh he was a guest in Edinburgh of the Royal Medical Society at their annual dinner. In his speech there he recalled the relationship of this, the oldest Medical Society in the English-speaking world, to the profession in the United States and Canada. He spoke of the notable Scots who had been members of the Society and who had greatly influenced American medicine. He told of how Rutherford had brought clinical teaching to the English schools " and what had been called the Edinburgh method dates from the introduction by Rutherford of practical classes in the Royal Infirmary. But we owe the method to the Dutch, who are Masters in this as in nearly all the advances in modern civilization. Rutherford and his colleagues, Plimmer, Sinclair and Innes, were pupils of Boerhaave, the Dutch Hippocrates, under whom the objective method of Sydenham reached its highest development, and out of which when united to the 'anatomical thinking' of Morgagni, and the new methods of physical diagnosis, modern clinical medicine has evolved." His own likeness to Boerhaave has impressed many physicians. The students in Edinburgh were enthused by him and gave him a great reception. The impression he made during this visit probably created in them the desire that he should be a candidate for the Lord Rectorship contest which was to take place a year later.

He was still worrying over the *System of Medicine;* it was coming along too slowly for his assistant editor; it always seemed to be the work waiting for Dr. Osler around the corner — and the only work he wanted to dodge. As a matter of fact he was constantly increasing his responsibilities; he accepted an appointment as consulting physician to the staff of the new King Edward Sanatorium for Tuberculosis at Midhurst, Surrey, and was punctiliously attending to his University posts. He was also professional representative on the Hebdomadal Council which met every Monday.

About this time the McGill Medical School and the Museum, which contained his old specimens, were burnt. The specimens fortunately were saved, but he did not know this till later. Ignoring his own apparent loss he wrote Dr. Abbott not to lose heart — that he felt sure the buildings would soon be replaced; but his optimism was practical; it took the form of interesting men of wealth to undertake the restoration. And as he himself always gave more than most people would think he should, his appeals were not often turned down. He was a very considerate beggar, never thinking he knew a man's purse and obligations better than the man knew them himself. It would be utterly inconceivable, his making anyone feel mortified because they wanted to give and could not. All these matters he approached in such a way that he left his victim a self-respecting door of escape; and in the history of his life, one gets the impression of the uncoerced generosity of rich and poor.

May, 1907, found him back again in America to attend the Triennial Congress of American Physicians and Surgeons. The subject for general discussion was " The historical development and relative value of laboratory and clinical methods of diagnosis." It is remarkable that Francis H. Williams's discussion of the X-ray as a method of diagnosing early pulmonary tuberculosis excited little interest.

Dr. Osler found Oxford, on his return, full of business in which he must have a hand. The Oxford University Appeal Fund was under way and later the first annual meeting of the Association of Physicians of Great Britain and Ireland took place. *The Quarterly Journal of Medicine* (Clarendon Press) was started with an editorial board, Dr. Osler, Chief. The Royal Society of Medicine had its initial meeting. It was the amalgamation of seventeen of the possible twenty-one organizations; but unfortunately the old London Medical Society held aloof. He threw himself into the new amalgamation with intense interest, never failing to drop into its rooms when in town; wrote countless letters about the library; arranged for speakers at the meetings. He was on its Council for the first three years and on the Library Committee until his death. His successful fight in the States against tuberculosis was continued in England and the anti-vivisectionists found his lance sharp against them. In his testimony before the Royal Commission on Vivisection, he told the story of yellow fever, how Walter Reed had conducted experiments on human volunteers; and he defended the use of animals for teaching men in surgical technique. He spoke of the humanity of the physiologists, and said that it was an insult to put vexatious restrictions upon them. And he gave his opinion that once a man had made a voluntary decision it was entirely moral for him to submit to experiments that might have bad consequences to himself; but highly immoral to experiment upon anyone without his uncoerced assent.

The interest in health measures had been speeding up rapidly everywhere. In Ireland the Woman's National Health Association was formed with the Countess of Aberdeen as President, and as tuberculosis among the Irish was rampant the quest of methods to prevent its ravages was imperative. In order to educate the people a tuberculosis exhibit was planned at the time of the International Exhibition in Dublin and a course of lectures was arranged for which Dr. Osler gave the inaugural address. It is difficult to realize how very little was known at that time of preventive measures. The world has so profited by the work of these health pioneers that now every schoolmistress and health officer in the land takes certain precautions as a matter of course. At the end of his address, or rather his call to common sense, he says: " In this crusade against tuberculosis there are two indispensable factors: enthusiasm for work, which should not be hard to maintain, since we are everywhere fighting a winning battle; and the second essential factor is perseverence. It is not a year's work; a decade will make a difference; a generation should see a reduction in the mortality of 50%; and your children and grandchildren should be able to point to a victory over tuberculosis as memorable as that which our fathers have won against typhus and typhoid fever."

Lady Aberdeen gave him a delicate task; she asked him to speak of the Irish climate. This is what he said: " People say sometimes that on this side of the Atlantic we have only weather and no climate. But peripatetic as I have been, living in many places, I have always regarded climate and

weather as two of the non-essentials, and I think the people who take that view of both climate and weather are
the only happy ones in life. But there is no reason whatever for you here in Ireland to growl about the weather.
It is quite good enough for you. And it is a first-rate climate for consumption. It is not a bit more moist in any
part of Ireland than it is in that tail-end of England, Cornwall. Yet in no climate do consumptives do better. I do
not know where this idea, that Ireland is a bad climate for
consumptives, comes from; certainly I cannot think it
comes from the profession. It is one of those fads possibly
women have encouraged. . . . Sunshine is not essential
for the cure of the disease. The things that are essential
are fresh air, good food, good houses and hope."

It seems long ago — all this — but it was in 1907; and
still longer ago seems the visit of the German Emperor and
Empress to England in November of that year. They were
the guests of King Edward and Queen Alexandra. There
was fear both in England and France lest the *entente cor-
diale* should be affected; but it was " How do you do? "
and " How do you do? " again, and " after you, my dear
Alphonse " — and everything was lovely. " God save the
King " and " Deutschland über Alles " were equally ap-
plauded, notwithstanding that the new German Naval
program was announced about the time of the Kaiser's
famous speech at the Guild Hall. " Mind your Manner "
was in the air. Oxford conferred on the Kaiser the degree
of D.C.L. Dr. Osler's account of the function, held at
Windsor, is amusing. " The deputation consisted of the
Chancellor, the Vice Chancellor, the Proctors, the Regius
Professors, Sir William Anson and the Registrar. We had
a special carriage and a room was arranged at the White
Hart for robing. At 4:45 carriages were sent from the
Castle and we drove to the State entrance. The Master of
Ceremonies took us up to one of the reception rooms

which was hung with pictures by Van Dyke, chiefly of Charles II. Lord Curzon came in with the faithful Moon (the University bedell) holding up his train. We were arranged in a semi-circle in order of precedence, the Chancellor in the middle and a little in front of us. The Emperor came in with a staff of eleven, among whom were the German ambassador and Lord Roberts. He looked a little nervous and did not know just how far away from the Chancellor he should stand. At first he did not look at all happy — as if bored or tired — and he seemed fagged and worried. Lord Curzon made a singularly felicitous speech, extempore. Only he said it was the degree of Common instead of Civil Law. And he made a cold shiver pass around the semi-circle when he said: ' And you remember, Sir, the telegram you sent ' — Everyone felt that it might be an awful break but was relieved when the Chancellor added — ' about the aquatic contests on the Thames,' referring to some incident in the races years ago." Somehow the little Kaiser in his red gown of an Oxford D.C.L. under which he wore the uniform of a British Field Marshal brings back very forcibly Thackeray's celebrated picture of George IV: ' I try and take him to pieces, and find silk stockings, padding, stays, a coat with frogs and a fur collar, a star and blue ribbon, a pocket-handkerchief prodigiously scented, one of Truefitt's best nutty brown wigs reeking with oil, a set of teeth and a huge black stock, underwaistcoats, more underwaistcoats, and then nothing."

Before this there had been quite a different order of pageant held during the summer in Christ Church Meadows with thousands taking part in it. The " Book of Words " described the scenes taken from the last ten centuries which were depicted by the pageant. It was a great success. On the day before it opened Lord Curzon's first *Encaenia* was held and the academic procession was something to remember. Among those up for degrees were General Booth, the Archbishop of Armagh, Rudyard Kipling and Mark Twain. Thackeray would have found a great deal of difficulty in describing what was under the caps and gowns of these men — no material for caricature there. But what a picture Dr. Osler might have given! for he saw men clearly and saw them whole. His habit of merely saying a word or two of praise, or saying nothing at all, merely obliterated personality. It is not to be commended even though prompted by a good heart. Kipling and his wife stayed with the Oslers during the pageant; and Dr. Osler tells us " they were so bright "; and of Mark Twain, " he was most amusing." From Mark Twain, however, we get a realistic touch; he tells us that during the pageant he met the greatest of all widowers, Henry VIII, in the street and found him a much more pleasant personality than he had expected.

Christmas 1907 was spent happily at No. 13 Norham Gardens. The house was now comfortable and his books in place; they were steadily increasing and when out of all bounds a shower of treasures fell upon his students and friends. In nearly every letter some mention is made of Revere, referred to as " Isaac " or " Ikey " or " Tommy " or " Egerton Jr."; of his sweetness of character. He adds a little regret that books are not in his line.

The dust of the past never got into his eyes or mind. The old books and the old physicians stepped out of their cerements and became a part of him. In his Linacre lecture which he gave at this time, while loving the humanitarian physician he does justice to the grammarian. He said: " Fed to inanition on the dry husks of grammar and with bitter memories of ' Farrar on the Greek Verb,' I can never pick up a text-book on the subject without a regret that the quickening spirit of Greece and Rome should have been for generations killed by the letter with which

alone these books are concerned. It has been a great comfort to know that neither ' Pindar nor Æschylus had the
faintest conception of these matters and neither knew
what was meant by an adverb or preposition, or the rules
of the Moods and Tenses ' (Gomperz). And to find out
who invented parts of speech and be able to curse Protagoras by his gods has been a source of inexpressible relief. But even with these feelings of hostility I find it impossible to pick up the larger work of Linacre without the
thrill that stirs one at the recognition of successful effort
— of years of persistent application. No teacher had had
such distinguished pupils — Prince Arthur, the Princess
Mary, Sir Thomas More, and Erasmus, the greatest scholar
of the age."

On the panel over his mantel hung portraits of Linacre,
Harvey and Sydenham; and many recall how quickly and
vividly Dr. Osler introduced them with a word, so that
they always afterwards thought of them as friends of Dr.
Osler's from the far past, living intimately with him in his
study.

On the fifth of August they took one of the very rare
trips *en famille*. Revere, Mrs. Osler and he went off for a
motor trip to Scotland by the Great North Road. He
wrote that it was such a happy time, their first long motor
trip together. Revere was to have some fishing and they
were to have just the ordinary delightful outing that so
many people constantly have and that singularly enough
was so unusual for them — just the three of them together. One seldom sees greater love than existed among
these three; but they were rarely alone, and in their active
life the outsider was never excluded. And there was seldom
a day when the affairs of many people were not being considered as vitally as their own. His comments on their trip
are hardly worth reading; his reactions, even to the gathering of a bit of grass from a mound in Wordsworth's

garden are most orthodox. But the rejuvenating effect of the trip made him eager for a still longer holiday; and though he had planned to be in America for the International Congress of Tuberculosis which met in Washington in the autumn, he suddenly decided to take a winter off. "After thirty-four years with harness on," he wrote, "I am going to steal a winter." France for three months, then Italy — and America, perhaps. He planned a Sabbatical Year.

Sabbatical Year & Baronetcy

For peregrinations charmes our senses with such unspeakable and sweet variety, that some count him unhappy that never travelled.

Burton.

CHAPTER X

SABBATICAL YEAR & BARONETCY

DR. CUSHING in his *Life of Sir William Osler* writes: "Having finished the Text Book revision, it was characteristic that he would unceremoniously walk out of the house on October first (1908) with nothing but a bag in his hand, as though prepared for a week-end sojourn rather than for the long absence necessary to secure a 'thorough brain dusting.'" This is described in such manlike fashion that it is well to inquire why he could leave for a long absence with only a bag. Mrs. Osler waited to put Revere into his school and close the house; and she unquestionably filled his bag in a very thorough and understanding fashion; then after all their affairs in Oxford had been put in shape she joined him in less than two weeks with doubtless a full supply of luggage. Mrs. Osler radiated an efficiency that made any man coming within her dominion feel that he was carefree in all mundane matters. There is no doubt whatever that, in the very depths of his nature, he was an adorable saint but there is also not the least doubt that he was an extraordinarily well-watched-over and well-looked-after saint — one who was tested in the furnace of good fortune. And it was due to Mrs. Osler and not to any simplicity of nature that he could walk off whistling for a year's sojourn with only a bag. A friend sitting beside Mrs. Osler one day in church suddenly felt her start, give a suppressed exclamation, and rush out of church. Her friend followed, thinking she had been taken ill, only to find that Dr. Osler was leaving for an out-of-town consultation and she suddenly remembered that she had forgotten to pack some item of his toilet. There was never a more smartly dressed man than Dr. Osler and he wore his flower in his buttonhole and carried his stick and yellow kid gloves with an air, but it was Mrs. Osler who saw that he had them.

In Paris they had a delightfully furnished apartment, servants and all put at their disposal. Their holiday began most auspiciously.

It is rarely interesting to hear of travellers' impressions unless something very out-of-the-ordinary occurs, and Dr. Osler so quickly harmonized himself with his surroundings that you do not ever catch from him the outsider's reaction of surprise to new manners, and customs and peoples. His real interests lay in his profession, and his winter was chiefly devoted to absorbing all he could of Paris and French medicine. He was *persona grata* everywhere; all doors were opened to him but he wished to avoid social functions, to be free to attend clinics and lectures; he had a special workroom given him at the library; he was elected a member of the Société des Hôpitaux; he became well acquainted with such men as Raymond, Marie, Dieulafoy, Vaquez; he haunted old bookshops; and of course, he put another wreath on Louis' tomb in Mount Parnasse.

Of the Paris medical student he wrote: " As I have seen him during the past three months at work in the hospitals, the Paris medical student is a very hard-working fellow, keenly alive to the importance of scientific and practical medicine and with a charming touch of human sympathy with the patients entrusted to his care." And again: " In the medical world of Paris at first glance the men only are recognizable; everything else is different, and so very different. But here is the charm and it does one good to get into an atmosphere charged with novelty, where the burning questions are for a time unintelligible. There are four factions of first importance: the medical school, the hospital, the medical societies and the Pasteur Institute." He rarely speaks of anything in regard to people as ' unintelligible ' and, as a matter of fact, he immediately makes it intelligible, and from a sympathetic point of view. The reverence of the French for their great men, their hero worship, found in him a kindred spirit. Indeed he might easily have made them feel a little cold in comparison. He tells us that all Paris is at Père Lachaise on All Saints Day, that hundreds of thousands visit the tombs there and literally cover the graves with flowers. He, belonging to what he calls the " cold-blooded Anglo-Saxon race," gives two days of ardent hero worship at the tombs of the illustrious dead. " I had a special mission," he said, " to see the tomb of that rare genius, Bichat, who started a revolution in medicine before he was thirty, and who died at thirty-two, leaving a name which is reverenced throughout the world. It was good to see that his simple grave was not neglected. A wreath, fresh flowers, and several plants, showed that his memory was still cherished, and I added a bunch of pansies for thoughts." Dr. Osler's life has been marked with pilgrimages of this order and he had an almost tiresome, certainly a tiring, way of incessantly starting up memorial meetings and extending them until they consummated in a portrait, or an endowed chair, or a volume of the works of the dead. No Frenchman on earth could excel him in such matters. And he was far from content to limit his respect and reverence to the great lights of the past. Whoever came near him and did any little thing in the least worth while for his profession always obtained his recognition for what he had done. He longed for everyone to get something out of life. So he kept bolstering up the youth who came near him; and as for his former teachers in Canada, the grave of every medical hero which he visits recalls to him some likeness in them to the illustrious dead — often with more gratitude than discrimination. Mrs. Osler was never unsympathetic with this aspect of his nature.

The first weeks in Paris were saddened by the news of Mr. Gilman's death. When people speak, as they often do, of Dr. Osler's success in life being due to his very fascinating personality (though physicians, familiar with his contributions to medicine, will make no such mistake), it is well to recall the fact that he was one of Mr. Gilman's chosen immortals, and that his fascination would not have stirred the beat of a pulse in Mr. Gilman. Any man, during his presidency, elected to a professorship in the Johns Hopkins must have guaranteed brains of a very high order. Mr. Gilman felt Dr. Osler's charm, but, if that had been his chief asset, he would have politely relegated him to the social tea parties. He might have overlooked some very respectable brains but no moderate one caught his official attention. Seeing his suave manner, his smile, a colleague might have approached him hopefully with a candidate or friend he wanted placed; but between that smiling face and himself would fall a steel shutter. The King's O.M. might be given for many delightful things but Mr. Gilman's meant just brains. After this cold appraisal had been given, however, and the young Canadian installed in office, Mr. Gilman joined the majority, and gave him his heart.

Dr. Osler wrote to Mrs. Gilman: " I have just seen in *The Times* the death of my dear friend — or rather Mrs. Osler read it out — and I exclaimed from my heart — My father! my father! The chariots of Israel and the horsemen thereof! " . . . It was a moment as well, of happy memories that swept over him — of years of unexampled achievement, made possible for himself and his colleagues by the most broad-minded and single-minded of directors.

A small disappointment came when he failed to win the

Lord Rectorship contest at Edinburgh. Professor G. A. Gibson wrote him: " I was away yesterday and therefore could not get a letter written to you about the result of the Rectorship Election. Your supporters made a splendid fight against the political odds and came within 200 of victory. A very little transference from Wyndham to yours would have made all the difference. I would like to congratulate you on the magic of your name and I do not believe any other human being standing as an independent candidate, could have shown anything like the same result. I have been wondering whether you would allow yourself to be put up next time as an independent conservative. If you did you would romp in." It was the very smallest of disappointments. It would have been only an honorary office, with a few Rectorial addresses; and that was unquestionably the reason he considered it at all.

While in Paris he read with delight all of Swinburne's poems. Those about children especially impressed him, which is strange; as Swinburne's infants *de luxe* have not much in common with his own flesh and blood children. But it is so delightful to see him for a moment without his persistent shadow, Æsculapius, that one is tempted to make much of it, perhaps too much; it is almost the only time in his Sabbatical Year (the time he is making his intimate acquaintance with Swinburne) that Æsculapius nods. But though Swinburne gives him a thrill, it is really Shelley, among the poets, who holds his heart. A tale is told of how, when some of his colleagues were tearing Shelley, the man, to pieces, Dr. Osler got up saying bitterly, " Shelley has been well hanged," and left the room abruptly without a good-bye to the company. Col. Garrison has said, " I feel sure his sentiments were those of Swinburne: ' *Otez à Shelley sa foi sublime, son dévouement héroïque, son amour du droit et de l'idéal, il sera toujours un des plus grands poètes de tous les siècles.*' "

Dr. Cushing found in the files of a medical journal some notes of Dr. Osler's appreciation of the French: " After a stay of three and a half months I am leaving Paris with many regrets. I am sorry not to be a member of the faculty of medicine. I should be glad to put after my name *Médecin des Hôpitaux;* the position of *Chef de Clinique* at the *Hotel Dieu* with Professor Dieulafoy would suit me admirably; I would be quite happy as an interne with Professor Raymond at Salpêtrière, or as an externe with Professor Pierre Marie at the Bicêtre or even as a *stagiaire* at the Cochin with Dr. Chauffard! Best of all, I should like to be a P. C. N. at the Jardin des Plantes, a student who is working at physics, chemistry, and natural history in the year preliminary to medicine. I should like to do the *vice versa* trick of Anstey's story, and change places with the young P. C. N. in this year's class who will go through the grades of my regrets just mentioned and who about the year 1940 will become Dean of this ancient and remarkable Medical School.

" It would be pleasant to see the superstructure which the next two generations will build on the scientific foundations of the nineteenth century — but these are fancies, not impressions. . . ."

About the middle of January they went to Rome, where the libraries and the bookshops were evidently far more in his mind than the ancient ruins. His exclamations of appreciation of old Rome were the same every tourist has uttered since the reign of tourists began. Have we not heard many times: " Rome at last! wonderful! — what pigmies we are in comparison with these old fellows! " That feeling expressed and honestly felt, he goes on to his real enthusiasm: " Splendid bookshops here. I have already got some treasures. Redi and Vallisneri — splendid editions! " He was no tourist or amateur when he approached the incunabula.

The work the Italians had accomplished on malaria was of intense interest. He sent a letter to *The Times* entitled, " Malaria in Italy, a lesson in practical Hygiene," which was a very comprehensive treatise in a short space, of a disease he could speak of with authority. It is his work on malaria, begun when in Philadelphia and carried on through his students at the Hopkins, that has been so rich in results. But books absorbed him. Every note to his friends and colleagues is filled with his glorious finds in the bookshops. After leaving Rome for Florence he was called back to an ill American stranded there and he writes: " I sanctified my fee by buying three copies of Vesal, 2nd edition, fine one for myself; a first for McGill (300 fr. was stiff, but it goes for 500) and another for the Frick library. I was sorry to miss the Rhazes, the Brussels library secured it. I have two copies also of the Venice edition of the Vesal. Have you one? I bought one *Imperialis* for the sake of the Vesal pictures — they have another which I will ask them to send. . . . I have a set of votives for the (Maryland) faculty — terra cotta arms, legs, breasts, eyes, ears, fingers — which the votaries hung in the Æsculapian temples in gratitude to the God — the modern R. C. ones are wretched (tin) imitations." And then followed many letters of the same order. No exclaiming " What pigmies we are in comparison with these old fellows! " Could the old fellows have walked again they would have wondered what order of creature this was who brightened up their old haunts; and the ghost of Æsculapius would have accorded him a seat of honour by his side. He would have had a less sympathetic time had the ghost of one of the Greek architects, or sculptors, been his guide: He would no doubt have cried at the end: " Alas! what I think best you declare worst." And if that latter-day, crossgrained saint, Ruskin, had been along, our beloved doctor would have had three pages of epithets hurled after him when he left Italy with:

" We came to the conclusion that about the best thing we saw in Italy was the last — Milan Cathedral." And he had been to Florence, Rome, Venice, Verona, Padua!

Books! The men of his profession, even the minutest dust of any one of them, who had bent his knee, or given his brains to the Æsculapian God, finds Dr. Osler stirring them into life and making the air vibrate with his enthusiasm the world over. Canada, America, England, all had to share his joy. And if he didn't understand overmuch about pictures or cathedrals, he never bored you in telling about them with more than a word or two; and he had the satisfaction of considering them fine affairs. One doesn't in the least regret the limitation, but one does regret his determination never to make an all-round characterization. He knew people and he came in contact with almost all the great men of his day and what sketches he could have given us if only he had not firmly covered every frailty he saw! In all his life he only gives one description that leaves you knowing the man, and that was of Walter Whitman whom he did not know. You do see the old poet in his study; but the others whom he met pass by as mere names on paper.

After his orgy of book hunting and book giving he went back to England for Easter, and was happy for a week or so with his boy, and then ends his Sabbatical Year with a visit to America. On arriving he went at once to Baltimore to be present at the dedication of the new building of the Maryland Medical and Chirurgical Faculty. It has been called the greatest day in the history of medicine in Maryland; and it was almost entirely due to Dr. Osler's work during his fifteen years in Baltimore that this achievement had been made possible. The hall was filled with notables. In the evening " Osler Hall " was dedicated and Dr. Osler made an address which ended with these words: " In one of his Hibbert Lectures last year at Oxford William James made a remark that clung — 'We live forward, we understand backwards. The philosophers tell us that there is no present, no now — the fleeting moment was as we try to catch it.' In the opening of this new building we have to-day made a happy addition to a happy past. Towards this day we have looked forward, and the future should still be in our thoughts. This old Faculty must continue to be our rallying ground — once inside its portals, schools, colleges, hospitals, societies, all other affiliations are absorbed in something vastly greater which includes all and claims from all devoted service, the united profession of the State."

This fourth visit to America seemed even more full of addresses and functions than any of the previous ones. The incessant practical activities that engaged him might be expected to disturb the scholar, but that was not the case. The mere physical strain, however, would seem appalling.

In Ontario he gave an address before the Ontario profession taking as his subject, *The Treatment of Disease*. It was a vivid address that the laity could understand and the profession value; but all his addresses are much on that order — they become literature, and very charming, arresting literature. The (London) *Lancet* of October 2, said of this address: " By his words and counsel and encouragement to the young practitioners, and of sympathy and understanding with the older, which have on many former occasions fallen from his lips, Professor Osler has well earned the title of the Nestor of British Medicine." He had unquestionably earned the analagous title in Canada and the States. He could never, as he grew older, have taken Emerson's advice to " leave the many and hold the few "; he kept his touch vitally with thousands until his death. In this supposed carefree holiday he is so concerned about the affairs of all his friends that whatever he feels or hears that could help them in any way, must be imparted to them post haste.

Innumerable people and libraries were made richer by the books he had collected during his holiday. And now on his return to Oxford the old routine was begun again, visitors flocking to the house, incessant calls on heart and mind and time. For the latter he observed a strict method; for the mind an intense concentration, and for the heart a limitless love. There is no doubt that he drove his machine too fast. It was probably the only way he could drive it, as he looked upon himself, in everything except his book collecting, as a sort of emergency ambulance. When you consider his life you get the impression of far too many functions, too much activity; in reading his essays you are in another realm, one of great peace and beauty and assurance — the assurance of the preacher with the tolerance of the scholar.

In his address, *The Nation and the Tropics,* after speaking of the responsibility of Empire and of its many sins against humanity he says: " But heap in one pan of the balance all the grievous tragedies of America and Australasia, the wholesale destruction of native races, all the bloodshed of India and the calamities of South Africa; and in the other pan put just one little word, ' order ' which has everywhere followed the flag and it alone makes the other kick the beam. . . . There may be a doubt as to the grafting of our manners, and still greater doubt as to the possibility of inculcating our morals, a doubt also as to the wisdom of trying everywhere to force upon them our religion; but you will, I think, agree that the second great function of the nation is to give the inhabitants of the dependencies, Europeans or native, good health — a freedom from plague, pestilence and famine. And this brings me to the main subject of my address, the Control of the Tropics by Sanitation." And then in glowing and feeling terms he told of the self-sacrifice of many investigators whose work resulted in the discovery of the transmission of malaria and yellow fever by mosquitoes, thus bringing these diseases under control. Without these discoveries the Panama Canal could not have been completed.

His interest as a bibliophile was steadily increasing, and no matter what other business was on hand, a book sale, if it seemed important, caught him; it was not only purchasing books; but everything connected with them was his concern. He was intensely interested in editions of Burton's works, and the books that Burton had owned; he gave much time assembling the copies scattered in the Christ Church Library, and had them arranged all together about a portrait of Burton himself. In an address before the Bibliographical Society on the " Library of Robert Burton," he said: " *The Anatomy of Melancholy* has not always been understood. It is much more than

> ' A mire, ankle-deep of deliberate confusion
> Made up of old jumbles of classic allusion.'

It is a great medical treatise (the greatest ever written by a layman), orderly in arrangement, intensely serious in purpose, and weighty beyond belief with authorities. The sources are to be found in sacred and profane literature, to the time of Burton. There is probably no English author who quotes from so many writers on so many subjects."

The years of Dr. Osler's life have been full so far of that rarest thing in the world, a happiness that steadily increases and becomes more and more beneficent. He was following the strong currents of events in the medical world. Not a creative genius in the science of medicine, he continued to be one in the art of medicine; and he was always strengthening its dignity and broadening its scope. The history of medicine was becoming his strongest oar now in his sixtieth year; though indeed his attitude of mind was always the historical one, unifying the past and the present. Anyone to-day can, looking through Dr. Osler's eyes, see the story of medicine in its wonderful advance through the ages, and its limitless possibilities.

He realized that important contributions to medicine had come from many sources, some apparently antagonistic; and he sought the good in them all. In dealing with modern factions he tried to bring them together by emphasizing their similarities instead of dwelling on their differences. Faith healing and Christian Science were having their day; and instead of decrying them he, after speaking with his usual felicity about their tenets, says: " My experience has been that of the unconscious rather than the deliberate faith healer. Phenomenal, even what could be called miraculous, cures are not very uncommon. Like others, I have had cases any one of which, under suitable conditions, could have been worthy of a shrine or made the germ of a pilgrimage. For more than ten years a girl lay paralyzed in a New Jersey town. A devoted mother and loving sisters had worn out their lives in her service. She had never been out of bed unless when lifted by one of her physicians, Dr. Longstreet and Dr. Shippen. The new surroundings of an hospital, the positive assurance that she could get well with a few simple measures, sufficed, and within a fortnight she walked round the hospital square. This is a type of modern miracle that makes one appreciate how readily well-meaning people may be deceived as to the true nature of the cure effected at the shrine of a saint. Who could deny the miracle? and miracle it was, but not brought about by any supernatural means."

In his most beautiful farewell address to the medical profession in the United States, *Unity, Peace and Concord,* after speaking of the ways of bringing these about, he held out his hand to the homeopath with these words: " Is it not too late in this day of scientific medicine to prattle of such antique nonsense as the ' pathics ' ? We have long got past the stage when any ' system ' can satisfy a rational practitioner, long past the time when a difference in the action of drugs — the most uncertain element in our art! — should be allowed to separate men with the same noble traditions, the same hopes, the same aims and ambitions. It is not as if our homeopathic brothers are asleep; far from it, they are awake — many of them at any rate — to the importance of the scientific study of disease, and all of them must realize the anomaly of their position. It is distressing to think that so many good men live isolated, in a measure, from the great body of the profession. The original grievous mistake was ours — to quarrel with our brothers over infinitesimals was a most unwise and stupid thing to do. That we quarrel with them now is solely on account of the old Shibboleth under which they practise. Homeopathy is as inconsistent with the new medicine as is the old-fashioned poly-pharmacy, to the destruction of which it contributed so much. The rent in the robe of Æsculapius, wider in this country than elsewhere, could be repaired by mutual concessions — on the one hand by the abandonment of special designations, and on the other by the intelligent toleration of therapeutical vagaries which in all ages have beset the profession, but which have been mere flies on the wheels of progress." At the beginning of the address he quoted from Emerson:

> " Life is too short to waste
> In critic peep or cynic bark,
> Quarrel or reprimand:
> 'Twill soon be dark;
> Up! Mind thine own aim,
> And God speed the mark! "

And feeling that with all his soul, he saw no reason why the Temple of Æsculapius should not hold under its vast canopy Christian Scientist, Faith Healer, Homeopathist, regular practitioner — provided (but this was a very definite proviso) they would all devote a few years to the study of pathology, and pass another goodly number in the hospitals. After that they might remain honest Christian Scientists but they would not be quacks.

But for the Spiritualist he had less sympathy — table rappings and such performances seemed to him irreligious.

Perhaps the most important event to Dr. Osler in 1910, far more so than the Lumleian Lectures, or even the fact that the last volume of the *System of Medicine* was being finished, was that Revere had gone to Winchester. He had entered the big impartial world of an English Public School, and he was no lover of books or of rough play — how would he fare? The majority of parents the world over feel exactly the same way when their children first leave the home; but he had consolations that few of them have. Instead of closing his heart around his own to the exclusion of other children, his love for his boy was additional fuel to warm his heart to every little child he met. The reactions of parents are not generally as noble as they are supposed to be. A good illustration is the story of a mother who said to her son, " Jack, are you not ashamed to let Billy J—— stand at the head of the class? You are making me wretched; I turn my head away whenever I see Mrs. J—— coming"; and the little wretch replied, " Wouldn't you rather have Billy's mother happy than be happy yourself? " That boy came to a bad end. The " Open Arms " was very wide open indeed to all children and youth; once within its shelter there was a riotous bliss for the babies and for others encouragement and inspiration. Though missing his boy, the day's work went on at full pace, halted hardly at all by a sharp attack of illness;

for the innumerable notes he wrote lying flat on his back are like a chronicle of medical events. In all Sir William's letters there is something said of Revere who is alternately called Tommy, or Ikey or Egerton Jr. In one: " Tommy writes in such good spirits from Winchester — no homesickness or worries. As a new boy he has to pay for his gallery (dormitory) and an early duty is to call boys at 6:30, go back to bed and call them at 6:35, 6:40 and 6:45. The boys have a special language of their own, nearly four hundred words, which a new boy, or rather man — as the boys are called men — has to learn within the first fortnight . . . he is assigned a senior boy as Pater or instructor and if at the end of a fortnight the words are not known, the Pater has the privilege of spanking the new boy." He motored to see Revere and was enchanted with the school; and then gave himself up to his work with mind and heart at ease — and evidently in the gayest of spirits. For he writes to a little girl, one of his playmates:

" My boy is so horrid — has turned into a Winchester man! he has just come home. I had to go on in ink as my fluffy-headed stenographer struck her fist on the table and said she did not come down here to take down nonsense — not she, not for any man! What do you think I said? Nothing — but I gave her a basilisk look, and she fainted dead away and is groaning with her fluffy head in the waste paper basket and there she can stay until I finish this. Mrs. Osler has gone to America, leaving me in charge of a black-eyed Canadian girl, my grand-daughter once removed, who is leading me a pretty dance.

Your affectionate friend
Wm. Osler

P.S. 1: My love and sympathy (to and with) your poor parents.

P.S. 2: The fluffy-headed vestal still groans. An envelope
and two sheets of paper protrude from her mouth
— the basket just fits her head.

P.S. 3: I have just had a photograph taken of her.

P.S. 4: She has recovered and I am leaving quick. Good
bye."

We are struck with what a sore trial he must have been
to Sargent; for ever after the painting of the Four Doctors,
he besieged him to make sketches of men he wished to
have honoured. A characteristic note like this would often
greet Sargent: " Could you arrange to do a black and white
of my friend Musser of the University of Pennsylvania?
he is at the Piccadilly Hotel for two days and could call
at any time? Send him a wire. . . . Do you think it would
be possible for you to give us a sketch for our tuberculosis
campaign that could be reproduced on a post card? Anything would do, from a caricature of J. William White to
the bacilli attacking a modern Mona Lisa. The general
verdict at the College is that you have hit off our good
friends to the life." It speaks volumes for his charm
that Sargent did not answer with a big Damn in red
— and it is rather nice to feel that Sargent did not
take himself seriously enough to resent the post card
suggestion.

In the spring of 1910 Theodore Roosevelt lectured at
the Sorbonne on the " Duties of the Citizen in a Republic "; and on May 5th gave his Nobel Lecture in which he
suggested a World Court, the checking of armaments and
a League of Peace; and a sinister fate laughed in its sleeve.
On May 6th, King Edward died and the Court went into
mourning, and all festivities and Congresses stopped for
a while. In the summer Roosevelt went up to Oxford for
the Romanes Lectures, where he was duly given his D.C.L.
Somewhere there was a caricature of Roosevelt on the

lecture stand, having twisted his doctor's robes about his neck and with clenched fists haranguing a startled crowd, while a great lion stood licking his lips with a wicked glint in his eyes and a bear was scratching his head ruminating and the dove of peace wept. There was an immense amount of fun and Oxford gave him a big day, the Oslers doing their part to make it a success.

Henry James was ill in London and Dr. Osler had written Dr. J. William White, who was in the Engadine to come to London and cheer James up. You cannot think of these men, Osler, James, White, Sargent and Roosevelt, without feeling the tremendous power of friendship they all had, and how most of them united in making a hero of Roosevelt. J. William White indeed exalted him into a god. Dr. Osler's hero worship was of a different order, the difference between reverence and adoration. He had a profound reverence for the qualities of his heroes and for what they had accomplished, but it was not an adoration of the man. With his old teachers in Canada, it was merely the exercise of a persistent gratitude with his eyes closed determinedly to any of their failings. We have only to read his biographical essays to see the order of his feeling for the medical heroes of the past. Of the living — his feeling for Dr. Edward Livingstone Trudeau illustrates the nature of his reverence. Dr. Trudeau, who was stricken with tuberculosis, checked the disease and gave his life to the care of tubercular patients in the Adirondacks. " Now and then," Dr. Osler writes, " men are fortunate enough to overcome the worst foes encountered in the battle of life — chronic ill health, and enforced residence in a paralyzing environment. The attitude of mind so splendidly expressed in Henley's verse: ' Out of the night that covers me,' scoffs at the menace of years, and unafraid, with unbowed head, the happy possessor of the unconquerable soul of this sort feels that

It matters not how strait the gate
How charged with punishment the scroll,
I am the master of my fate;
I am the Captain of my soul.

And this is the lesson of Edward Trudeau's life — the lesson of a long and successfully fought campaign. An impeccable foe, entrenched within his own citadel, has been brought to terms of truce, never wholly conquered.

" I like now to admit to the select company on my shelves only the literature that has a personal interest to me, or epoch-making works of the masters of medicine. When the 25th Annual Report of the Sanitarium appeared, I had it bound, and it reposes in my library between a work of Laennec, and the story of the early days of the Johns Hopkins Hospital. I wrote on the fly leaf: ' A triumph of optimism. This shows what a badly crippled man may do single-handed, once let him gain the confidence of his brethren, medical and lay.' Trudeau had the good fortune to be made of the stuff that attracts to himself only the best, as a magnet picks out iron. Of an unselfish, sympathetic disposition, he secured the devotion of his patients, to whom he was at once a tower of strength and a splendid example." To hearten on his suffering way so great a benefactor as Dr. Trudeau is perhaps like adding force to great causes, but along with that Dr. Osler took time just to cheer some fellow creatures whose lives did not extend beyond their own firesides. He once ran into the room of a woman who had become blind with, " How I wished for you in Italy! You have seen more with your eyes than anyone I know and you could have told me where to look." And when he left her she sat dreaming over her fireside with the inner light all aglow.

As far as his personal interest was concerned it was as if he had never left either Canada or the United States

and when trouble or good fortune came to either place
he was all sympathy, though medical questions were the
most important to him. At this time in the States they
were usurping the head lines. Abraham Flexner's report
on Medical Schools had made the low-grade schools exceedingly wroth; he held up the Johns Hopkins as a
model; and though much good was done, it was exceedingly trying, as superiority always is when self-conscious.
The main thing, however, that concerned Dr. Osler was
the question of full time positions for clinical teachers.
Upon this question he had very definite opinions. In a
letter to President Remsen, of the Johns Hopkins University, he wrote: " The subject of whole-time clinical
teachers, on which I send you the promised note, is one of
great importance, not only to universities, but to the profession and to the public at large. It is a big question with
two sides. I have tried to see both, as I have lived both,
and as much perhaps as any one can, appreciate both. Let
me thank you, first, for Mr. Flexner's report. As an angel of
Bethesda he has done much good in troubling our fish-
pond, as well as the general pool. The Report as a whole
shows the advantage of approaching a problem with an
unbiassed mind, but there are many mistakes from which
a man who knows the profession from the outside only
could not possibly escape." And after a heart-searching
review of what he thought a hospital clinician should be
and do, he ended with: " These are some of the reasons
why I am opposed to the plan as likely to spell ruin to the
type of school I have always felt the Hospital should be
and which we tried to make it — a place of refuge for the
sick poor of the city — a place where the best that is known
is taught to a group of the best students — a place where
new thought is materialized in research — a school where
men are encouraged to base the art upon the science of
medicine — a fountain to which teachers in every subject

could come for inspiration — a place with a hearty welcome to every practitioner who seeks help — a consulting centre for the whole country in cases of obscurity. And it may be said, all these are possible with whole-time clinical professors. I doubt it. The ideals would change and I fear lest the broad open spirit which has characterized the school should narrow, as teacher and student chased each other down the fascinating road of research, forgetful of those wider interests to which a great hospital must minister." Two years later the question came up in England and his opinion was still the same; but his confidence in Dr. W. H. Welch, who was in favour of full-time professors, made him a little distrustful of his own judgment. The years have straightened out the tangle, and apparently Dr. Osler came over to Dr. Welch's opinion, but it was a burning matter then.

> " Little of all we value here
> Wakes on the morn of its hundredth year
> Without both feeling and looking queer.
> In fact there is nothing that keeps its youth
> So far as I know but a tree and truth."

Unfortunately, they don't either. At the present rate of progress it takes only twenty years and not a hundred to make what seems an established point of view obsolete.

Upon the methods in medical schools Dr. Osler had very positive opinions. He was entirely out of sympathy with the prevailing system of examinations in England; his sympathy was with the student. " The student," he said, "needs more time for quiet study, fewer classes, fewer lectures, and above all, the incubus of examinations should be lifted from his soul. To replace the Chinese by the Greek spirit would enable him to seek knowledge for itself without a thought of the end, tested and taught day by day, the pupil and teacher working together on the same lines, only one a little ahead of the other. This is the ideal towards which we should move. The pity of it all is that we should have made an intolerable burden of the study of one of the most attractive of the professions, but the reform is in our own hands, and should not be put off. A paragraph in an address of the late Dr. Stokes contains the pith of my remarks: ' Let us emancipate the student, and give him time and opportunity for the cultivation of his mind, so that in his pupilage he shall not be a puppet in the hands of others, but rather a self-relying and reflecting being.' " His influence in all these matters was, if possible, greater in England than it had been in America. Mr. Fisher who was President of the Board of Education under the Coalition Cabinet of Lloyd George speaking of Sir William said: " His remarkable evidence given before the Royal Commission on London University was specially important as helping a professional opinion in favour of the clinical unit system of teaching which he had himself perfected at Johns Hopkins, and is sufficient to give him an enduring importance in the history of English Medical teaching. Until his death he was a distinguished member of the two committees which successfully advised the board of education and the Treasury in the distribution of State grants to the universities, and was thus brought into contact with all the medical work of an academic character which was proceeding in the country. In the end I doubt whether there were many men in Europe or America who had so good a synoptic view of the contemporary state of medical education in the world at large."

The Life of Pasteur, with his introduction, the edition financed by Mr. Henry Phipps, had proved a great success. The biography was distributed to all Anglo-American medical-school libraries and it is among the most service-worn on their shelves. Dr. Osler's *Aequanimitas with other*

Addresses, published in 1904, and his *Alabama Student and other Biographical Essays,* published in 1908, show from their thumb marks the favour they have found with medical students; and in many lay libraries, these books have their place side by side with Oliver Wendell Holmes's *Breakfast Table* Series, and Sir Thomas Browne's *Religio.* And his text-book! an honourable first in all the great and little medical-school libraries; and in many a private library in his old home in Maryland it will be found standing in the proximity of bound copies of the *Ladies Home Journal.*

In February 1911 he seems to have been especially low in pocket; and consequently aching for incunabula. Outside of that things were going fairly well in the world. Ireland, to be sure, was causing a stir, and the anti-vivisectionists were, as always, irritating; but the big lights in the land were being so reasonable that surely the little ones would become so too. The warlike Mr. Roosevelt was advocating peaceful means of settling disputes. Mr. Carnegie was building a Peace Palace; and it seemed the right moment for Dr. Osler's brother, Sir Edmund Osler, to induce him to join his party in a six-weeks holiday in Egypt. And from his landing in Cairo to his return his letters are full of enthusiasm. In Cairo, he, of course, went at once to the Khedival Library and to the hospitals. Then the party went up river. In this trip through Egypt, though the medical side and the books are never neglected, as appears from his later addresses, there are long days when just Egypt fills his imagination. And when, after seeing Denderah and the Temple of Hathor, he exclaims: "Heavens, what feeble pigmies we are! even with steam and electricity and the Panama Canal!!! " the exclamation comes with a very different note to the one heard in Rome. Now his very spirit is caught up in wonder; the realization of what men were six thousand years ago overwhelms him, and he wrote: " I am a bit bewildered." Of course, he pays reverence to *Imhotep* " the first physician with a distinct personality to stand out in the mists of antiquity." Every word he wrote makes you long for that strange land. It is perhaps the only time in his life that he finds himself drawn into a lazy mood.

While he was away Mrs. Osler " read letters," she said " from young doctors, old doctors, men of all ages, which made me feel how wonderful an influence Dr. Osler has been in the profession. How proud I am of him no one can believe (excuse this outburst but you both understand) ."

When he returned to England London was in a whirl of business getting ready for the coronation of George V. He showed Mrs. Osler a letter from 10 Downing Street, marked confidential. It notified him that his name was down on the list of coronation honours for a baronetcy; and her quick remark was: " What excuse are you going to give for declining it? You always have said you would." And he replied: " I think I'll have to accept — Canada will be so pleased. There is only one Canadian baronet." Mrs. Osler was indifferent to the honour. It may seem a very little thing to comment upon; but the majority of women will realize how fine it was and how amazingly unusual. They tried to keep the news secret but it got out, and the house was besieged by telegraph boys. There was an avalanche of cables, telegrams, letters. The impressions made upon him are shown in a letter to his sister:

" Dear Chattie:

You must have had a shock yesterday morning when you saw Bill's name in the coronation honour list. We had word about ten days ago from Mr. Asquith, but nothing could be said. I did not know when it was to come out. I thought not until after the coronation, but yesterday before I was out of bed the telegrams began to rain in and there has been a perfect stream — more than 100 from England and 49 cables, U. S. and Canada; 2 from India. Letters galore. . . . I have had rather more than my share but these court honours mean so much here. And when in the swim we must take what comes. These things have never bothered me, and we have had so much, and been so happy, that we really did not need it as much as some poor fellow who has done more but has not caught the public eye. I am glad for the family. I wish father and mother had been alive and poor B. B. and Nellie. It is wonderful how a bad boy (who could chop off his sister's fingers) may fool his fellows if he once gets to work. Ask Bill Lyon how he accounts for it. The girls are greatly excited. Nona looks so well. Her presentation picture is so good and as for Grace — it was her royal appearance that settled George R. Love to Charley and the girls.

Your affect. bro.
Sir Billy!!!!! "

Of more consequence to him really was that the Payne Collection of books was on sale which he wanted for the Johns Hopkins, and the baronetcy held one grievance. " I shall be heartbroken if we do not get it " (the Payne Collection) he wrote a friend, " purse-broken, too, as there are three or four items I must bid for — though I believe these baronetcy fees are ruinous and may take all my spare cash."

The far-reaching activities of his life could only have been accomplished, even given the will and the wisdom and the vitality, by a man who had few personal worries and who had means. Had he come home to a wife worn out with home duties, and to children who were wringing his heart, with no money to lighten the burden, he could not possibly have done what he did. He realized his good fortune to the full. But neither good fortune nor ill would have influenced by a hair's breadth his human and spiritual side; and so when reading his essays, hearing his addresses and, above all, when coming in contact with him, the man under the wheel of dire circumstances was not envious, but comforted. He knew to a certainty that here was one who having great possessions gave all that he had. And to repeat what has already been said, it was the unfortunate who were his chief concern. He had something in him like Robert E. Lee, who in the midst of a battle, seeing a little bird had fallen in the line of fire, stepped out without thinking, exposing himself, to pick it up. No one could have condemned such an act more than Lee, but it was instinctive. And with Dr. Osler the little insignificant person obstructing his pathway would have been very gently put on a safe path of his own, just as he took off his overcoat to give it to the old beggar when he was a young man in Montreal, with no other coat for himself to replace it; and just as he stopped on the way to a dinner in all his gay rags to pick up a dirty little boy who had been hurt, and let him dry his eyes on his breast, comforted; that was William Osler's way.

It might seem at first glance staggeringly absurd to say that Robert E. Lee and William Osler were made in the same crucible. Their tastes, except in their love for children, unlike; their vocations at the opposite poles. From their manner and appearance they might have come from a different race. But cut through the rind of all this and you will find the idol of the South and the idol of the physicians amazingly alike. Each in a crisis would have acted in the same way. The adoration Lee received and the adoration Osler received had nothing to do with the reserve and seriousness of the one, or with the gaiety and easy approach of the other, but with what was below the surface in both. Their characters were as clear as squares of crystals. With integrity and magnanimity, a stern sense of duty and truth, a brilliant intellectual grasp of their professions and unfailing good judgment, they were human and compassionate, with simple, sweet and gentle natures, and entirely unselfish. Their religion without fanaticism, was the most vital influence in their lives. Both men served only one Master; His message to them was the same — Charity — and when a man serves only one master he is never taken by surprise. These two were great enough for their fellow-men to trust them absolutely with their lives. Both had caught a glimpse of the divine love, and it radiated from their presence. The long bitter road and defeat of the one, the sunlit path of the other, only served to bring out in each his innate nobility.

Dr. Osler was very happy over the fact that a fund of £200,000 had been collected by the Executive Committee of the Welsh Memorial to King Edward to be devoted to a campaign against consumption. The fight against tuberculosis that he had so persistently carried on was, at last, firing the imagination of the public. It would seem that one might reasonably be optimistic about the world, for the important men were continuing to propose most pacific measures. Mr. Taft witnessed the signing of the arbitration treaty with England and the United States. Lord Haldane was delivering an address in Oxford, " Great Britain and Germany: A Study in Ethnology." He tried to explain the misunderstandings and show how they could be cleared and lightened; Mr. Carnegie was making a peace speech at Liverpool. To be sure Lloyd George's insurance bill was before parliament and the dock labourers were on a strike. And thunder was in the air! But men who were steadily reducing pain and overcoming disease had neither ears nor time to hear the slow approach of war.

Lister's death must have brought to the medical world a fascinating retrospect. " I have just come from the Abbey service," Sir William writes, "the most splendid tribute ever paid to our profession, and so richly deserved in the person of Joseph Lister, one of our greatest benefactors of humanity. Voltaire saw Newton buried like a king in the same Abbey and ever after esteemed it one of the glories of England that she was able to recognize a king among men. . . . Only those who lived in pre-Listerian days can appreciate the revolution which has taken place in surgery. . . . As with everything else that is worth preserving in this life there has been evolution; but from the great underlying principle on which Lister acted there has been no departure." And perhaps as he walked away from the Abbey these words, that he used later in one of his addresses, may have taken birth in his mind: " What has been accomplished is only an earnest of what shall be done in the future. Upon our heels a fresh perfection must tread, born of us, fated to excel us. We have but served and have but seen a beginning."

He was interested in Woodrow Wilson's campaign for the presidency in 1912, and wrote to a friend: " We are all very excited about Woodrow Wilson of whom I am very fond. He is sure to catch many mugwumps. I am sorry for Taft and still more sorry that Roosevelt should have treated him so badly." The peace dove must have felt hysterical over that.

The Phipps Psychiatric building at the Johns Hopkins was completed. There the mentally sick were to be given quarters equal to any that were provided for other diseases, and this was the first time such a thing had been done. It was Sir William Osler who had interested Mr. Phipps in this matter; and with Dr. Adolf Meyer, these three brought about the change in attitude toward, and treatment of, the insane. To give the opening address at the clinic, and to give the Silliman lectures at Yale, his last trip to America was taken in the spring of 1913. His visit to America became almost a lecture tour. His address at the opening of the Phipps Clinic, *Specialism in the General Hospital,* told of a desire accomplished. We know now what was undertaken and what has been accomplished; but on that spring day, lovely with flowers and hope, only the fine start had been made. In his address Sir William brought before those present the ideals for which they must strive. His address caused a good deal of emotion, he was so greatly loved in Baltimore. One of the newspapers expressed in an editorial what many felt: " One sees now, if he never realized it before that Dr. Osler would have been great in any field — in the pulpit, in politics, in literature, in journalism — because God gave him a great and exceptional mind, and a spirit which such minds often lack — the inspiration, the courage, and the honesty of the prophet who has walked on the mountain top and swept the whole world with his eyes, and who can deliver a message that is as unbounded as his vision." He would unquestionably have smiled a little whimsically at all this. God gave him a mind that knew what he could do and what he could not, and no enthusiasm of his friends would have made him undertake another man's mission. And that alone is enough to make him stand out from the majority. It is a common everyday story that a man who can do one thing supremely well believes, and his friends believe, that he is fit for anything; and so we have the most inartistic of plain business men selecting our monuments.

Sir William was in Baltimore only a few days. Fortunately for their peace of mind his friends had no conception that this was to be his last visit to America.

From Baltimore he went to Yale to deliver the Silliman lectures on *The Evolution of Modern Medicine.* His conquest of the undergraduates was instant; they at once fell under the spell of his fascination. A faculty reception had been arranged for the evening of his arrival but he suggested: " If you don't mind I would prefer meeting the undergraduates. I see Dons every day at Oxford but not enough undergraduates from America." So the reception was changed to an undergraduate tea.

It was a gay preliminary to the following evening when he addressed the undergraduates on *A Way of Life*. The tenor of that address may be found near its end. " The day of a man's salvation is now — the life of the present, of to-day, lived earnestly, intently, without a forward-looking thought, is the only insurance for the future. . . . Begin the day with Christ, and His prayer. . . . You need no other. Creedless, with it, you have religion; creed-stuffed, it will leaven any theological dough in which you stick. The quiet life in daytight compartments will help you to bear your own and other's burdens with a light heart. Pay no heed to the Batrachians who sit croaking idly by the stream. Life is a straight plain business, but the way is clear, blazed for you by generations of strong men, into whose labours you enter and whose ideals must be your inspiration." Their buoyant acquaintance of the day before had become a prophet but it did not seem incongruous to these lads, for there was no pose in either mood, and both the light mood and the grave completely harmonized in his personality. The lectures on the Silliman foundation followed. Unfortunately he delayed getting them into shape for publication; the war came and his mind was absorbed by other things. Many years later in 1921 his notes were recovered in somewhat imperfect form and the reconstructed lectures were published by the Yale Press. In the preface the editor, Col. Fielding H. Garrison writes, " Osler describes these lectures as ' an aeroplane flight over the progress of medicine through the ages.' They are in effect a sweeping panoramic survey of the whole vast field, covering wide areas at a rapid pace with an extraordinary variety of detail. The slow painful character of the evolution of medicine from the fearsome, superstitious mental complex of primitive man, with his amulets, healing gods and disease demons, to the ideal of a clear-eyed rationalism, is traced with faith and a serene sense of continuity." And Col. Garrison ends his preface with, " The editors have no hesitation in presenting these lectures to the profession and to the reading public as one of the most characteristic productions of the best-balanced, best-equipped, most sagacious and most lovable of all modern physicians."

On his return to England shortly after, he found preparations under way for the great International Medical Congress which was to be held in London in August of that year, and he was made chairman of the medical section. It was to be a tremendous affair not unlike in bulk and ambition the one he had attended thirty-two years before, when Sir James Paget was president. The royalty at that famous Congress had been the Prince of Wales and the Crown Prince of Prussia. The immortals were Pasteur, Bastian, Huxley, Lister, Virchow, Koch — though dead, yet they live. The later Congress produced as brilliant a scenic effect as its predecessor; the Albert Hall was packed to its utmost limit. Prince Arthur of Connaught, speaking for the King, opened the Congress, and Sir Edward Grey spoke for the Government. But who were there to equal those creative geniuses of 1881? " Comparable to these," Dr. Cushing writes, " there were no outstanding figures at the second London Congress, whose transactions comprising a staggering list of subjects, may be said to have been based almost entirely upon the further development of the researches of these giants. There was one exception, perhaps: the most picturesque figure of the Congress, a German, Paul Ehrlich, the discoverer of salvarsan, whose brilliant career was to end two years later." Nevertheless the whole level of the medical world had risen to a height which these great men, who fought for their ideas, could hardly have foreseen. Indeed, the thirty odd years between these two great assemblies was a most momentous period; there had been almost a revolution in all Science. Sir William, in his address at the opening of the Phipps Clinic, described the impression made on him by these changes: " I am sorry for you, young men of this generation. You will do great things. You will have great victories, and standing on our shoulders, you will see far, but you can never have our sensations. To have lived through a revolution, to have seen a new birth of science, a new dispensation of health, reorganized medical schools, remodeled hospitals, a new outlook for humanity, is not given to every generation." But if no new revolutionary discoveries were reported at the Congress, still its members had builded marvelously on the old.

After a round of festivities and work he and Lady Osler ran off to recuperate in Scotland, and he wrote from Lochinvar: " We have had a deuce of a business with this Congress and only just escaped with our lives." But no one knowing his predilection can fail to realize that he had a passion for medical congresses and functions. A friend who knew him well, says: " He often looks as though he would just adore to fool away his time but it's a sort of mirage he deceives you with. He simply adores work."

Christmas was a very happy one; and to his great store of good fortune one final joy was to be added. Revere was beginning to show a love for literature and had sent in his first bid to Sotheby's, £1, for Landor's *Pericles and Aspasia,* " and got it," his father triumphantly exclaimed. His boy was to be not in the least a duffer with his books. There was something in the sensitive high-bred boy that was like his father, but it was the part of him you only met at moments of quiet. He would never have taken to the profession of medicine; he would have devoted friends;

but they would be of the few, not of the many; even as a child he had his father's invincible integrity, tenderness of heart and lack of egotism. There had been nothing about him from his great good looks to his sweet nature that any parent would not rejoice over, except that fishing and sketching, not books, had held his interest; and now, it was to be books as well! All through the boy's life until now his father spoke of this lack of scholarly appreciation with a little sigh of regret; now in every letter there is a note of joy. " He is taking such an interest in good literature." Between the father and the son there had always been perfect love; and now there was to be congeniality of taste — not a matter of supreme importance, one might think, but it filled his father's cup of joy to overflowing.

The War

" *God, whose law is that he who learns must suffer. And even in our sleep pain, that cannot forget, falls drop by drop upon the heart and in our own despites, against our will, comes wisdom to us by the awful grace of God.*"

Æschylus.

CHAPTER XI

THE WAR

FEW saw the tragic mask the New Year held under his cowl, even though in this year, 1914, the militant suffragettes were on the rampage causing a tremendous ado. A bomb was let off in the Abbey; railway stations were burned; valuable pictures destroyed; they slashed up Sargent's great portrait of Henry James, and heaven only knows why they did that; fortunately, Sargent was able to repair it. And James, who was ill, and whom none but an insane mob would want to hurt either in person or in effigy, had the comfort of knowing that it was not ruined. He had an almost naïve pleasure in this portrait of himself done by the friend he loved. But far more serious than anything else, the Ulster crisis was at hand and it seemed that Home Rule would be enforced by arms and then Civil War would follow. All this did not seem greatly to concern Sir William Osler. His reaction to the suffragettes was shown in his answer to a request by a colleague to bring reason or medicine to bear upon an American woman who was running wild in London. He wrote: " W—— says she is not certifiable, so what are we to do? I have written to her brother urging him to come over and take her out of the country. These ancient cynophilic vestals should be segregated by an act of Parliament. The government should buy Iceland from Denmark and deport them there automatically at the menopause." Though they might irritate him he did not take them seriously; nor would it seem that he thought the situation in Ireland alarming.

During the summer the death of Lord Strathcona, whom he had known since his early youth, must have brought vividly before the world a remarkable career. Lord Strathcona was born in Scotland in 1820. At first known in Canada as plain Donald Smith, counting muskrats' skins as a vocation, he later became factor of the Hudson Bay Company and now at the end of a long life, his obsequies attended by the great of the nation, he had become Lord Strathcona Mount Royal Chancellor of the Universities of Montreal and Aberdeen, High Commissioner of Canada, and one of the bulwarks of the British Empire. All this may not have mattered so much to Sir William's colleagues as the fact that when, in need of a valuable book for the Bodleian or help to replace a burned building, they would never again hear from Sir William " have you asked Strathcona? " or " I'll ask Strathcona," and " Wasn't it splendid of Strathcona? " You get the impression of a man of great generosity and are terribly sorry that you are never again to hear " Ask Strathcona."

It would be illuminating to Communists to read the lives of men like Lord Strathcona, Andrew Carnegie, John D. Rockefeller, Henry Phipps and many others. Quite a big library could be made of biographies of rich men whose lives unquestionably will pass through the eye of the needle.

Another death nearer to his heart was that of Weir Mitchell of whom he said: " Had I been a son he could not have been kinder to me during the five years of my life in Philadelphia." The great American neurologist and Sir William had this in common — neither ever lost a friendship once begun.

In July Sir William went to Cambridge to preside over a meeting of the Bibliographical Society of which he was president. While there he spent much time working over the Pepys library. It was then that the idea of the *Bibliotheca Osleriana* was elaborated. From this time on the cataloguing of his library became his chief interest. The Catalogue was to be much more than an impersonal list of books; it was to follow somewhat the features that Conrad Gesner, the father of bibliography, had put into his *Bibliotheca Universalis* and Sir William was greatly influenced by the *Bibliotheca Chemica* of John Ferguson, Professor of Chemistry at Glasgow.

He wrote to Professor Birkett at McGill: " As I daresay you know my collection of books will go to the College. It will be particularly rich in historical works and original editions of the old Masters of the first rank. Of course, many of these rarer things I could not myself have afforded to buy but my brother E. B. has given me in the past two years about £1000 for the purpose of purchasing incunabula and the more expensive editions."

While his mind was full of the most peaceful projects no note was taken of the strained relations between Austria and Serbia. And on the day that Winston Churchill was having a test mobilization of the British fleet at Spithead, Sir William and Professor Margoliouth were attending a meeting of the Persian Society in London and discussing a plan to repair Avicenna's tomb. He wrote: " I cannot get away on account of some local meetings." And again: " I wish you could see our roses which Grace gathers by the bushel." It seems incredible — roses — local meetings — the tomb of Avicenna; and in a short time the youth of the land were to find their graves in any available mudhole in the fields of France. But only a very few saw the stealthy, sinister approach of war, and they simply could not impress upon the world what they saw.

Absorbed in their own profession a crowd of physicians and surgeons held a meeting in London late in July and, at the same time, the British Association met at Aberdeen. A number of American surgeons and other foreigners attended the latter meeting, among them some notable Austrians. At the annual dinner given to the Congress no one seemed to notice that the Austrians had been recalled. Sir William was there, very gay. Lady Osler and Revere had gone ahead of him to America and he was to join them in a week or so. After the dinner he went off without a glance at the newspapers, to the island of Colonsay for a few days' rest and amusement. It is only fair to say that neither the ministers nor ambassadors were over-alarmed. It was not that they would not believe — they did not believe that such an evil could not be averted. It is ironic — everywhere American tourists, enjoying their sightseeing, rushed to the Continent; and England, content, carefree and prosperous, in what was considered a time of ultra-civilization. On the 29th Austria declared war against Serbia; on the 31st came the Russian mobilization; on August 1st, Germany's declaration of war; on August 3rd, her troops entered Belgium. On August 4th came England's declaration of war. Fast and furious came the storm, so much so that its very violence made many feel it would soon pass over.

Sir William and his friends, caught napping on the island of Colonsay, had some difficulty in getting off. They found Oxford a changed world. It must have seemed to them like the change of scene on a modern stage. The dance is on; then a moment of darkness, which lifts to show the world turned into a great plan for emergency work. The insignia on Devonshire House, the Red Cross; and the Red Cross workers moving quietly about; everyone grave but no excitement, no disorder; even the swarms of American tourists were considered and what help they needed was systematically given; their hysterical rush for safety — and their baggage — was not scoffed at, merely quietly attended to, and order established. The militant suffragette had thrown aside her personal cause and was working heart and soul for her country. It was a wonderful sight, seen as a whole, but a heart-breaking sight, when you saw into the hearts of the individuals. The profession of medicine at once entered the field; and none other gave so brilliant an account of itself as the great army of physicians. A War Emergency Committee was formed to organize the profession in England, Wales and Ireland so that the government could use every practitioner to serve the country in such a manner as to turn his qualification to the best possible use. Osler's name headed the list of those appointed by the War Emergency Committee of the British Medical Association. He was made Honorary Colonel of the Oxfordshire Regiment; consulting physician to a hospital in Devon, which was supported by Lady Randolph Churchill and other Americans; also to a Canadian hospital supported by Canadians near Netley. He sent his American friends his regrets that he must miss his visit to them, " a small matter compared to the tragedies that were inevitable in the families of friends. I have to help organize the medical department of the Territorial force. Grace and Revere sailed on the 31st (July). She will be furious to have the ocean between us and she has been on the committee of the Nursing department. . . . It all seems so unnecessary, but the nations are still in the nursery stage squabbling and fighting like children." It seemed to him hideously stupid, but he did (what every man and woman in England did) his best. " An order was given and they obeyed." As always, his work was within the scope of his profession; the wards were his campaign ground; and he only wore his Colonel's uniform, as required by regulations, when he visited them; deadlier than bullets, he believed, were the diseases that might attack the troops.

Lady Osler returned immediately, and wasted not a moment but rushed into work. " The examination rooms," she wrote, " have been turned into a thoroughly equipped hospital — operating room, post mortem room, chapel and every detail complete. . . . Everyone has come home; all heads of Colleges but Brasenose, who is lost in Germany. All helping, all working like slaves. These military hospitals have been established all over the country — 3000 beds in Cambridge, *etc.* Willie says that the quiet, calm way in which it has been done could never be believed without seeing it." Fortunately a great number of Americans did see it, and when safe at home, remembered their experiences and sent checks, boxes of clothing, *etc.* What neither government neutrality nor pro-German propaganda could obliterate, was the indignant fury of the small souls who had been hustled out of Germany. They however only caused a flutter in the air; those who had actually lived in the atmosphere of Viscount Grey's defeated peace proposals, his desperate efforts for a peace conference, were greatly impressed. Sir William either smiled or sighed and turned quickly away. When the government did not touch his vocation it was not his affair but when the government either failed to extend help or retard it in the medical world then indeed it was his business; and he was instant in writing to *The Times:* " In the war the microbe kills more than the bullet. Malaria, cholera, typhus, typhoid and dysentery have been the scourges of armies. From the first three our soldiers are not likely to suffer; but it will be difficult to prevent outbreaks of dysentery or of typhoid fever, of which, in the South African war, more men died than were killed in action. Against this we must possess an effective vaccine; and I write to urge that the anti-typhoid vaccination should be made compulsory in the army. Pending the issue of a compulsory order, it is the duty of the medical officers of the Territorials to urge as many men as possible to be vaccinated." The anti-vaccinationists and the anti-vivisectionists were violently opposed to any compulsory legislation of this kind. So Osler went from camp to camp urging the men to take the precaution. He brought before them the South African War with its 57,000 cases of typhoid fever and he told them of the Spanish-American War and of what vaccination had meant, and how Almroth Wright's discovery of the advantages of inoculation had been used in all countries but their own. In many instances it was like St. Anthony's address to the fishes — "Much delighted were they, but preferred their own way."

In these early days of the war, forgetting their national quarrel, Sir William wrote without a thought of bitterness to his friend Paul Ehrlich: "Do you think it would be possible to arrange for the manufacture of salvarsan in the United States under your direction? I have had letters and have been asked to communicate with you through the American Ambassador in Berlin. Perhaps Flexner has already communicated with you. No doubt the Rockefeller Institute would undertake the control, and arrange that your financial interests were protected." He enclosed this letter to Mr. Page asking him to forward it to Professor Ehrlich — that it was a matter of national importance; and a year later when Ehrlich died, he wrote: "With death war dies." And of another young German, "It was a noble motive that prompted the Warden and Fellows of New College to put upon the roll of honour in their hall the name of a German Rhodes scholar, one of her sons, though an enemy, who had fallen in battle for his country, an action resented by certain narrow-minded Philistines in the Press. I should like to pay a last tribute of words to Paul Ehrlich, one of the Masters of Science, who has recently passed away. . . . The brilliant labours

of such a man transcend national limitations and his name
will go down to posterity with those of his countrymen
Virchow and Koch, as one of the creators of modern
pathology."

In a London address he spoke feelingly of " the brave
young fellows, allies and foes alike "; and when the in-
flux of Belgians was upon them in their destitute condition he even then tried to look at all things dispassion-
ately. The situation was bad enough, but he would not
have it distorted, nor would he permit anyone the dissipation of talking of horrors in his presence. He longed to
find his foes misjudged. " I have been looking over photographs of atrocities," he wrote, " and of mutilations, and
have asked in the various hospitals, and one can never
get anything closer than the damned third person, whom
I should like to mutilate personally. I suppose there have
been atrocities, particularly in the sack of Louvain; but
in other parts they have been grossly exaggerated. . . .
There have been all sorts of rumours and statements but
I do not believe there has been a single case of mutilation
brought to this country. I am sick to death of newspapers.
I wish the government would suppress them during the
war and issue a weekly bulletin." As Colonel Garrison
writes: " During the war, Osler's attitude was that of a
first-class military man — the impersonal ' hostile view '
rather than the hysterical ' hostile feeling ' of the hymns
of hate." But with much indignation Dr. Osler exclaimed:
" What a cursed act of vandalism to destroy Louvain! "
And immediately we see him trying to help. " Do you
think that we (the Bibliographical Society) should do
something about the Louvain outrage in the way of sending an official letter of sympathy; and when matters quiet
down I am going to suggest that we help them in a small
way in the restoration of the library. I would like to undertake with some friends to replace the books of Vesalius

who, perhaps after Erasmus, is the greatest name on their lists." An army never followed up the retreating enemy more assiduously than he followed up a humanitarian impulse towards friend or foe. Though his official area was in Oxfordshire his services were called for in every part of the country. The Canadian hospital was started in London by Canadians and Anglo-Canadians; and he was needed there. The Queen's Canadian Military Hospital was established at Beachborough Park, Shorncliffe near Folkestone; and he was physician-in-chief there until the end. The American Woman's War Relief Fund was organized, and maintained as an auxiliary hospital of 250 beds at Paignton, and later opened up an Officers' Hospital at Lancaster Gate; he was consultant at both these places. One who came in contact with him there wrote: " To everyone in medical offices, matron, nursing staff and patients, his visits were like a ray of sunshine. His oversight was what made us efficient; his sympathy and enthusiasm smoothed our path."

The scope of his activities is so wide that we can only mention a few of the hospitals he habitually attended. In addition to those already mentioned he visited regularly each week throughout the war the Daughters of the Empire Hospital for Canadian officers, and the Duchess of Connaught's Canadian Red Cross Hospital at Taplow. All the men and women in England throughout the war worked hard and did their best to encourage those about them; but he had preëminently the power of inspiration. Indeed the atmosphere he brought was so radiant that few realized the fear that was eating his own heart — his boy was approaching the horrors of war and he could not save him at the expense of his conscience. Very often he quoted these verses of Clough's poem, *Say not the struggle naught availeth:*

" For while the tired waves vainly breaking
Seem here no painful inch to gain
Far back through creeks and inlets making
Comes silent flooding in, the main.

And not by eastern windows only
When daylight comes, comes in the light,
In front the sun climbs slow, how slowly —
But westward look, the land is bright! "

But what he refrained from saying was that he knew that when the day did break it would not be for his generation or his boy.

With a certain amazed scorn he heard women say they were glad to send their sons. No, he was not glad to send his son, nor to see other men's sons go — they must because it was right that they should. For the peace of his soul he felt their cause a righteous one, but " glad " ! they who said that had only goaded themselves up with vengeance and the lust of hate. Many of the women would truly have preferred to go to the front, or thought they would, instead of making mufflers and bandages at home, but as long as they did stay at home it was rather fearful, their willingness to see their boys go. Poor things! they suffered enough; only many were intoxicated with the excitement. Sir William had no such relief; he would not follow the war news; he would not permit the talk of horrors in his house. What this house was is hard to describe. It was to many, oh, so very many, the shadow of a great rock in a desert land. No one entered its doors either in body or spirit, and left it unaided. Nor ever after could they feel themselves homeless. Lady Osler's working hours, almost the whole day, were inspiring. The Belgians' peaceful invasion of Oxford found in her a general of the first order. She collected funds, and she found homes and food

and occupation for them. She was then — and throughout the entire war — a bracing tonic to whoever came near
her; though she, too, was keeping a dreadful fear in her
heart. In a note to an American friend she gave a glimpse
into that strong heart where fear had rarely entered: " It
was very nice hearing from you and I am sure that you are
all so English your sympathy goes out most sincerely to us
in the midst of this awful war. Every morning we read
of friends being mown down, all the youth and glory of
the country, the young men we have known up here; and
our only boy training in the park under our eyes — except
that I can't look. Work is the only salvation and I keep at
it from 9 A.M. to 11 P.M. W. O. is busy and trying to be
cheerful; hard work sometimes." And at another time
she wrote: " The Regius is keeping up; he inspects, and
writes and preaches — and hopes."

In the early days of the war twelve Belgian professors
with their families, refugees, were supported at Oxford;
they were sixty-one persons in all, many of them destitute.
" This Belgian business," he wrote, " is an awful tragedy.
I was at Folkestone yesterday and saw the horror of it on
the station platform — old men, women, children, all
with their little possessions tied up in bundles, the whole
town full. Fortunately they are being well cared for." It is
comforting to many Americans, looking back, to realize
how very much they did to help at that wretched time.
Rockefeller came to the rescue and Dr. J. William White
almost killed himself with his ardour. Individual Americans gave their money freely with no thought of return —
to whichever side held their sympathies. The map of the
world could not have been drawn in clear constructive
lines, but in colours of emotion. America was not in the
least neutral. She was violently pro-Ally or pro-German,
except in the Middle West, where many felt indifferent
rather than neutral; but in the White House the President

put his feet firmly on the rock of neutrality, to the fury of some and the complaisance of others. He was a little like a man who locks and bars the front of his house against burglars and forgets to close the back door. The pro-Germans and the pro-English kept creeping through the back door, disturbing the neutral atmosphere. England was uneasy over the American notes — an uneasiness Mr. Page tried to dispel; and Sir William, believing in America even more than its ambassador did, never failed to say some word that he thought would bring about understanding between the countries he loved.

The President of the United States desperately wanted peace, and so did Sir William; but the former's idea of peace was something quite different from the latter's. The affairs of other nations were his affairs. To " Am I my brother's keeper? " his answer would have been, " Most certainly you are! " The cause of the Allies was, in his opinion, a righteous cause and for them to gain would mean benefit to all humanity; to his friends, the Germans, equally with the rest. " Good will come out of all this horror," he wrote, " if it wrecks forever the cursed militarism of Germany." That was where he placed the blame, on the German militarists.

To some peace resolutions, however, passed by the Federation of American Biologists, in which is expressed the hope for an early and enduring peace, without permanent cause of rancour, ensuring to each nation the glories of scientific and humanitarian achievement, he replied: " It is a pious wish, but there is an intellectual gulf wider and deeper than the Atlantic being built between Germany and this country. It is very sad and it is hard to know just what to do about old friends. I never saw that copy of Müller's letter; I should like very much to read what he said. I suppose in a way it is most fortunate that they can get into such a mental attitude. After all it would be a terrible tragedy if they did not believe their own country was right. It is a job — to try to get any truth between the two sides." And, " I wish they could hang a few of the newspaper editors," was often his pious exclamation even though he rarely read the papers. " We can't help feeling very sad about our old German friends. . . . Of course the atrocities have been grossly exaggerated. Klebs tells me just the same stories about English troops. Unfortunately, there seems to be no question about the Belgian horrors. And one of the tragedies is really the mental attitude of our German friends. Still I suppose one has to stand by one's country, right or wrong; but there is the plain fact, Germany has been progressively preparing for this conflict for twenty years." But he did not want to hear about it and Lady Osler wrote: " All the horrors and war talks nearly kill him and he looks ill and worn."

Revere's entrance into College brings from Lady Osler this sad little note: " My heart is aching for him, he is not doing what he thought would be better — but he has not complained once, only said, ' I will do what Dad thinks best and train here this term.' Willie runs if I speak of it." Revere would soon be nineteen and then what would he do? You cannot help feeling that in Sir William's play for time, he never really deceived himself; he knew with certainty that there would be only one thing that he and his boy could do, being what they were. And Lady Osler was terribly afraid either way. Every household in England that had a son felt much the same way, only Sir William's gaiety of manner and Lady Osler's dominant bearing, made everyone go to them for courage, failing to realize that these two could also be afraid. The midnight ride of Paul Revere seems a small episode beside the steady drive of his great granddaughter during these black years that were upon the world. She as well as he had a way of whistling along the road. " Of course we feel terribly about

Antwerp," she writes, " and Winston Churchill has been blamed for sending our marines — however, one can't tell. We have got ourselves schooled now and don't listen when people tell tales — or try to — and believe nothing but official statements. We expect the worst and try not to think about it. I allow no one to abuse Kitchener or the Admiralty to me and find these rules make life much less fatiguing; I no longer mind when women put on shirt sleeves hind side before."

The number of night shirts that had to be made was immense — and certainly it was enough to make a sewing woman wonder why humanity was made so inadequately protected against atmospheric conditions. But Lady Osler was not of a speculative turn of mind, fortunately for all concerned; and her house was converted into a Mothers' Meeting Sewing Rooms for the Belgian women, where they made mostly baby clothes; the refugees were a prolific race.

Sir William in a letter to a friend, wrote: " We see too much of the tragedies of life to be very happy. I wish you could look in our drawing room turned into a Galleries Lafayette for the wives of the Belgian professors, who work at their clothing every morning from nine to one. Grace has a dressmaker for them and a half-dozen machines. We have nearly one hundred in sixteen families. Poor things! it is an appalling tragedy for them and there are such nice women among them. Then G. bosses one of the big laboratories with fifty University women working for the soldiers. These (New) England women are full of vitality. . . . I am very sad about all my good German friends. I wonder where truth is? at bottom of an artesian well these times! " But even with their drawing room turned over to the Belgian women the house was a home of peace and beauty and order for the recuperating soldiers, or the tired nurses, or for the unofficial venturers from over the seas. Sir William would have no heroics, no feeling of wounds; he would not read the papers or follow the armies on the map. His whole mind was put on what good he could bring out of all this evil; how he could, being a physician and lover of men, relieve wounds of body and soul. So his regular work went on at the Radcliffe; his Sunday and Tuesday clinics were held — and he was full of the idea of making a collection of army medical statistics; making more complete records of the sick and wounded than the staff could do while prosecuting war; to accomplish that would be permanent good work. His health campaigns were spirited, warring against " These sons of Belial, the Anti's." The Anti's had put up recruiting posters: " Men of the Empire enlist, but refuse to be inoculated." That was wholesome food for his rages — far more to his taste than abusing the Germans.

Revere's heart was not in the drill and yet when failing to get his commission — " Too immature " the O.T.C. reported — he felt that the only right thing for him to do was to enlist in the ranks. It was a sad business for his mother who wrote to her sister: " Revere has had his nineteenth birthday and has made up his mind about the first step to take. He simply can't talk with his father but talked wisely — oh, so wisely, with me. To-day he brought home his books from Christ Church and his lovely room must be dismantled. What a strange fate after our fear that he might never get in! So that is done for and the only hope is that the war may some day be over and he can return. Of course, dear sister, it is useless to say ' Don't worry for us ' because I know you will feel it terribly, but with you to look up to and the women I was brought up among, I shall do my utmost to hold out and have a cheerful face for the poor dear unselfish angel who is breaking his heart over giving up his boy to this awful risk — that's all."

And at the same time Sir William wrote to a friend: " I wish you could see the wonderful activity in this old land — everyone working and so hopeful. Revere is leaving College and going into the Universities Public School Regiment at first as a private so as to know the drill and then he will apply for a commission. I hate to have him go and it's a shame to have his training here interrupted just as he was developing so splendidly."

Lady Osler's letter gives a true perspective, and his is only the defense he puts up to " keep the light from his eyes." For a little while destiny held her hand; Colonel Birkett of the McGill unit cabled from Montreal asking that Revere act as his orderly; the offer was at once accepted and for a time Revere's conscience was satisfied and his father could draw an easy breath; and he wrote: " Very busy and very hopeful. Ike in the training Corps. Grace working like a galley slave and I knocking about and seeing much of interest." Lady Osler's next letter to her sister has a brighter ring: " His interest even in wounds and the results of wounds is intense and I think the new edition of the *Practice of Medicine* will be a war book. He is all the time urging men on about the case histories and is conducting a campaign on typhoid inoculation." Everything that affected the medical side of the army was of absorbing interest; there he could give expert help. He was happier far than some of the Americans who were miserable because they could not help.

For some time there had been a desire by a number of people to have representatives from the U. S. Army and Navy Medical Services come over and study the problems brought up by the war, and Mrs. Whitelaw Reid offered to pay the expenses of two or three men from each service. It seemed an opportunity that should not be lost. Sir Alfred Keogh, the Director General of the Army Medical Service, was in sympathy with the plan; but nothing had been accomplished nor would they have been able to impress the authorities at Washington if Sir William had not written a personal note to President Wilson strongly urging that this chance be given the medical officers of the United States; and the President acceded to his request because of the great admiration he felt for the writer. It was a very important step with far-reaching effects.

The American Ambulance at Neuilly, Paris, had been established and arrangements had been made to have one of the hospital services taken over by successive groups of surgeons and nurses from some of the American Medical Schools. Dr. Crile, from the Western Reserve, was there and he was to be followed in three months by a unit from Harvard and then another from the University of Pennsylvania — and even at this distance and time, you heave a sigh of relief that that valiant man, J. William White, could release some of his pent-up fervour. It was a cruel fate for him to see the American notes and to hear that he should be neutral. Neutrality and White would be an impossible combination. And so it would be with Roosevelt or poor Henry James, and very many others. The President of the United States had an unruly handful among the men of the country.

And the American women too were, many of them, doing all they could; only it was exceedingly different to love *all* your neighbours as yourself — a feat they could not accomplish, but on one side or the other, they were helping.

" We have got twenty-two Belgian professors here and their families all living on your American money. . . . What a tragedy for them! " With their families they amounted to 153. But Lady Osler could write humorously of the departure of a Belgian family for Holland: " They insisted on going, and said they could not stay on charity any longer. And 9:30 Thursday morning I was to be seen in the car going to the station with nine P——s and their bags — followed by a cart full of luggage and another Belgian with a male and female bicycle. I should think it had been a prosperous year for the P——s. They came with five children and two Gladstone bags. They left with six (one in a hat box) ; four trunks, a cradle, and two bicycles. The N——s have left too. My wee house is empty now but we shall put some others in soon, I think." Her sympathy never gave out, nor her purse, as she and he were not only giving all they could themselves but were drawing on their American friends who responded generously. He said over and over again: " I do not know what we could do without American help "; and he often said at that time: " It is better for us that America is neutral." Lady Osler felt differently. Her spirit was more in sympathy with Roosevelt's.

Sir William tried to turn his mind away from the happenings in Flanders. He hoped — and paradoxically expected the worst. His book collecting and cataloguing and his library, were his greatest consolations. As the dead list slowly came in and he learnt that his young friends were mown down he tightened his belt and worked! Fortunately, his days were filled to their utmost. The sinking of the *Lusitania* and later the development of chemical warfare by the Germans roused the whole nation to a high state of bitterness, and there was a cry for reprisals — then he wrote a fierce note to the *Athenaeum:* " The cry for reprisals illustrates the exquisitely hellish state of mind into which war plunges sensible men. Not a pacifist but a ' last ditcher,' yet I refuse to believe that as a nation, how bitter soever the provocation, we shall stain our hands in the blood of the innocents. In this matter let us be free from blood-guiltiness and let not the undying reproach of humanity rest on us as on the Germans."

" The pluck of the women is wonderful," he wrote, " and the burden of the loss falls on them." The story of the war has been written from all sides with all manner of motives and emotions guiding the pen. His immense tolerance is free from all pettiness and his vast pity put him in a class apart, in a small minority. With all the youth he loved at the front he could write: " I have just been reading Henry Osborn Taylor's last book *Deliverance* in which he sketches the ways in which our ancestors of all times and countries have adapted themselves to the fears and hopes of their nature. From such a story of incessant and successful adjustments one may take a Pisgah sight of a day when nation shall not lift up the sword against nation, neither shall they learn war any more."

Had he been a youth he would have gone into battle though he hated strife — and his boy was walking in the steps he would have walked in. Revere, at Camiers with the McGill unit, saw the wounded as they were brought into the hospital — 200,000 casualties — and the grave-soaked field of Flanders, and he felt too safe. He must take some of the risks his friends were taking; so he determined to exchange to the artillery. While waiting for his papers he and his father had a great time over their books. His mother writes that " he and his dad were glued to old books all the time he was here, and reading to each other every evening." Always in that house, or in Sir William's neighbourhood, the young soldiers found themselves talking of other things than the war; never pessimistic, steadying their nerves with wholesome surroundings, yet knowing that he knew the exact truth of what they had endured — and that he cared. Edith Cavell had been condemned and executed. " This Cavell business has been a great aid to recruiting," he wrote. That was all; but we knew it must have wrung his heart. How stupid it was! The Germans, by this ruthless deed, threw a battalion of hate into their enemies' hands.

It would be interesting to follow the fortunes of war even in its appalling horrors, but we are considering the life of a man who would not follow it for anything; we must stay in England where, when he is not fighting microbes, or cheering the wounded and the workers in the hospital, he is hunting incunabula or working over his catalogue. " The Zeppelins," he wrote, " do much good in stirring up the people and bring home the realities of war. 'Tis sad to have the poor women and children butchered. A bad business and old humanity should be ashamed of itself." The Zeppelins evidently did not upset his equanimity, for Lady Osler wrote, after describing an excited night, " W. O. of course remains peacefully in bed and reads. He keeps steadily writing about his books or some medical problem." He and some others started a big Army Heart Hospital at Hampstead. " Allbutt, Mackenzie and I have the selecting of the staff, *etc.*" To every Canadian hospital that was established in England he, by common consent, became the practical head. The letters written of him by his old students and friends are what we know they would be — full of the power of his love and the charm of his presence. We start our life labelled with our personality and with our little bundle of characteristics to help or hinder us on our round. And when we have made the circle of our days and return to the point where we entered mortality we meet ourselves again plus or minus many things — but the same person. To read the stories written of Sir William at that time is to meet him again as he was when a young professor at McGill. He writes to a bereaved mother of her son's death, how the night before he died the boy asked that he might be alone with him; and he continues, " Poor fellow! I did what I could to comfort him. . . . I can realize what you feel. Our boy will be at the front very soon and we shall have to steel our hearts." Are we not back with him in the smallpox hospital in Montreal? Only now, death is the order of the day and the rush of work far greater; but it is the same power that he always possessed of attending to all and specializing with each.

Fifty men among his own relatives and connection were at the front; among them nephews to whom he had been a father — Norman and Campbell Gwyn, his sister's sons, and Dr. W. W. Francis, his " little doctur " " Willum." All of them came back to the Open Arms when on leave — some with wounds and all with tales of the trenches. But Sir William refused to listen to these tales, and somehow kept pessimism away. Revere's battery had been ordered to France; and Lady Osler wrote Dr. Francis: " I have only two duties in life: to keep on cheering the wounded, and to keep W. O. fit for his tremendous amount of work and strong enough to bear the parting with Revere." And to her sister: " I do not know when Revere goes. He should have four days before reporting at Southampton but sometimes they don't get that. It will be hard if we don't see him again. Willie is with him now. He went to Newcastle last Wednesday for the British Association and has to stay with the Bishop. I was asked but I knew I should hate it and only have glimpses of Revere. He is very busy; has had command of the battery several days since he went back. They are going farther north with a literary friend to see some famous old library, so they have been happy together." And Sir William when the parting was so near, wrote cheerily to others of their affairs — and only alludes casually to his own suffering in such words as " Revere goes over in a few weeks to take his chance with the rest. He likes the artillery." When Revere left, the battle of the Somme had been going on since July 31st. He reached France in October and was at once sent to the front with an ammunition column and was soon ordered to join a battery of Field Artillery with which he was in the thick of the fighting in the last stage of that great battle. And at home his parents went cheerily and busily on, living as they had always lived. Later to Dr. W. S. Thayer Sir William wrote: " Revere is in the thick of it — in the last push on the Ancre. He is in the 59th Brigade, Battery A. Dirty business for a decent lad but they have to go through with it. Of course we are terribly anxious but the seen arrow slackens its flight, as Dante says and we are steeling our hearts for anything that may happen." Fortunately his hobby had become an avocation. He did not take up book collecting and his catalogue to relieve his mind as a needed relaxation; it was his delight. He did not read up about the old physician and medical history in order to write about them; he read because he must — and wrote from an overflow of knowledge absorbingly gained. There have been many bibliophiles but never one that we know of so cheery as he; not a solitary thinker, but gathering into his net all who came his way, sharing every find. This and his incessant companionship with children — finding a playmate in the nurseries of every friend he had — were his salvation while the war was raging.

Just before Christmas this tragic year of 1916 found him in bed with one of his sharp attacks of broncho-pneumonia, and sending from his bed Christmas greetings to his friends. " Every month of the past two years seems a year in itself — and the end is not in sight. There will be an appalling mass of battered humanity to be taken care of. Without any big battle the wounded continued to pour in. We have 1500 beds here — always full. I expect a group of sixty-eight American doctors next week. We have asked for 250 young men who will be placed in the various military hospitals and relieve men who can go to the front. It is marvellous how much comes into the country every week from the United States. . . . Uncle Sam is doing more than he knows." And each note with his Christmas greeting tells also of his books. " Have the library all arranged and shelf-marked and the catalogue up to date. My secretary is still away but Hill from the Bodley comes every evening and a vestal who has been helping me with my incunabula, with a view to printing (ultimately) ." . . . Weak from his illness President Wilson's note, Peace without Victory, was unusually trying. " Bad time over here for the Dove of Peace. I wish Wilson's note (arrived this A.M.) had been shot on the way. Peace at this time would mean another big war within ten years. We must go through with this one now to the bitter end and either come out on top or go under and leave the future of Democracy to the United States. I think we can hold out another $1\frac{1}{2}$ years or longer. The country is at last alive to the business." And, " Poor Wilson's peace kite has come a cropper. I am so sorry he sent it just now. I hope he will be answered with Abe Lincoln's word — wonderful how Father Abe is quoted here and his example held up as a model! "

Probably inspired by the thought of his own lad, and the others he loves so dearly, being, it would seem, wantonly sacrificed, he tried to ease his own soul and those of others with a Christmas message to *Lloyd's Weekly*, called *The Silent Unit*. " There was a famous paradox in antiquity — a grain of wheat falls noiselessly to the ground, the same thing happens with the second, the third, the fourth, and so on — for the thousands of grains that make up a bushel. But collect the grains again, and drop the whole bushel and behold! a great noise. It seems difficult to explain how the sum of many thousands of silences could result in one great sound. The silent unit, the single grain, will win the war. In the world's crisis it is the spirit of the individual worker — in trench or camp, factory or farm, that keeps the mouth shut, the heart fixed, the hand steady.

"The call is for silent sacrifice, of time, of habits, of comforts, of friends, and of those dearer than life itself — the sacrifice of sanctification in the old Hebrew sense. It has come. Do we not feel in our heart of hearts that only a rich anointing of the spirit of the Fathers could have so stirred the Empire from the Centre to the Circle? My blood was thrilled the other day by the Honor Roll of the Consumers' Gas Company of Toronto, 386 men of the Colors from one corporation, of whom 25 have been killed, 37 wounded, and 8 taken prisoners! Why? The answer is in the words of the Prophet-Poet of Great Britain:

'Because ye are sons of the Blood
And call me Mother still.'

Let this message be heard above the din of battle and clash of machinery; The Silent Unit will win — in quietness and confidence will be your strength."

There was a full house at Christmas — and while Lady Osler was at the Hospital helping with the Christmas dinners, he writes his notes; and no doubt anyone coming in heard him whistling, as he always did when tears were near his eyes; for after all is said his natural instinct, where war was concerned, would have been that of little Wilhelmine:

"Why, 'tis a very wicked thing,
Said little Wilhelmine."

And some moments later we hear him saying of Germany: "What a cruel shame that her rulers have made outlaws of such good people as we know, at least in the profession."

The Peace Dove was being very trying. Reluctantly,

with an agony few people understood, the President of the United States realized he had failed and turned from the dove to the eagle. On April 2, 1917, Mr. Wilson sent his message to Congress: " The present German warfare against commerce is warfare against all nations " and asked for an immediate declaration of war. " This is a wildly excited household to-night," Sir William wrote. " I have just returned from town and found the houses bedecked with the Union Jack and the Stars and Stripes, the Revere girls dancing for joy. Wilson's speech is A 1. . . . America has already done splendidly over here. I wish you could have visited with me to-day the American Women's War Hospital for Officers — room for fifty, and so well arranged." Waving the flag was not very congenial to him; but the Allies had their backs to the wall and he felt with the others a sense of relief when America entered. " The moral support will be immense and I feel we shall need all the financial and physical help possible before the ghastly business is over — " " I have spent the first unhappy Easter of my life," he wrote, " No letter from Revere and his battery ' on the move.' So that we cannot but be worried. Still we keep up our courage and hope for the best." Then to his great joy Revere broke in upon him. Hardened in body but his spirit just the same. He had been granted ten days' leave. No talking of war if it could be avoided — just angling on the river or sitting close to his Dad, their heads bent together over some volume of forgotten lore — and triumphing over his wonderful treasures just bought — Philemon Holland's, 1603, *Plutarch's Morals*, a great book.

The ten days passed quickly and his boy was off again — and at 13 Norham Gardens all was outwardly cheerful, busy, inspiring; and the day's work went on quickly until in the latter part of May the vanguard of the American Expeditionary Force, mostly medical officers and engineers, arrived. Certain base hospital units came first and all of them officered by old-time friends of the Oslers, and Norham Gardens was their objective. Every little thing that concerned them was the concern of Lady Osler and himself. And he acted as an intermediary between the raw officers and the War Office. . . . He wrote *A note of warning to Examiners of Recruits* for the journal of the *American Medical Association*. It tells of " the unfit who furnish a large contingent in our hospitals and a needless burden of transport, care and pension — the mouth-breathers, the neurasthenics, thin-chested. Cut out un-sparingly the owners of these. If lungs and heart are not in good case the head is of no use in War . . . [this] is the experience of one whose work has been largely with the wastage of the recruiting office."

The stream of American officers began at once; the pa-rade of American troops in London took place; he and Lady Osler were alternately advisers or consolers — and slaves all the time; though he does take an hour or so to give a lecture and a wholly delightful one on the *School of the Book*. Though he speaks of the seen arrow slacken-ing in its flight, Pandora has really left a little hope in his heart and his consuming zeal for others would always keep him from impotently turning on himself.

Revere was safe on the 14th of August. Lady Osler wrote: " How badly you would feel *if* you saw him brought in wounded; but what a mercy it would be for him. He is near St. Julien, I believe. One of his men passed through the McGill Hospital, wounded, and Billy Francis saw him. His Captain is in the hospital in London. They are terribly busy, and the weather has been too aw-ful — Mud as bad as the Somme, and no dry days for days on end. Poor W. O. is almost a skeleton and keeps busy every moment but sometimes can't sleep; and it makes one very anxious. I dread the winter for him, to say nothing of Revere if it is as bad as last year." For those who had a martial spirit these days held the excitement that spirits of such calibre must often experience, but for a man of Sir William's type consolation could only be found in carrying-on.

The End

Ye old, old dead, and ye of yesternight,
Chieftains, and bards, and keepers of the sheep,
By every cup of sorrow that you had,
Loose me from tears, and make me see aright
How each hath back what once he stayed to weep;
Homer his sight, David his little lad!

Lizette Woodworth Reese.

CHAPTER XII

THE END

ON August 29, 1917, Lieutenant Osler (Revere), while advancing his battery in the Ypres salient, was struck by a piece of a bursting shell.

To the lasting comfort of those who loved the boy, when at the dressing station he opened his eyes, he looked into those of his own and his father's dear friend, Dr. Cushing. All that mortal could do was done but he was wounded beyond help and in a little while was at peace and the high hope of his father's life was over.

Dr. Cushing writes: " We saw him buried in the early morning. A soggy Flanders field beside a little oak grove to the rear of the Dosingham group — an overcast, windy, autumnal day — the long rows of simple wooden crosses — the new ditches half-full of water being dug by Chinese coolies wearing tin helmets — the boy wrapped in an army blanket and covered by a weather-worn Union Jack carried on the shoulders by four slipping stretcher-bearers. A strange scene — the great great grandson of Paul Revere under a British flag and awaiting him a group of six or eight American medical officers — saddened with thoughts of his father. Happily it was fairly dry at this end of the trench, and some green branches were thrown in for him to lie on. The Padre recited the usual service. A bugler gave the ' Last Post ' and we went about our duties. Plot 4, No. 7." And the two in Oxford whose hearts bled inwardly until the Last Post was sounded for them, lifted their heads and went about their duties.

" I was sitting in my library," Sir William had written in his note-book, " working on the new edition of my Text Book when a telegram was brought in. ' Revere dangerously wounded; comfortable and conscious, condition not hopeless.' I knew this was the end. We had expected it. The Fates do not allow the good fortune that has followed me to go with one to the grave. Call no man happy till he dies. The War Office telephoned at nine in the evening that he was dead. A sweeter laddie never lived, with a gentle loving nature. He had developed a rare taste in literature and was devoted to all my old friends in the spirit — Plutarch, Montaigne, Browne, Fuller, and above all, Izaak Walton, whose *Compleat Angler* he knew by heart and whose *Lives* he loved. We are heart broken, but thankful to have the precious memory of his loving life."

In a letter to Mrs. Cushing Lady Osler wrote:

" . . . thank God for two things — your Harvey was with him and he has gone to a peaceful spot. I feel sure of that — and we are rather old and may go too, very soon — We hope so — just fancy Harvey being with him — We are waiting and waiting for his letter and I am sure he will come here on his first leave — and perhaps bring some messages he couldn't even write. I can only see Revere lying on his stretcher with Harvey holding his dear, dirty hand . . ."

Every woman in the world will understand these words, and feel closer to her. Later, in this poignant letter, we see her in her unusual unselfishness and faith:

" . . . My poor man is heartbroken. I feel very anxious for him — he puts up a bluff in the daytime but the nights — three nights — have been torture — and I am watching near his door now — in case he needs me. . . . Before closing this — I want to tell you that in it all I feel grateful for the years we have had him and rejoice that he did his duty so pluckily — and believe he is with his many young friends waiting to see his ' Dad and Muz.' "

Major Davidson wrote of Revere to a friend, never knowing the Oslers would see the note: " Osler was the personification of purity, unsordidness and unselfishness. It is the killing of such a boy that makes me *loathe war.*" The ravages of humanity in the mass would leave us hopeless but for the miracle of the unit.

Innumerable men and women in the world were carrying their grief with a controlled and unconquered spirit — and many had to meet a tragedy far greater than theirs; and yet so greatly was he loved that everywhere people felt it their personal sorrow. The explanation in part was that no friend at any time had ever been excluded from the inner circle of their hearts and now, though their hearts were broken, their friends were not excluded. Whatever the cause, everywhere people felt that for Sir William Osler to lose his boy was intolerable to them. Everyone was leading a double life in England — the gay word — the stiff upper lip — and the chill of death at their hearts — but few had in their hearts, without bitterness or envy, such unutterable sweetness that they could find consolation in other children when their own had gone. The little Max Müller boys, with whom Sir William played, would never have guessed their playmate had received a mortal blow.

" Dear Laddie," he writes in one of his hundreds of letters, " he loathed the whole business of war and I daresay is glad to be at peace out of the hell of the past six months. . . . We are taking the only medicine for sorrow — time and hard work." When the American mail came — it had been delayed a month — it came in masses. He must have felt the whole world was with him beside his boy's grave in Flanders; but the living needed him and in less than a week he was back visiting his hospitals and he continued to work on his Text Book.

A great wave of spiritualism had swept over England — such longing possessed people to have back their dead; but Sir William felt it almost offensive and pasted in his copy of Sir Oliver Lodge's book, *Raymond,*

> " Have we not earned our rest? Oh, hear them plead
> Whom death hath drawn across the dividing line!
> You should have kept their memory as a shrine
> A holy place, where he who runs may read
> The lovely record of a noble deed! "

He was a shadow of himself and Lady Osler seemed to forget her own grief in her care for him. To his sister he wrote: " We are desolate at heart but keeping up the old ways — as there are so many to help and make as happy as possible. She is splendid (Lady Osler) and has stood the trial so well. It is a great thing to be busy. 'Twill be a sad Christmas for us all with our laddies lost and gone."

As usual Christmas found the house full of guests; among them fourteen American doctors. " Such nice boys," he writes, " it was a pleasure to have them." And one of these nice boys wrote of the day: " We were at the Oslers at our first Christmas night overseas, a great crowd of us and Sir William was very lively and entertaining." And perhaps, when alone, he took from against his heart a letter written to him from his boy on his 21st birthday, which ends with these words: " I can't help feeling that at this time next year we will all be together again. I hope Lloyd George doesn't stop us buying books! I am very happy considering it is my birthday. I have no regrets except for my own shortcomings, only endless love and gratitude for you both." Might he not well have said after reading these words from his boy: " O death where is thy

sting? O grave where is thy victory? " He had consolation
beyond most men even in the sorrow that broke his heart.
For many a man throughout the land was uttering the bitter cry of David: " Oh, Absalom, my son, my son! " And
he recognized this, for some months later he wrote to one
of his colleagues who was in bitter grief:

" Dearest —— Your letter of October 18th has just
come. We have been wondering and worrying and sorrow-
ing not a little about you. . . . For one thing you must
feel thankful that she had from you all the affection and
care that any woman could desire. That must be a comfort. None of those terrible regrets that add so much to
the bitterness of death. We have that comfort, too, about
our dear Isaac. He and I never had a disagreement and I
never had to say a harsh word to him. Poor laddie, the
war was an awful trial. He had not the heart to shoot a
partridge and the terrible scenes of the year at the front
must have been a perpetual agony. He kept it all from us
but I knew how he felt. The men and horses were his only
solace, trying to make their situation less hard. I wish you
could have seen him of late years as his mental development was remarkable and in the directions which were a
delight to me. Such love for all that was best in literature
and art, and he had developed a singularly sound judgment for a lad of his years. It is a hard blow for us. Grace
is splendid, and we both keep up, as he would have wished,
our old life. There is so much to be done that we can't
brood over our sorrows. What a wonderful experience you
must have had! Poor Russia! Fortunately America takes
her place and is really now the hope of humanity, but a
heavy task is ahead. Courage and patience will be needed."

He was losing in weight, and try as he might to staunch
the wound in his heart, it kept bleeding. Work was increasing for him; he saw to that; but as he was completing

the circle of his life he became more in spirit as he was when with Father Johnson at Weston. "The consuming zeal for others" was, if possible, stronger than ever, and the order of thought, induced by the *Religio,* was more in evidence. At the hospitals, and meetings, and Clubs, wherever he touched, few saw the change in the spontaneity of his banter or the break in the elasticity of his step. But Lady Osler saw it and was fearful.

In Dr. Cushing's *Life of Sir William Osler* is the beautiful picture of him at the bedside of a little girl whose mother writes: "He visited our little Janet twice every day from the middle of October until her death a month later, and these visits she looked forward to with a pathetic eagerness and joy. There would be a little tap low down on the door which would be pushed open and a crouching figure playing goblin would come in, and in a high pitched voice would ask if the fairy godmother was at home and could he have a bit of tea. Instantly the sick-room was turned into a fairyland, and in fairy language he would talk about the flowers, the birds, and the dolls who sat at the foot of the bed who were always greeted with 'Well, all ye loves!' In the course of this he would manage to find out all he wanted to know about the little patient. . . .

"The most exquisite moment came one cold, raw November morning when the end was near, and he mysteriously brought out from his inside pocket a beautiful red rose carefully wrapped in paper, and told how he had watched the last rose of summer growing in his garden and how the rose had called out to him as he passed by, that she wished to go along with him to see his little lassie. That evening we all had a fairy tea party at a tiny tea table by the bed. Sir William talking to the rose, his little lassie, and her mother in the most exquisite way; and presently he slipped out of the room just as mysteriously as he had entered it, all crouched down on his heels; and the little girl understood that neither the fairies nor people could always have the color of a red rose in their cheeks, or stay as long as they wanted in one place, but that they nevertheless would be very happy in another home and must not let the people they left behind, particularly their parents, feel badly about it; and the little girl understood and was not unhappy."

There was only boundless love in his broken heart; there was no room for bitterness or revenge. When things seemed very dark indeed in the spring of 1918, Lady Osler wrote: " The conditions in France have depressed him greatly and I think he has been very pessimistic. We talk quite freely of visits from the Müllers and Ewalds. Should the Huns reach England, I daresay he would welcome them kindly — saint that he is." After the war some Germans did come to England and put wreaths near his urn.

For the individual all things come to an end — even sorrow, we hope. But for the nations, though the war was indubitably drawing to a close, it was to be far from the end of their folly. Almost all that could be destroyed had been destroyed. Sir William had far too much the Greek mind to call evil good, and good evil; or to cry " Peace! " when there was no peace; but revenge he would not have. From all the waste and misery he sought the good that could be rescued; every readjustment must be an advance towards permanent peace, and the torch which his beloved young dead were to hold up, and he to carry, was not one to show the horrors or the glory of war. And their sacrifice must save other youths and bring to the world a greater civilization. Pending demobilization the physicians and surgeons organized, and faced the problems of the future; there was to be no armistice for them. Sir William writes: " All here are so enthusiastic about the United States and Mr. Wilson. What a wonderful change

in a few months! there may be at last a great peace! "
But he knew that it was to benefit other generations; a
long mortgage had been put upon prosperity, health and
faith. Organizations and societies were cropping up everywhere; resolutions were passed and everyone, except the
physicians, was talking of things he did not understand.
Before the demobilization, it was a mad world, a heart-
breaking world, fed on artificial stimulus for consolation
or excitement; now the dull treadmill of paying the piper
was to begin. At first the thought of a great peace was
thrilling — that passed soon. Looking over vast accounts
and deciding who made the bills and who must pay them,
when there had been a raid on all banks, is far from heroic
work, and not material for poems. The herculean task of
reconstruction had to be faced. A meeting was to be held
in Oxford to consider the War Memorial. Sir William
wrote to the Mayor: " Sorry I cannot be at the meeting
about the War Memorial. Put every half-penny you get
into decent houses for the poor."

The Peace Congress was becoming very worrying to one
who loved simple truth and his fellow men everywhere.
In February 1919 the blockade was still on; and a British
Military Commission had been sent to Austria to look into
the reports of what had been said to be its desperate condition. Sir William wrote Professor Wenckebach, who
had held the premier chair of medicine in Vienna, " Lord
Parmoor's committee is anxious to have first-hand evidence with reference to the food conditions in Vienna,
particularly among the poor. Could you let me have as
soon as possible your impressions. The people in this
country are most anxious to do everything possible to
relieve the suffering in Vienna which they feel must be
very severe. I hope all goes well with you."

He did not receive an answer to this for two months,
and when it came with the news that in Vienna they were

nearly starving, he cabled and then wrote: " Dear
Wenckebach, Yours of the 4th of March came to-day and I
have sent it at once to the Foreign Office. I telephoned at
once to one of the Secretaries to ask what the action had
been and he said food was being hurried through. I am
trying to arrange with friends in Schweiz to forward some
supplies directly to you. I shall try too to get a telegram
through to you if possible. I have asked the Foreign Office
if they would like to have a special interview with you in
Schweiz. It made me very sad to hear of all your sufferings. We lost our dear boy in Flanders." Professor
Wenckebach said this was the historic letter that brought
the Viennese the first gleam of hope. Sir William brought
the conditions in Vienna before the public and started the
relief work. It was a difficult job. Many still felt Austria
the enemy, but to talk of enemies when children were
starving was intolerable to him; and the Government's
haggling with peace terms tried him sorely, but he kept
steadily at the work until something was done.

" It was in the summer of 1919," Dr. Alice Hamilton
writes, " the latter part of June, I think, that I went from
London to Oxford to see Sir William and had an hour or
so with him in his home. I told him that I was about to
go into Germany with Jane Addams and some Quakers,
at the request of Herbert Hoover, to report on the condition of the people there, after the long starvation of the
war and the armistice. Sir William responded with eager
approval. ' I am so glad to hear it,' he said. ' I received a
report by some Dutch physicians and I was shocked at the
picture they drew. And those cows that they say are to be
delivered to the French. Really that must not be; they
must be kept for the German children who have little
enough. I have just been writing Robert Cecil about it.'
As I said Goodbye he asked me to do him a favour. ' When
you are in Berlin I wish you would call up Frau Ewald

and give her my love. We were such good friends, she and her husband and I, before the war, and now her husband is dead and all these years of the war I have not been able to get a word to her. Tell her that her husband's death made me very sad.' Perhaps this does not sound so extraordinary now; but in those days of quite undiminished hate of all Germans, babies and all, even on the part of those who had lost none in the war, this attitude of a man who had lost his only son and who had seen the sufferings of the wounded and the wrecked soldiers, was so unusual that it did move me very deeply."

Now and then some honours came to Sir William that gave him very genuine pleasure. One of them was his election to the Presidency of the Classical Association which led to his delivering a very notable address on *The Old Humanities and the New Science*. Dr. W. H. Welch fortunately chanced to be in Oxford at that time. He sat by Lady Osler during the address and at the end turned to her and said: " That was Dr. Osler at his best." And later he wrote: " There have been physicians, especially in England, well known for their attainments as classical scholars, but I am not aware that since Linacre there has come to a member of the medical profession distinction in this field comparable to Osler's election to the Presidency of the British Classical Association. It was in recognition not merely of his sympathetic interest in classical studies and intimate association with classical scholars, but also of his mastery of certain phases of the subject, especially the bibliographical and historical sides, and the relation of the work and thought of classical antiquity to the development of medicine, science and culture.

" Osler told me that he had never given so much time and thought to the preparation of an address as he did to this one. The occasion and the whole setting were to me most interesting and impressive. At noon the audience of distinguished scholars and guests assembled in the Divinity School. At one end of the hall the Vice Chancellor of the University presided, and half-way down one of the sides was the high seat of the orator. The distinguished company, the brightly coloured academic gowns and hoods, the traditional ceremonies for such an occasion in Oxford, the figure of Osler himself, the charm and interest of the address and the cordial appreciation and reception by the audience, all combined to make a scene of brilliancy and delight which I shall always carry in my memory. . . ."

Lady Osler described the scene " with the sun filtering through the Exeter trees and those ancient windows; Willie standing in that black oak pulpit, and, in his scarlet gown and velvet cap, looking medieval and wonderful."

Many friends had been secretly planning a great celebration for him on July 12, 1919, his seventieth birthday. And he was touched that in all this time of sorrow and anxiety they should take trouble to think of him. He was surprised by the outburst of affection from all over the country. The journals in the United States, Great Britain and her dominions issued special Osler numbers. A special volume was brought out as a memorial with tributes from his old friends and pupils; The *Johns Hopkins Hospital Bulletin* had a series of twenty papers written by the members of the different departments; and Miss Blogg compiled his bibliography. This last greatly amused him; he handed it to Dr. Cowley, Bodley's librarian, saying: " Here is a tragic record. I should like to have it buried in the Bodleian."

" That a well-ordered seventieth birthday," he wrote, " may have all the advantages of the final exitus is shown by the July number of *The Johns Hopkins Hospital Bulletin* which leaves nothing to be said. The end of the number brought the thrill of the day, when I saw revealed the utter shamelessness of my life — and the true reason of our Secretary's attachment to me! A bibliography of my writings extending to 730 articles! An illuminated address from the staff at Bodley (not to have worshipped at whose shrine I count the day lost) the promise of a medico-literary anthology in my honour, with greetings from scores of dear friends helped to complete a very happy day." All notes and cables and tributes had to be acknowledged. To Dr. W. S. Thayer he wrote: " Very special thanks for that beautiful tribute. You only of the old boys could have done it. The verses were splendid. I have had such a happy time. Only after the presentation of the volumes by Allbutt I did not feel very well and have been laid up ever since with bronchitis." But the day saw the beginning of his breakdown in health. As Colonel Garrison writes: " his intimates began to realize that he had 'trod the upward and the downward slope' and was done with life."

After Revere's death they took steps to make their house in Oxford a freehold and it was to be left to Christ Church as a permanent home for the future Regius Professors. The Memorial to Revere was to be the establishment of a Tudor and Stuart Club at the Johns Hopkins University similar to the Elizabethan Club at Yale. The dedication of Edward Revere Osler Memorial Fund was " in grateful recognition of the happy years we spent in Baltimore "; and its purpose was " to encourage the study of English literature of the Tudor and Stuart periods." Revere's collection of books was to be the nucleus and the fund was to be expended " for the purchase of further books relating to these periods, and in the promotion of good fellowship and a love of literature among the members." His own books were to go to McGill — except the non-medical ones — the Shelleys, Fullers, Keats — which were to be added to Revere's collection. Though making all these arrangements for the final disposition of his books, the collecting was going on very steadily. " Something new in every day — three nice original Pasteur papers from Strong this week." And: " Sir William says it's a cold day when he doesn't add something to his library."

The steady entertaining fell largely on Lady Osler. Americans were pouring in and he wanted to see them all. Just before his seventieth birthday they had a great function at All Souls and Lady Osler's account of it permits us to be present: " We were in an uncertainty about the Hoovers as no message came about Mrs. Hoover but his wires said *we,* so were supposed it was Mrs. Hoover but she is in California and did not come. I was glad to think I needn't go, and asked Nancy Astor to take my place, but the Vice Chancellor sent another ticket and asked me to be there. So I went of course. Pershing with General Biddle and three aides arrived at 10:45; also Colonel Lloyd Griscom with an aide; also Mr. Hoover with a Captain Somebody; three big United States Army cars. Also an orderly to polish up the General. You would have laughed to see the blue room and your bath room. Twice during the day General Pershing was brushed and polished. It was a very cold morning and I had a nice wood fire in the drawing room over which we all hung gratefully. There were sandwiches, coffee and drinks in the dining room and they had a good meal as they left town at eight o'clock. Nancy arrived in the midst of it, kissed the General affectionately and said: ' Do let's dance; you are the best dancer in the American Army! ' We dressed the degree people up — scarlet gowns and velvet hats — and all went down in cars. Wanda had a seat with me. It was really a wonderful sight. Lord Curzon was gorgeous. The prince did not come, but the degree was given *in absentia.* Pershing had a splendid reception, as did Mr. Hoover; but Haig was the hero. I never heard such a racket. Joffre looks old and sad; worn out, I fancy. As the big doors were

opened at the Sheldonian, ' God save the King' was played
and as Joffre, the first to enter, stepped in he saluted. And
one could see all the others in procession behind him; it
was a gorgeous mass of scarlet and black, with touches of
blue from the French uniforms, and M. A. hoods. After
the ceremony the All Souls guests walked across the street
into the big quad. At the gate the plan of the table was
handed you, and you can fancy my surprise when I saw Sir
Douglas Haig was to take me in, and Sir David Beatty on
my right. I said I felt I must be Great Britain, I was so
well protected — Army and Navy on either side and
France and America in front. I got on very well with my
friends. General Haig said everything that was charming
about Bob Bacon. He said he had just had a letter from
Billie H. telling him everything, and appreciated so much
his writing. Then I had such a delightful time — the best
of the day. Wright, our All Souls friend, stood just behind
us, looking after the wines. I told Sir Douglas there had
not been a better warrior in the army's forces, so when we
got up Sir Douglas spoke to him; shook hands and thanked
him. Wright nearly cried and I did — I could see him
carrying those poor things down the hospital steps. It
is an awful thing to say but I was much happier when the
war was on and I was really helping. Now everything is
upset, and fuss on all sides; strikes and fights and daily
horrors in Europe. Mr. Hoover was most depressing about
the winter outlook and had to leave directly after luncheon as he was called back — Huns holding up food in
Poland. After the luncheon General Pershing dashed over
to Blenheim to see the Palace, *etc.,* then back to the University garden party at Wadham, then for a walk, and back
here. He said he would like a nap, so I tucked him up on
the blue room sofa; an aide on the bed; and Griscom in
your bed. At 7:30, having been dusted and polished again
they all went to dine at Christ Church and left by motor

for London at 10. And back to France at dawn. So that's all. Such a business! " No woman could have better fitted into such a scene. She was herself a good deal of a Commander with a martial spirit. Her sense of duty, impregnable; her conscience, very exacting; but she was not in the least a slave to those often dulling qualities, but a general marshalling her troops in dress parade with the effect of flags flying and music, entirely up to the mark — yet compassionate and very tired.

After the strain of so many functions, especially the birthday excitements, Sir William was taken with a sharp attack of broncho-pneumonia; he seemed to recover from this after a short rest at the seashore; but exposure on a journey taken during the railroad strike, brought on another attack and from this there was no rebound. The spirit of fun was in full force during the early days of his illness; all who entered his room must be cheered. His irrepressible spirits had been used all his life to protect him from showing the depth of his feeling — but

" Show me the books he loves and I shall know
  The man far better than through mortal friends."

A jest for everyone, but when too ill to read himself, these are the books he wanted read to him: Plato, Sir Thomas Browne, Walter Pater's *Marius,* the Peach Blossom and Wine Chapter in *Gaston de la Tour,* Bridges' Anthology, *The Spirit of Man.* And he often asked to have sung to him the twelfth century hymn of the great Peter Abelard, " *O quanta qualia* " which is known to most in the English translation " O what the joy and glory must be! "

It had been so much the habit of his lifetime to see other persons in the camera, and not himself, that it was not until very near the end that he realized his heart was filled with joy for himself, the only selfish joy he had ever known; for the portal he was entering was the only one through which he could meet his boy. On a slip of paper was found, written during the last days of his life, these words: " The Harbour almost reached after a splendid voyage with such companions all the way and my boy awaiting me."

On the last night of his life, Dr. Francis, whom he had called, in his childhood, his " little doctur " and who had always been to him a well-loved and adoring child, sat by his bed, and Sir William asked him to read from *The Spirit of Man,* and some verses from *The Ancient Mariner.* Dr. Francis writes: " When I took leave of him he said to me as though I were still a child ' nighty-night, a-darling.' " The end came for him quietly and peacefully on the afternoon of December 29th. He left us in the certain faith of a joyous resurrection. Many cannot have that faith; and to them who knew him he is himself their " lamp in darkness."

Into Christ Church Cathedral, followed by a great assemblage of mourners, they carried his bier. On it lay a single sheaf of lilies and his favourite copy of the *Religio.* When the last words of the burial of the dead had been said she, who had so loved and cared for him and his profession, turned quietly back to their home to continue the service until her death in 1928.

His library was to go to McGill but he was anxious before the books were sent that his *Catalogue* should be finished which, he said, " would still require ten years of not too senile work." To the accomplishment of this wish Lady Osler gave her life, encouraging the editors, financing the cataloguing and establishing a fund of £10000 for the maintenance of the library. When the work was almost done and the books quite ready to be packed, she died. He had written: " I like to think of my books in an alcove of a fireproof library in some institution that I love; at the back of the alcove an open fireplace and a few easy chairs, and on the mantel piece an urn with my ashes, through which my astral self could peek at the books I have loved, and enjoy the delight with which kindred souls still in the flesh would handle them." His library and his Catalogue are in the McGill University in a beautiful room in the fire proof Strathcona building. At the end of the room in the centre of an alcove is a bronze medallion bearing his portrait behind which are his ashes; and the librarian, his cousin, Dr. Francis — making in all a strangely restful picture of fulfilled desire.

In Sir William's life you catch the effect of a great symphony conceived in its entirety. The noble theme sweeping on without a conflicting motive. During the Baltimore years it reaches its height in a flood of action, and then slowing down in rapidity but deepening in depth and colour, the final chords are struck with a profound and beautiful authority.

What has he done to escape oblivion now that his amazing personality is no longer felt by actual contact? What shall we say to those who did not know him? He perhaps would answer in the words of Sir Thomas Browne: " The greatest part must be content to be as though they had not been, to be found in the register of God, not in the record of men." Let us give the answer to these questions in the words of a distinguished physician, Professor Adami, of Liverpool: " ' So passed into history, untimely, even though he had attained unto the allotted span, the greatest physician in history.' I confess that this characterization arrested me when I read it. We are not accustomed to measure up our friends against the giants that have been. And above all it is as a friend that during his lifetime we regarded Osler; as one who possessed the genius of friendship to a greater degree than any one of our generation. It was his wonderful interest in all of us that was the outstanding feature. Above all others the Angel might write him as one who loved his fellow men, placing him foremost among those whom God had blessed. It was from his humanity, his extraordinary interest in his fellows, that all his other powers seemed to flow. On thinking over these other powers, while we admit freely that there have been greater medical men — Harvey, for example, Vesalius, John Hunter, Claude Bernard, Lister, yet when we pass in review the great physicians, those who by their lives, their practice, their teaching, and their writings, have exercised the greatest influence over the greatest number of their fellows, putting together all those powers which make the complete physician, Osler must be awarded the first place. Hippocrates, while farthest away, perhaps comes nearest, yet he is largely mythical; Galen, high as were his aspirations, had but limited knowledge and could not escape from the trammels of tradition; Boerhaave, great as a teacher and clinician, was also under the trammels of authority, and in his writings did not advance his subject; Sydenham was a clinician of notable powers of observation and independence, but was no teacher and incapable of founding a school. Think of those years at Johns Hopkins, when Osler revolutionized the teaching of medicine and of clinical medicine in a community of seventy millions. Think of the influence wielded by his text-book, not merely among English-speaking people, but the world over, even to China and Japan. There is no physician who during his lifetime has had so profound an influence upon so great a number; no one individual who has done so much to advance the practice of scientific medicine, no one whose personal intimacy with his fellows in the profession has covered so wide an area — Canada, the United States, Great and Greater Britain and the leaders in medicine the world over: no one, in short, who has combined in the same degree the study, practice, and teaching — the science and the art of medicine."

Where that swift spirit has gone we do not know; but to those he cared for on earth he brought life. We will look back and remember that for us was the high privilege of having seen and felt power without evil — a transcendently beautiful life.

> " They walk in the City
> That they have builded
> The city of God
> From evil shielded."

INDEX